LOCAL HISTORY

HOW TO GATHER IT, WRITE IT, AND PUBLISH IT

By DONALD DEAN PARKER

Head of the Department of History and Political Science
South Dakota State College of Agriculture
and Mechanic Arts

Revised and Edited by

BERTHA E. JOSEPHSON

for the
Committee on Guide for Study of Local History
of
The Social Science Research Council

GREENWOOD PRESS, PUBLISHERS
WESTPORT, CONNECTICUT

Library of Congress Cataloging in Publication Data

Parker, Donald Dean, 1899-
    Local history.

    Reprint of the 1944 ed. published by Social Science
Research Council, New York.
    Bibliography: p.
    Includes indexes.
    1. United States--Historiography. 2. Local
history. 3. United States--History, Local--Sources.
I. Josephson, Bertha E. II. Social Science Research
Council. Committee on Guide for Study of Local
History. III. Title.
E175.7.P3 1979   808'.066'9   78-11873
ISBN 0-313-21100-0

808. 0669
P238

Originally published in 1944 by the Social Science Research
Council, New York, N.Y.

Reprinted in 1979 by Greenwood Press, Inc.,
51 Riverside Avenue, Westport, CT 06880

Printed in the United States of America

10 9 8 7 6 5 4 3 2 1

CONTENTS

	Page
FOREWORD	vii
PREFACE	ix
INTRODUCTION	xi

PART I

GATHERING MATERIAL FOR LOCAL HISTORY

CHAPTER

I. SOURCES OF INFORMATION FOR LOCAL HISTORY AND WHERE TO FIND THEM	3
Library and general sources	4
Village, town, and city histories	5
County histories	8
State and regional histories	9
Sociological material	11
Family histories and biographies	12
Military records	13
Directories	15
Maps	17
Atlases and gazetteers	19
Accounts of travelers	20
Anniversary addresses and sermons	21
Photographs and pictures	21
II. OTHER SOURCES OF INFORMATION	24
Old residents	24
Private letters	32
Diaries	33
Account books	34
Keepsakes, heirlooms and relics	35
III. NEWSPAPERS AND PERIODICALS	37
IV. PUBLIC RECORDS	48
Census reports	48
Abstracts of title and title deeds	51
Surveyors' notes	52
Public school records	54
Other public records	54
County archives	55
Town records	62
State public records	65
Pension bureau	67
New planning agencies: national and state	68
V. BUSINESS RECORDS	70
VI. CHURCH RECORDS AND CEMETERY INSCRIPTIONS	80

PART II

WRITING LOCAL HISTORY

VII. THE TECHNIQUE OF GATHERING AND ORGANIZING LOCAL HISTORICAL
       MATERIAL 93
       Bibliography slips or cards 93
       Note-slips or cards 94
       Notes on printed works 95
       Notes on manuscripts and special materials 98
       Notes on maps and illustrations 99
VIII. A MODEL OUTLINE FOR A LOCAL HISTORY 102
IX. COMPOSITION AND TECHNICAL DETAILS IN HISTORICAL WRITING . 124
       General Suggestions 124
       Repetition of words 125
       Clarity without repetition 125
       Conciseness without drabness 126
       Paraphrases and quotations 127
       Identification of persons 131
       Indication for footnotes 131
       The component parts of a local history 132
       The footnotes 133
X. BIBLIOGRAPHY, ADDENDA AND INDEX 138

PART III

PUBLISHING LOCAL HISTORY

XI. VARIOUS MEANS OF PUBLISHING LOCAL HISTORY 149
       Printing 149
       Lithoprinting and planographing 155
       Mimeographing 156
       Hectographing 158
XII. COOPERATIVE LOCAL HISTORY 160
       The local historical society as a cooperative enterprise . . . 160
       School-sponsored cooperation 162
       Library-sponsored cooperation 164
       Community-sponsored cooperation 165
       Newspaper-sponsored cooperation 165
       Club-sponsored cooperation 166
       Church-sponsored cooperation 168
       Anniversary-inspired cooperation 169
APPENDIX—Writing the War History of Communities 171
BIBLIOGRAPHY 179

FOREWORD

GOOD local history is one of the most effective contributions that can be made to social science. Current problems, if studied only by the method of contemporary observation, lack perspective. The essential problems of social science do not always manifest themselves on large national canvases, nor do the fundamental processes which direct social evolution often originate in capitols and legislative bodies or in national associations. These problems and these processes generally emerge in localities, in communities, and their nature, operation, and influence can be studied most effectively only there. No isolated problem or process can be truly understood without a complete and accurate picture of the complex which makes up the environment.

The effective study of local history is an essential of social science. Without it, primary information of the utmost importance will be unobtainable and, to the degree of that omission, all results will be incomplete. Much local history is being studied and written, many people are interested in it, but so huge is the task that many more are needed. In order to have adequate samplings, prepared with the basic needs of social science in mind, a much larger staff of workers is needed. It is hoped this volume will stimulate new interest and guide the labors of many in this fruitful vineyard. Indeed a main purpose of this Guide is to suggest to workers in local history both general ideas and specific aids in the exploration of this important field.

The Social Science Research Council began the study of this problem in a series of conferences which resulted in the appointment of the Committee on the Guide for the Study of Local History. This committee secured the cooperation of Dr. Donald D. Parker who had already prepared a manuscript on the subject. A subcommittee, composed of Messrs. Crittenden, Merk, Nichols, Schlesinger and Shryock, was organized to edit and revise Dr. Parker's manuscript. They had the benefit of the criticism of Dr. Constance McLaughlin Green of Smith College, Dr. Bayrd Still of Duke University and Dr. Kimball Young of Queens College. Dr. Rodney Loehr of the University of Minnesota prepared chapter V. Dr. Jeremiah P. Shalloo of the University of Pennsylvania supplied sociological data. Dr. Richard H. Shryock of the University of Pennsylvania radically re-drafted chapter VIII. The entire volume was edited, without proof reading responsibility, by Miss Bertha E. Josephson of the Ohio State Archeological and Historical Society and a member of the editorial board of the American Association for State and Local History. In the course of editing and revising she wrote the latter half of chapter III and chapters VII, IX and X. Dr. Lester J. Cappon of the University of Virginia prepared the Appendix. Permission to quote has been granted by the D. Appleton-Century Company, The Macmillan Company, the McGraw-Hill Book Company, Inc., Prentice-Hall Inc., and the University of Chicago Press.

The committee expresses its indebtedness to these various cooperators.

C. C. CRITTENDEN
FREDERICK EGGAN
HERBERT HEATON
FREDERICK MERK
ARTHUR M. SCHLESINGER
RICHARD II. SHRYOCK
LEONARD D. WHITE
LOUIS WIRTH
ROY F. NICHOLS, *chairman*

viii

PREFACE

THE study and writing of local history receives attention from three classes of people: students, teachers, and adults not connected with educational institutions. Each of these has its own approach. For the first, local history is an excellent, but too little used, introduction to the whole field of history. It affords contact with original, primary sources of information, it calls for exploration and discovery in untrodden areas, and it prevents the misconception that history is merely something already written in books. For teachers it offers the opportunity, also, of putting scientific training to the service of the community and of avoiding the endless repetition of stale information. To men and women not connected professionally with schools, it presents an excellent field for the exercise of a lively intellectual curiosity, and provides a safeguard against the leadership of ignorance; it gives the individual, humble or noted, a place in the development of knowledge and wisdom.

Professional historians are critical of the product of nonprofessional study of local history, often justly so. Its defects, however, are due in part to defective training received in schools and in part to the failure to grasp the importance of widespread work in local history. The appearance of guides for the amateur local historian, the multiplication and growth of historical societies, and the establishment of higher standards for publication are remedying the first of these evils. The importance of more widespread study of local history needs emphasis. While it cannot be maintained that state, national, and general history is the sum of local history, generalizations cannot safely be made without taking local developments into account. There is a necessity, then, for mass production of historical writing in which the participation of many people everywhere is required. One can never tell what locality and what circumstance, which has seemed not at all out of the ordinary, may assume a peculiar importance. Professional historians now find William Bradford's *History of Plymouth Plantation* of greater value than many of the more ambitious historical writings of the time. Should someone find the record of a thorough-going local historian covering the Lincoln neighborhood of southwestern Indiana between 1816 and 1830, or New Salem, Illinois, between 1830 and 1836, the importance of the discovery would be unquestionable.

Interest in local history finds countless channels for useful activity. A detailed history of the development of a community must cover political, economic, and social development from the first migrations to the diversified activities of the present. Narrower subjects such as the movements of a single family, the growth of a single business firm, the history of a church, or the life of an individual are worthwhile subjects for careful study. Waste of effort on nonessentials is easily prevented by keeping before one the question: What would an intelligent outsider want to know about this community or about this subject? If the student of local history keeps this question in mind and works honestly upon his subject, he will have the satisfaction of knowing that the product of his work is a useful contribution to the goal of all historical effort—the understanding of the world in which we live.

CHRISTOPHER B. COLEMAN
Indiana Historical Bureau

INTRODUCTION

THIS book is not intended for the person who has been fortunate enough to receive graduate training in the study and writing of history, though it is hoped that even such an individual may, perhaps, find useful suggestions in the chapters that follow. Neither is it primarily for the sociologist or the genealogist, though each may find it serviceable, for they, like the local historian, will have to go to the same sources for their information about local conditions in the past.

It is, instead, meant to give to the individual of intelligence, with more than average educational advantages, the necessary information for gathering, writing, and publishing the history of his own community— his village, town, city, or county. It is hoped that such a serious-minded graduate of a high school or college will find in it useful instruction in the technique of gathering, writing, and publishing local history.

It is not, after all, the highly trained historian who will write the local history of each community in this vast country. Not only is the field too great but usually the trained historian is primarily interested in larger areas of research, such as state, regional, and national history. If the local history of the United States is to be written at all, it will have to be done by an interested, if amateur, citizen or group of citizens in each community.

To those inclined to underestimate their own ability a historian named Goss offers encouragement:

It is not necessary to go to great libraries to write history; it is not necessary to go abroad for inspiration. It is not necessary to become a student in an advanced class of a great university . . . to learn how to use original sources and obtain a literary style; it is not absolutely necessary to sit at the feet of the great masters; all these are aids, but if you wish to study and write about local affairs, paraphrase the good old motto of Michigan, 'If you would write good local history, look about you.'[1]

Too often history has been regarded as merely the record of distant celebrities and of great but far off events. These have their place, but the history of a nation is incomplete which fails to give an account of the ordinary man and woman, their affairs and interests. In this respect the local historian has a golden opportunity, for he can enter more fully into these everyday events about everyday people. Nor is local history isolated; it is part of the history of the state, the nation, and the world. Indeed, good national history cannot be written without sufficient reference to local history. The local historian, therefore, definitely aids the state or national historian in his work.

---

[1] Dwight Goss, "Methods of Securing Information for Local History," *Collections of the Michigan Pioneer and Historical Society* (Lansing), XXXVIII, 1912, p. 59.

Someone has compared a community which does not know its own history to a man who has lost his memory. Your task will be well worthwhile if you can succeed in restoring and strengthening a sense of tradition and continuity in your community.

You may think that your particular village, town, city, county, or region has no history. Perish the thought! It can always be said, as it was two generations ago: "There is scarcely a town or city in the land that has not its records and its public documents, its newspaper files and its Fourth-of-July orations—all replete with information waiting for the historian."[2] You need but scratch the surface in your own community to find that this is true. Every locality is teeming with interest and historical information, only waiting to be revealed by well directed enthusiasm.

One word of warning! Do not undertake the writing of local history with the expectation of making a small fortune from the publication of your book. People are interested in the history of their own locality— their village, town, city, county, or region—but not often are they interested to such an extent that the sale of your book will pay you fully in dollars and cents for the time, effort, and expense involved in preparing it. You will have, however, the satisfaction of being the most recent—perhaps the only—chronicler of that bit of American soil you call "home." You will be a public benefactor of first importance. The community will be indebted to you for all time. In addition to being a benefactor you may also be called a small scale philanthropist, for the publication of your history, once it is completed, may, instead of making a profit, actually cost you money.

The materialist will ask, "Why do people write local history, knowing in advance that it will take hours upon hours of research, and in the end produce no income?" The materialist, however, can hardly be expected to appreciate the answer that some local historians have given to the question of the why, when, and how of writing local history. A British writer of local history has summed up this "urge":

I am often asked the question: How does one begin to write the history of a village? And to this I give a very plain and direct answer, which is—To begin when you have fallen in love with a village and not before. You can fall in love with a pretty or attractive village just as you can, if you are a man, fall in love with a pretty or attractive woman. . . . In other words, the writing of a village history is an entirely high-class love-affair. . . . Do not think you will make money by compiling a village history: most historians live in an attic or cellar, sell matches in the street, and die in the workhouse, but do not despair. The fun of it is, simply enormous, and when once you get going it chases cross-word puzzles, the various football competitions and, dare I say it? bridge as well off the field. . . .

I hope to persuade you that the investigation of the history of any one of our

---

[2] Robert Luce, "Town and City Histories," *Granite Monthly* (Concord, N. H.), VII, 1884, pp. 306–327.

old villages, and the reconstruction of its past, is one of the most pleasant of pastimes, and one which can be worked at all the year round. It is not the high-brow affair you may think, and at the back of it lies love of home and country and the healthy desire to know something about them. . . .

It is, of course, by far the best if you write of your native village, or of one with which you have some family ties. If not your native village, it may be the old home of your wife, or even of your mother-in-law, or your best-loved aunt. Do not mind if it is a very small village, and do not say: 'I am sure this place has no history, because it is so small.' Every village has its history, and it is far better to select one about which little or nothing has so far been written.[3]

Another writer on the same subject suggests that

you take a house or bit of land, a road or a river or Indian treaty, as a nucleus; and as you read old books, newspapers, and letters; examine old maps, plans, and pictures; and as you talk with old residents—your facts form layer after layer around your centre; and as you compare and generalize and let your imagination flow over all, your house or bit of land, or road, or river, or Indian treaty grows and crystallizes into a shapely, lasting concretion of local history.

In choosing some nucleus for a study of local history, one cannot do better than begin with one's house or yard. One should trace back the several owner-ships to the original grant, discover what other buildings were ever on the place, with something about the earlier people who lived there: if Indians ever hunted on it or soldiers tramped on it; changes of topography; when adjacent roads were opened; and one's own family traditions. One incident will inevitably lead to another, fascinating facts will peep from every cover, and conversation will fol-low the trend. All one's finds should be firmly held in place by the little rivets of accurate names and dates.[4]

Almost any local history, just so it is carefully and accurately put together, is worth doing and preserving. A fine thing about writing a local history is that it can be as thorough or as sketchy as the compiler desires. No matter whether you perform your task completely or partially, you will find, as you progress, the satisfaction which comes from facts dove-tailing one another "until the whole narrative emerges, clear, compact and concrete, and becomes surrounded by memories and traditions asso-ciated with the poetry and emotions of the home."[5]

It is not intended that the writer of local history should follow blindly the suggested procedure in chapter VIII—"One has to cut one's coat according to one's cloth." You may be interested in a particular phase of local history—economic, social, religious, educational, or what not. Nevertheless, you should give sufficient attention to what might be called the general history of your community to provide a fitting back-ground for the special aspect which interests you and you should have some sort of a guide to direct your steps toward that end.

---

[3] A. L. Humphreys, *How to Write a Village History* (Reading, England, 1930), 7–8.
[4] Editorial, *Scribner's Magazine* (New York), XLVIII, 1910, p. 250.
[5] Humphreys, *Village History*, 39.

It is hoped that the following pages will tempt you to venture along the enchanting byways of your local history. Should you feel that you would like the help of others in your adventure, you will find some suggestions at the end of the volume which may assist you in securing such aid.

PART I

GATHERING MATERIAL
FOR LOCAL HISTORY

Chapter I

SOURCES OF INFORMATION FOR LOCAL HISTORY AND WHERE TO FIND THEM

Historians like to talk about original and secondary sources. These are no mysterious or frightful bugbears. Original sources include all material which has been preserved from the period you wish to study—written or printed documents, conversations with people who actually lived at the time you are describing, and physical survivals such as mounds, buildings, and relics. Secondary sources are those written by individuals who have studied the original sources.

It is obvious that the original sources, if one can find them, are more nearly accurate than later writings based upon them. They may, however, be more difficult to understand and often will have less meaning than the secondary material, which is, after all, a more finished product on which the other fellow has already done the spade work. The danger in using the secondary material alone is that it represents someone else's interpretation of the original and this may or may not be a correct interpretation. Even with original sources one must sift and weigh and take into account "the probable opportunity of the author to know his facts, his liability to prejudice, etc. In the use of secondary sources, still greater caution is necessary, for here we have merely an interpretation of the originals, and all men" are apt to err—to misinterpret, either consciously or unconsciously to "understate or exaggerate."[1]

It is well, therefore, to bear in mind the distinction between original and secondary sources. It is also well to remember that for general background, secondary sources such as national, regional or state histories, or even articles in the *Encyclopedia Britannica* and the *Dictionary of American History* will serve as excellent introductions to your subject and help you place dates and events in their proper sequence.

Before reading on in this chapter you are advised to examine carefully chapter VIII entitled "A Model Outline for Local History." This will give some idea of the field you will have to cover and will suggest many of the possible sources of information which you will need to look for.

Among the chief sources for your information will be (1) published histories of your locality and nearby localities, whether village, town, city, county, region, or state, (2) family histories and biographies, (3) military records, (4) directories, whether county, city, telephone, commercial, or fraternal, (5) maps, (6) atlases and gazetteers, (7) accounts of

---

[1] "Suggestions to Local Historians," State Historical Society of Wisconsin, *Bulletin of Information* No. 12, December, 1899, p. 2.

travelers, (8) anniversary addresses and sermons, (9) photographs, (10) the stories and reminiscences of old residents, (11) private letters, diaries, and account books, (12) keepsakes, heirlooms, and relics, (13) local newspapers and periodicals, (14) census reports, (15) abstracts and title deeds, (16) surveyors' notes, (17) school records, (18) public records of all sorts —village, town, city, county, and state, (19) business records, (20) church registers, denominational minutes and reports, and (21) cemetery inscriptions. These may be either published or unpublished materials.

An examination of this list reveals the fact that items 1 through 9 might be called library and general sources, and are to be found, for the most part, either in the local library or in the possession of persons and organizations in the community. They will be discussed in this chapter. Items 10 through 12, which are in some way related to old residents, are considered in the next chapter. Item 13, the local newspaper and the periodical, is treated in a separate chapter. Items 14 through 18 deal with government affairs or public records and are discussed in chapter IV. The remaining three, 19, 20, and 21, are considered last.

LIBRARY AND GENERAL SOURCES

At an early date you should consult your local library or historical society library, if one exists in your vicinity. When once your purpose is made known the resources of the library will usually be placed at your service. Often librarians have had requests of the same kind from others who have desired to investigate some phase of the history of the locality. If your library has been in existence for some years and if it has had farsighted librarians, no doubt it will have a collection of books, newspapers, clippings, reports, and the like which can easily become your initial nest egg. Prepare to do a lot of examining of the library catalogue, a great deal of leafing through volumes, and a long process of note taking. Having absorbed some information on the subject, you will begin to be able to speak intelligently of your community's past. From this beginning you will perhaps also have gained some idea of the location of other sources of information and about this, your librarian may be able to give you sound advice. A librarian is, or should be, more than a mere custodian of books. Approach your librarian considerately and tactfully and ask his or her advice with regard to all possible material. He or she will be glad to help you.

Whenever you get a "lead" or a suggestion as to where further material can be found, write it down in a notebook (preferably a loose-leaf one that can be later arranged alphabetically) or on cards. It is better to write things down immediately instead of wondering later, "Was it John Brown or James Brown who wrote that? And was it page twenty-seven or seventy?" It is best to use but one size of paper in taking notes or copying excerpts. Specific directions regarding this important phase of gather-

4

ing material will be found in chapter VII.[2] Above all, remember that you will have to read a great deal more than you will want to record and much more than you will later use, but since it is easier to discard than to backtrack and fill in, the formula of too much is preferable to the one of not enough.

VILLAGE, TOWN, AND CITY HISTORIES

You should early become acquainted with what your like-minded predecessors have written and published on your own locality or nearby localities. Such material of previous gleaners in the field may be in printed form, in books, pamphlets, periodicals, or newspaper articles, or even still in manuscript. Do not be discouraged if you find nothing devoted exclusively to your own community. Look for the history of a town a few miles away for it may contain revealing paragraphs about your own town or county. It may point out, for example, that the early residents of your locality, lacking certain trading facilities at home, drove ten or twenty miles to the nearby town to do their shopping. Your town may be compared with the nearby town. From reading the local history of a nearby town you may learn, to your surprise, that the pioneers of the neighboring town regarded the pioneers of your town—perhaps your own ancestors— as cranks, gamblers, and drunkards, headed straight for perdition. Don't become unduly alarmed. Remember that everything in print is not necessarily true. Make a note of the statement, and attempt to discover whether it is based on fact. Remember, too, that where there was so much smoke there may also have been a little fire.

Perhaps the difference of opinion arose because of jealousy, perhaps because your town many years ago got the county seat and courthouse after a long and bitter struggle with your mud-slinging neighbor. Some of the pioneers were especially adept at name-calling and contemporary journalism was filled with it. In 1872 the editor of the Leavenworth *Commercial* referred to Kansas City, his down-river rival, as "that blustering, impotent Sodom at the mouth of the Kaw, that over-grown village whose every foot of territory is carpeted with three-ply mortgages, that night-old fungus whose whole life is bound up in moneyed exhalations of an Eastern dung-hill, and which . . . is rapidly passing into that decay which presages death."[3]

Town histories are most numerous in the older parts of our country, though certain Middle Western states are not far behind. By 1900 New England alone had about 1,100 town and county histories published. By 1915 Michigan had about 175 state, county, and local histories. It is too bad that there are so few bibliographies of local history and none which is complete. Some ancient ones have been prepared by the New

---

[2] See below, pages 93–101.
[3] Kansas City *Times*, July 25, 1872.

York State Library for Maine, Connecticut and New York. Major Otis G. Hammond, Director of the Historical Society of New Hampshire has compiled an excellent bibliography of the histories of New Hampshire towns. Would that there were more such.[4]

To help you learn what town, county, or family histories exist, it is advisable for you to become acquainted with the various bibliographies and printed catalogues on this subject. You can secure from Goodspeed's Bookshop, 18 Beacon Street, Boston, Massachusetts, a *Catalogue of Genealogies and Local History*. This is issued every two or three years and lists only the books which the famous bookstore has in stock at the time. Their stock is very large, however, as is shown in the catalogue, which generally lists thousands of family and local histories. By studying this catalogue you will find numerous suggested titles to aid you in your local research.

Genealogists and writers of family histories have contributed a great deal to the writing of local history and to compiling bibliographies on the subject. The *New England Historical and Genealogical Register*, begun in 1847, has published more than ninety volumes. It is not confined to New England alone as its title might indicate. Here and there can be found occasional valuable items of a local history nature. The Index to Genealogical Periodicals[5] indexes local histories as well. Doane lists a number of other genealogical periodicals and indexes which may be consulted for local history items. Many of these, however, can be consulted only in libraries containing large genealogical collections, such as Washington, D. C., New York, Philadelphia, Boston, Chicago, Seattle, San Francisco, Los Angeles, Denver, and other large cities.[6]

You may find local history books and articles indexed in *Writings on American History*, begun in 1904 by Ernest C. Richardson and Anson E. Morse for the year 1902, continued the following year for 1903 by Andrew C. McLaughlin, William A. Slade, and Ernest D. Lewis, and then con-

---

[4] Gilbert H. Doane, *Searching for Your Ancestors* (New York, 1937), 69.

[5] Edited by Donald L. Jacobus and published in 1932 at New Haven. *The American Genealogist* continues the Jacobus index and keeps it up to date.

[6] A few of the more important genealogical indexes are: (1) Munsell *List of Titles of Genealogical Articles in American Periodicals and Kindred Works*, 165 pages, 1899; (2) *Alphabetical Index of American Genealogies and Pedigrees*, 245 pages, 1886; (3) *Index to American Genealogies and Genealogical Material Contained in all Works such as Town Histories, Local Histories, Historical Societies, Publications, Biographies, Historical Periodicals and Kindred Works, Alphabetically Arranged*, by Daniel S. Durrie, published at Albany in five editions, 1868, 1878, 1886, 1895, and 1900; (4) *Munsell's Genealogical Index*, 1933 and later, which is really the sixth edition of Durrie's work; (5) *The Grafton Index of Books and Magazine Articles on History, Genealogy, and Biography Printed in the United States on American Subjects during the Year 1909* (New York, 1910); other good indexes are by Savage, Farmer, and Pope.

In addition to the genealogical periodicals given above, the following are very good: (1) *New York Genealogical and Biographical Record*, 1870 to date; (2) and for the South, the *Virginia Magazine of History and Biography* and the *William and Mary College Quarterly*.

tinuing annually from 1908 on by Grace Gardner Griffin under the auspices of the American Historical Association. Each volume contains thousands of items gathered from printed sources throughout the country. This index is undoubtedly the best in its field, but it goes back only to 1902.

A. P. C. Griffin has an excellent bibliography of American Historical Societies which indexes articles in magazines and proceedings. This was originally published with the 1905 *Annual Report of the American Historical Association*. Another work, the Channing, Hart, and Turner *Guide*, by no means so inclusive, can be consulted in most small libraries.[7] Many state historical societies publish magazines and these often print, at least annually, a cumulative table of contents of the articles which have appeared in the various issues. Such a table can sometimes be secured for the asking. Obtain one if possible, for it may be of great help in finding articles about localities and topics in which you may be interested. If not consult the catalogue of your historical society library. It may have these articles listed even if it has no printed table of contents or complete index. Sooner or later you will probably come to the point where you will agree with the historian, Dixon Ryan Fox, who wrote: "The bibliographical guides to local history in the United States are not so numerous or so complete as one might wish."[8]

You may be annoyed when you discover titles of books you want to consult and find that your local library cannot supply them. If this is the case you will find it advisable to join some one or more of the historical and genealogical societies of your state or even a society somewhat distant from your home. Many such societies allow their members the privilege of borrowing books. One writer on this problem offers the following assurance:

Membership fees are not high in these societies, considering the advantages which are offered. The New England Historical and Genealogical Society offers the use of its library, one of the largest of the kind in the country, to its membership, and books may be borrowed by mail by payment of postage both ways, which, under library privileges with the Post Office Department, is a small amount. This offers the facilities of this large library to any member, and though

---

[7] Edward Channing, Albert Hart, and Frederick J. Turner, *Guide to the Study and Reading of American History* (Revised . . . edition. Boston, 1912). This contains bibliographies on local and state history, biographies, gazetteers, travel, etc. Even the small local library or high school library is likely to have this volume, as it is widely used.

[8] Fox, "Local Historical Societies in the United States," *Canadian Historical Review* VIII, 1932, p. 267. Fox mentions Franklin F. Holbrook, *Survey . . .* as a good index.

Other general historical indexes might be mentioned: (1) Edith M. Coulter, *Guide to Historical Bibliographies* (University of Chicago Press, 1927), 104 pages; (2) Edith M. Coulter and M. Gerstenfeld, *Historical Bibliographies* (University of California Press, 1935), 206 pages; and (3) Henry P. Beers, *Bibliographies in American History: Guide to Materials for Research* (New York, 1942), 487 pages.

For other data about historical magazines and periodicals see chapter III.

he may live in the most isolated section of the nation he is as near a first class library as he is to his mail box.

Not all books of course are open to borrowing privileges. Some are too valuable to be sent out and, in the case of reference books, the call for their use is too constant to allow their being taken from the library. But the number of borrowable books is great. . . .[9]

If this idea appeals to you, it is best to approach your own state historical society first, since it probably has the largest collection of books unobtainable in your local library. Occasionally distant libraries are unwilling to loan books to individuals, but are willing to loan them to libraries in your community which in turn allow them to be used in the building or even taken home. This inter-library loan system, as it is called, is very extensive, especially among university and college libraries. If you are unable to get the books you need, consult your local librarian about this system.[10]

COUNTY HISTORIES

County history has perhaps come in for more condemnation than any other type of historical writing. There are several reasons for this. One is that the sources are not easy to secure because of the haphazard method in which public records have been kept. The more important reason is that county histories have been, almost without exception, the products of commercial enterprise, exhibiting "the marked defects characteristic of that type of publication."[11] Fox states that "throughout the country unnumbered tons of county histories weigh down the library shelves, but they are much too often the work of commercial companies employing cheap literary labour to accumulate impressive bulk . . . ."[12]

About fifty years ago many county histories began to be published. In fact, these were published wherever the promoters felt the population was "dense" enough (giving the word *dense* either of its meanings) to provide a good buying public. Works of this sort are easily identified by the space they devote to the "leading citizens" of the period (leading only, quite often, because each of them had the ready cash to pay for the page or two devoted to himself).

In spite of the low esteem in which county histories of the commercial sort are held, you may, nevertheless, consider yourself fortunate if your county was dense enough thirty to fifty years ago to have had one published. Along with the unfortunate chaff which such a work is likely to contain, will also be found a great deal that is worthwhile. If it proves to

---

[9] Oscar F. Stetson, *The Art of Ancestor Hunting* (Brattleboro, Vermont, 1936), 50.

[10] Another means of securing distant material through the use of photography will be discussed later in the section dealing with public records. See below, pages 48–69.

[11] Franklin F. Holbrook, "Some Possibilities of Historical Field Work," *Minnesota History Bulletin* (St. Paul), II, 1917, p. 77 n.

[12] Fox, "Local Historical Societies," 267.

be entirely worthless, at least you will have examined a horrible example and know what to avoid. If you do use such a history you must remember that all statements, dates, biographies, etc., will have to be verified before you accept them. Do not take too seriously the eulogistic statements made of the "leading citizens" of an earlier generation.[13] Yet even their lives will be found useful for portraying a fairly reliable picture of early pioneer conditions, reasons for migrating, political sidelights, social conditions, and customs.

As with village, town, and city histories, try to locate the neighboring county histories for an area of twenty to fifty miles on all sides of your own county. The one to the south may have nothing to say of your community, but the one to the north may devote many pages to it. The histories of counties older than your own should be of more value than those of younger counties. Unless the pioneers of your community were of a racial or language stock different from that of their neighbors, it will often be found that the early social, economic, political, and religious conditions of the entire area were very much the same. Nearby county histories may give you this background, though you should not take for granted the common background without verifying it.

STATE AND REGIONAL HISTORIES

A Wisconsin historian says that it is "the absence of a feeling for general historical results, on the part of workers in the local field, which makes so much local history work comparatively barren."[14] It is to avoid this criticism that you should read widely in the histories of your state and region. When you discuss in your local history the part your community took in regional, state, or perhaps national affairs, you should know whether or not it tallies with what the reliable general histories of your state have to say on the matter. Discussions of great movements such as those concerned with the slavery question, woman suffrage, or prohibition, which may have disrupted your community, will be found in the state and regional histories. There you will gain an understanding of the local situation by reading about the particular movement in its wider aspects. If you discover after diligent search, that your community took quite a different attitude on a question of regional, state, or national importance from that which prevailed nearby, try to account for the difference in viewpoint by looking for local statements and utterances on the subject. Things of this sort are what make your community "different" and, whenever differences are to be found, they should be

---

[13] Doane warns against compilations of biographical sketches made for subscribers. Some of these works have much good material in them, but unfortunately it is impossible to depend upon them. There are many such in most libraries. *Searching for Your Ancestors*, preface, x.

[14] Joseph Schafer, "Documenting Local History," *Wisconsin Magazine of History* (Madison), V, 1921, p. 3.

enlarged upon and an attempt made to explain the how, when, where and why of the special situation. Sometimes the origin of the difference may be traced to some racial, linguistic, or religious factor.[15]

Good histories of your state should be easy to locate. Find out from your librarian or your local high school history teacher which one or ones are considered the best. The teacher, especially, should be qualified to know, for many states, particularly in the Middle West, require the teaching of the history of the state in the public high schools.[16] Regional histories may be more difficult to locate, but histories have been written of natural areas, such as the Old Northwest, the Pacific Northwest, the Pacific Coast, the Great Plains, the Old South, the Old West, and New England.[17]

Closely akin to state and regional histories, and equally important, are the histories of movements, institutions, and periods. Delve into a good history of colonial social institutions, Indian relations, the slavery question, the settlement of the West, the Missouri Compromise, and the border warfare, overland trade, the Civil War, Carpetbag and Negro rule, the mining frontier, the building of the railroads, transportation, steamboating, the Granger movement, capital and labor, immigration, or any one of a number of different topics closely related to your locality, and you will obtain an understanding and background of these movements, institutions, and periods as they affected your community. As Joseph Schafer says, you will be obtaining "a feeling for general historical results" and be able to relate your local history to state and national history.[18]

---

[15] Schafer, in a study of Wisconsin history, states: "The correlation of economic, social, racial, religious, and political factors yields some striking results. For example, the conversion of German Democrats to Republicanism proceeded rapidly in communities of Protestants, slowly in Catholic neighborhoods. The explanation is, the attitude of American Know Nothings toward Catholics and the persistence of the fear that Republicanism harbored a Know Nothing element." Schafer writes also of a town which shifted abruptly from Democratic in 1856 to Republican in 1860 because it "had received during these years about one hundred Bohemian families who were readers of *Slavie*, Carl Jonas' newspaper published at Racine in the Lincoln interest. Previously its German and Irish families, combined, constituted a majority over the American, English, and Welsh families, who were prevailingly Republican." Both quotations are from Joseph Schafer, "A Rural Life Survey of a Western State," *The Trans-Mississippi West, Papers Read at a Conference Held at the University of Colorado, June 18–June 21, 1929* (Boulder, 1930), 303–304, 304–305.

[16] This movement began about the time of the World War. In 1924 a chronicler of the subject wrote that state and local history courses had been introduced into the high schools of many states, especially those of the Mississippi Valley, including Texas, Arkansas, Kansas, North and South Dakota, Minnesota, Michigan, Wisconsin, Ohio, Indiana, Illinois, and Missouri. By 1924, Missouri had done more than any other state and three-fourths of its high schools had such courses. Bruce E. Mahan, *State and Local History in the High Schools*, State Historical Society of Iowa, *Bulletin of Information Series*, No. 12 (1924). The state of New York has an extensive ten volume history and Ohio is completing the publication of a six volume series, *The History of the State of Ohio*. In Pennsylvania candidates for teaching certificates must present a course in Pennsylvania history.

[17] An example is Walter P. Webb, *The Great Plains* (Boston, 1931).

Another and more colorful, though less accurate, method of obtaining the desired background is through the reading of historical novels which deal with these subjects. Of the making of books there is no end, and this applies especially to historical novels. Your librarian will indicate some of the better ones or may show you his index of fiction which lists historical novels.

SOCIOLOGICAL MATERIAL

While the local historian is primarily interested in recreating his home town as it used to be in terms of streets, buildings, organizations, important persons, and the changes that have taken place as new people, new industries, and changes in relation to other towns have influenced its development, the sociologist, while interested in the same questions, is more concerned with why these changes took place when they did, what underlying processes and causes brought them into the picture of a changing community. The sociologist is interested in the family, in groups and classes, in the attitudes and prejudices of people and their influence upon the "mental mobility" of communities, i.e., whether they accept or resist social change, whether they have difficulty in adjusting to the new and strange. He studies much the same material and his work is helpful. He perhaps does more interviewing. He studies names of peoples, folk-lore and legends, peculiar social customs and how they have become a part of habit without leaving any clear trace of their origins.

A sociological analysis of the history of a town is therefore concerned with meanings and processes as inferred from attitudes which themselves must be understood as growing out of the relationships among and between groups and persons who have status and prestige. An important person, or event, in a river town does not give rise to the same immediate and perceptible actions as the same type of person or event would in a seaport or isolated rural community. The social changes whether in attitudes, or in the general "personality," that is, importance of the town in the eyes of its own people or in the eyes of rival communities, must always be related to such things as social mobility, culture contact, and forces making for conservatism or liberalism which in turn are related to accessibility as in the valley, or isolation, as in the hills.

The local historian can profit by reading some sociological works. We are supplying a list in the following paragraphs. This is a long one so we suggest that you sample. Two excellent works are J. M. Williams, *An American Town* (1906) and the articles in W. F. Ogburn, ed., *American Society in Wartime* (1944).

A few hints and many illustrations of the methods which will aid the local historian to analyze the influences, forces, and processes, which contributed to development of his community may be found in such socio-

---

[18] The Channing, Hart, and Turner, *Guide* . . . , has extensive bibliographies in each of the fields mentioned above and in others as well.

logical works as: J. M. Williams, *An American Town*, A Sociological Analysis (1906); J. M. Williams, *The Expansion of Rural Life* (1926); Frank Goodwin, The Eastern Shore (Ph. D. Thesis MS., University of Pennsylvania, 1944); W. F. Ogburn, *Social Change* (1928); A. W. Calhoun, *A Social History of the American Family from Colonial Times to the Present* (1919); Donald Young, *American Minority Peoples* (1932); Walter Burr, *Community Leadership* (1929), especially chapter II; Allison Davis, Burleigh B. Gardner, Mary R. Gardner, *Deep South*, A Social Anthropological Study of Caste and Class, (1941), chapters IV, V, VI, VII, VIII; Clifford Shaw, *The Natural History of a Delinquent Career* (1931); Harry E. Barnes, *Society in Transition* (1939), chapters 12, 13; Dwight Sanderson, *The Rural Community* (1932); N. L. Sims (ed.) *The Rural Community, Ancient and Modern* (1920); J. M. Williams *Our Rural Heritage* (1925); R. D. McKenzie, *The Metropolitan Community* (1933); R. E. Park, E. W. Burgess, *The City* (1925); Albert Blumenthal, *Small Town Stuff* (1932); C. C. Zimmerman, *The Changing Community* (1938); Robert S. and Helen M. Lynd, *Middletown*, 2 vols. (1929, 1937); John Dollard, *Caste and Class in a Southern Town* (1937); Harvey W. Zorbaugh, *The Gold Coast and the Slum* (1929); Jesse Steiner, *The American Community in Action* (1928); W. F. Ogburn, M. Nimkoff, *Sociology* (1940), chapters 11, 12, 13, 14, 17; A. H. Hobbs, *Differentials in Internal Migration* (1941), chapter VIII; Clifford R. Shaw and Henry D. McKay, *Juvenile Delinquency and Urban Areas* (1942); W. Wallace Weaver, *West Philadelphia*, A Study of Natural Social Areas (1930); Kimball Young (ed.) *Social Attitudes* (1931); C. J. Galpin, *The Social Anatomy of a Rural Community* (1915); W. Lloyd Warner, "The American Town"; Louis Wirth, "The Urban Community"; Lowry Nelson, "Farms and Farming Communities," found in W. F. Ogburn (ed.) *American Society in Wartime* (1944).

This selected list of references is meant merely to orient the local historian in ways *sociologists* have tried to utilize historical materials, and is not to be regarded as an exhaustive bibliography. Such journals as the *American Journal of Sociology, Social Forces*, The *American Sociological Review, Rural Sociology*, and *Sociology and Social Research* will acquaint the writer of local history with intensive analytical studies of contemporary, and, occasionally, historical, community problems.

FAMILY HISTORIES AND BIOGRAPHIES

You are writing local history, not family history. Nevertheless, you will find that family histories and genealogies, if available, may be drawn upon for a good deal of information. Family histories are of all sorts and of all degrees of accuracy. Doane warns against the genealogies, some of them very pretentious, which have been gotten up often at great expense to satisfy family pride but without much regard for accuracy. Such books are never to be judged by their bindings or their size. A little checking will soon make it possible for you to judge their accuracy. Many small unpretentious genealogical pamphlets are more valuable than elaborate volumes with royal pedigrees and the pictures of crowned heads.[19]

Very few families of your community have family histories in published form. If you discover some they are likely to fall into one of two classes: a genealogical statement giving the bare facts of birth, marriage, residence, occupation, children, and death, or, and this is far more valuable, a rather complete sketch of each individual, especially those of the older generation, in addition to the bare facts. Here you may find considerable information about certain early pioneers or about persons of a later generation.

Fortunately some family historians and genealogists are excellent local historians and incorporate much community history in their works. If you are interested in writing local biography, family history, or genealogy as well as discovering data for histories of their localities, you might well consult as examples and illustrations of method Herbert B. Howe, *Jedediah Barber* (N. Y., 1939); Jeannette P. Nichols, *James Styles of Kingston and George Stuart of Schoolcraft* (Swarthmore, Pa., 1936); or Edward P. Cheyney, "Thomas Cheyney, A Chester County Squire: His Lesson for Genealogists," *Pennsylvania Magazine of History and Biography* (Philadelphia), LX, 1936, pp. 209–228.

If your community, like Topsy, "just growed" without any particular person or family taking an outstanding part, you may not want to go into any detail regarding individuals or families. If, however, your town or city had a recognized "founder" who played an active part in civic affairs, you may want to devote a chapter to him and his family.

Perhaps your community has had some man prominent enough in state or national affairs to have had a biography written about him, or he may have written and published an account of his own life. In either case, he is likely to have devoted several pages or even chapters to his parentage, his boyhood, and the part the community played in his active adult life. An autobiography is closer to the subject and background than a biography if the writer has not tried to gloss over unfavorable episodes or gild his own reputation.

MILITARY RECORDS

You will want to include an account of the part your community played in the wars of our country. Some of this information may be obtained from old settlers, but there are other sources where it can be gathered. Certain states, especially in the eastern half of our country, have attempted to gather the military records of former soldiers of the

---

[19] Doane, *Searching for Your Ancestors*, 64.

American Revolution who lived at some time within their boundaries.[20] Revolutionary records for most of the states may now be secured in printed forms, as may also many of the papers held by historical and genealogical societies.[21] In a number of cases these will contain information of a military nature as well as the rosters of soldiers.[22]

Information regarding the government departments and their published materials will be found in the section dealing with public records. Among non-official sources of information, are the publications of the Daughters of the American Revolution, who have been active since their organization in 1890 in gathering the records of Revolutionary soldiers and their descendants. One writer tells us that more than 200,000 lineages have been filed in D.A.R. headquarters showing descent from Revolutionary soldier ancestors. The D.A.R. *Lineage Books* now number more than 150 volumes, each containing a thousand lineages. Indexes have been issued for the first eighty volumes and others, no doubt, will eventually be published.[23] Since these *Lineage Books* can be consulted in many large libraries, you may be able to find the service which each known Revolutionary soldier of your community rendered from 1775 to 1783. In addition, many state branches of the D.A.R., as well as certain individual chapters have published books containing data about the Revolutionary ancestors of their members. Many of these works have lists of the soldiers and of their burial places, also abstracts of their wills and much valuable collateral material. The various state societies in many instances have complete records. In some cases they have sent typewritten copies to the Washington headquarters of the D.A.R. and to the library of their state. Since 1892 the National Society of the Daughters of the American Revolution has published a magazine known until 1913 as the *American Monthly Magazine*, and after that as the *Daughters of the American Revolution Magazine*. Almost every number contains material of interest, biographies of the soldiers, descriptions of memorials, transcripts of marriage records, obituary indexes, probate records and the like.[24]

---

[20] Indiana has recently published a *Roster of Soldiers and Patriots of the American Revolution Buried in Indiana*, compiled and edited by Mrs. Roscoe C. O'Byrne, and 407 pages in length. No less than 1,394 such soldiers are buried in Indiana. *The Official Roster of the Soldiers of the American Revolution Buried in the State of Ohio* was compiled under the direction of the D.A.R. of Ohio in 1929 and is one volume, which is 447 pages in length, and a second, entitled *The Official Roster of the Soldiers of the American Revolution Who Lived in the State of Ohio*, compiled by Mrs. Orville D. Dailey in 1938, which is 436 pages long. See Doane, *Searching for Your Ancestors*, 236–242 for a bibliography of lists and rosters of Revolutionary soldiers.

[21] Frank Allaben, *Concerning Genealogies* (New York, 1904), 21.

[22] Little has been done, however, with the records of the wars following the Revolution "because soldiers and sailors in the later wars were more standardized and are more easily ascertained from the files of the various government departments, such as those of the War and Navy and the Pension Office at Washington." Stetson, *Art of Ancestor Hunting*, 46.

[23] Doane, *Searching for Your Ancestors*, 158, 172.

[24] *Ibid.*, 173–176.

Besides the D.A.R. the past half century has seen the birth of many other patriotic organizations and hereditary societies with local or national membership. Prominent among these are the Colonial Dames of America, the Sons of the American Revolution, the Daughters of the Revolution, the Sons of the Revolution, the Society of the Colonial Wars, the Daughters of Founders and Patriots, the Society of Mayflower Descendants, the United Daughters of the Confederacy, the United Spanish War Veterans, the Veterans of Foreign Wars, and the American Legion. Some of these publish yearbooks and magazines which may contain occasional articles of military interest.

There may still be some Civil War veterans living in your neighborhood and they or their children may be able to tell you where you can secure the records of local veterans. The local organization which has charge of decorating the soldiers' graves on Decoration or Memorial Day may have detailed records. Many veterans of the subsequent wars will still be living and only need to be consulted. Some posts may have had their records published. A number of the states have set up headquarters for veterans and patriotic organizations at their state capitals and such headquarters are in a position to supply information. Still other states, such as Texas and California, have patriotic organizations which perpetuate the memory of great events in their own state history. Several states have published special bulletins on the subject of that community or locality's participation in the First World War.[25] To be complete such a record should supply the names of men and women who went away to fight or to work in various capacities, the names of those who gave their lives, the effect of the war on the agricultural, commercial, and industrial life of the community, any special war work that was done, the local regulation of food supplies and its observance by the people, and some mention of the manner in which news of the Armistice was celebrated.

If in your research you should discover that your community was at any time the scene of a battle, large or small, you may want to devote considerable space to it, especially if the events have not been written up by other historians. From the various sources of these wars, and especially from the many volumes of the *Official Records of the War of the Rebellion*, you may be able to do a valuable piece of original research.

DIRECTORIES

What would you not give for a directory of your town, city, or county when it was five, ten or twenty years old? A complete list of all citizens, together with their occupations and addresses, would be invaluable. Un-

---

[25] *Bulletin* No. 10 (1919) of the Michigan Historical Commission gives an outline (pages 16–30), to be followed on the subject of "Our County in the Great War." Similar bulletins were published immediately after the war by the Indiana Historical Commission and the Pennsylvania War Historical Commission. See Appendix.

fortunately, directories were not published until the population had grown to considerable size, organizations had grown up, commerce had developed, and telephones were introduced. Such publications are of all sorts—state, county, city, commercial, fraternal, or telephone. The older directories are useful in determining addresses of prominent people, their years of residence in the locality, their occupations, the business firms of earlier years, areas developed for residence purposes, transportation facilities of the local and nearby towns and villages. They often contain paid advertisements which reveal much of the business, economic, and social life of previous decades. Old county and city directories may be located often in the offices of banks, lawyers, real estate men, and abstractors of titles. The library, too, generally has a collection.

Commercial, fraternal, and religious organizations may have published directories of their memberships at various times. These are most likely to be found in the hands of the secretaries of the organizations concerned though old volumes are apt to turn up almost anywhere and certain ones may be preserved by your historical society.

The telephone, which was the sensation of the Centennial Exhibition at Philadelphia in 1876 where it was first displayed, began to be introduced in large cities within a year or two later. Kansas City, for example, began to use telephones in September, 1877. By the end of 1879 it had about 50 telephones while New York at the time had about 250. In 1884 there were 427 phones in Kansas City while St. Louis had 1,195.[26] Since the telephone directory goes back only a few decades, most telephone exchanges keep a file of their old directories; some libraries also have such a file.

Many states issue, officially or otherwise, rosters or directories in which all state and county officials are listed. Often these can be obtained for the asking by writing to the office of the secretary of state. Your local library, bank, or newspaper office, however, is almost certain to have one. In this you will find definite information about where and to whom to write for historical data you may want from officials. Usually these state directories are not so comprehensive as the one for Vermont which supplies alphabetically arranged descriptions of all the communities in the state, including the names of the principal citizens and officers and their occupations.[27]

Other sources for directories are in the old county atlases and plat books. In these individual biographical sketches of the "leading citizens" are generally of the county history type and should be accepted in a critical spirit.

[26] Roy Ellis, *A Civic History of Kansas City, Missouri* (Springfield, Missouri, 1930), 120–122 and *passim*.
[27] Doane, *Searching for Your Ancestors*, 130.

MAPS

Before you have gone very far in your research you will have discovered a need for maps to locate unfamiliar places and to help supply you with a fuller significance of what you have read. You will also find yourself on the lookout for good maps with which to illustrate your own book. Often the older the map is, the better it will serve your purpose.

Your state historical society, the state library, or the university library no doubt, has a large collection of maps. The North Carolina Historical Commission, for example, possesses more than 1,700 maps, for the state as a whole, for each of the 100 counties, various towns, roads, canals, and railroads, for the boundary lines between North Carolina and other states and between various counties, the coast, and for other subjects, dating from the sixteenth century to the present. Some of these are especially useful in historical research. For instance, John Collet's map of North and South Carolina, 1770, not only shows the coast, rivers, mountains, counties, towns, roads, and other items you would expect to find, but also includes churches, many of the more important plantations (including the names of the planters), and other valuable information. If practicable, make a personal visit to see what maps, suitable for your purpose, are available in such collections. If you cannot go, write for your information, asking the cost of photostats. While you probably will not be able to afford the cost of photostats of complete large-scale maps of the entire state, it may be possible to secure at small cost photostats of merely those sections which include your own locality.

In addition to the map collections located in university libraries, state libraries, and state historical societies, both the Library of Congress and the National Archives have large map collections which should be consulted.

Then there is the Director of the United States Geological Survey, Washington, D.C., who has for sale large topographic maps on a scale of about one inch to the mile. These show altitudes, contours, drainage, streams, lakes, ponds, roads, farmhouses, churches, cemeteries, schools, private roads, railroads, county, township and U. S. section lines, triangulation stations, bench marks, and other information. These are beautifully and accurately gotten up and are usually in two or three colors. If you write for a map be sure to say exactly what you want, indicating the state, county or part of the county. It may be advisable to write first and inquire what maps are available for the state in which you live. In answer, you will receive a folded map which indicates the counties and areas where surveys have already been made. Geologic folios of certain regions are available. Each folio includes maps showing the topography, geology, underground structure, and mineral deposits of the area mapped and several pages of descriptive text. Most of the topographic maps are on sheets about $16\frac{1}{2}$ by 20 inches in size. The scale varies from

17

one inch to the half-mile, one inch to the mile, to one inch to two miles. Although topographic maps are not available for all areas of the United States, they can be supplied for most.

Often your state geological survey at the state capital can furnish you with information about county topographic maps which the state may have made. The state government often makes special maps of metropolitan areas and of certain mineral regions.

Aside from these, there are various other maps which may be consulted or obtained. The local real estate firms, banks, the public library, and lawyers' offices are good places to go for consultation. If there are none in these places, probably the abstractors will show you their maps or inform you of where they can be bought or borrowed. County and township maps are frequently mounted to hang on the wall and are a yard or so square. They show land ownership of the time the map was printed. Such maps are published at intervals of from ten to twenty years at which time the information is brought up to date. The older ones are often rolled up and put away when the new one is bought, but for your purpose the older maps are the most valuable.

In metropolitan or city areas it is often possible to obtain maps which show highways and main arteries, bridges, railroads and railroad yards, electric lines, parks, cemeteries, universities, and other main physical structures as well as natural geographic features such as hills, rivers, and lakes, Maps of this sort can be bought, but much the same information can be found on the enlarged road maps of large cities and their environs, which may be obtained free at any filling station.

Aside from locating unfamiliar places, you should know how to interpret a map in your local history research. An authority asserts that he who would write the history of a community "must master its geological formation and note the influence of this on the soil and on other matters which bear on the lives of men."[28] Such natural features as hills, valleys, swamps, mountains, rivers, lakes, and streams are generally the original force which determines the location of villages and towns. Their influence is, of course, being constantly modified by man's increasing control over the natural environment. For example, pioneer cabins were built in the shadow of hills to provide protection against the elements, but with the improved methods for heating, houses can now be built and comfortably heated on the top of a hill. An examination of the topographic map of your community suggests why the settlement began as it did. Villages tended to grow up where transportation by land or water was readily available. When buying land, settlers were primarily interested in opportunities to market such products as the land would grow.

The natural physical features of a region often determined the type of settler attracted. Four Wisconsin counties, stretching seventy-two miles

---

[28] John Fortescue, *The Writing of History* (New York, 1926), 4.

from the Illinois boundary along the shore of Lake Michigan, have been intensively studied. The southern two counties had open land for the most part while the northern two were mostly heavily wooded. This fact proved to be a persistent, deep-running influence in the history of the region. The author of this study shows how the early settlers, Yankees from western New York and Vermont went into the prairie interior, while later German immigrants undertook the gruelling labor of the wooded regions rather than running the risk of being marooned in the interior. The result was that the Yankees became prosperous while their German neighbors, for a number of years, remained poor.[29]

This study illustrates the importance of topography upon land settle-ment. It indicates, too, how topography has persistently influenced the later history of the area, even to its participation in the Civil War.

With a thorough knowledge of the natural physical features, revealed by a topographic map, you can enter imaginatively into the human motives which governed the process of settlement and farm-making fifty, or a hundred, years ago. Thus the miller might have been attracted by a falls in a stream while a site on a favorable riverside probably drew the trader. In Wisconsin, perhaps as elsewhere, open land attracted the Yankee while the immigrants took what was left.

Study a map of a town or city and you will see how the topography determined the location of roads, bridges, railroads, electric lines, rail-road yards, industrial property, residential sections, and parks. These man-made physical structures, as the sociologist will tell you, have been of great importance in dividing the community into cultural areas, nationality areas, racial areas, and the like. Cultural areas are usually designated by changing boundaries. What was Quality Row fifty years ago may be Poverty Row today. You will not do your local history jus-tice until you understand how your community has been affected by geo-graphic factors, such as soil and other natural resources, climatic condi-tions, topography and elevation contour, and geographic location. Much of this can be learned from a wise use of maps.

ATLASES AND GAZETTEERS

Closely akin to maps are county and township atlases and plat books. These are still being published, but like maps, the older they are the better they are for your use. In addition to their large-scale maps, these volumes often contain historical statements about the township, village, and county which are valuable. Like the county history, many of these

---

[29] Schafer, *Trans-Mississippi West*, 300–303. Schafer draws his conclusions from a very thorough and "scientific" study, *Four Wisconsin Counties, Prairie and Forest* (1927). In making the study, "the hope was entertained that, by placing a small community 'under the microscope' historical processes of general interpretative value might be identified, much as the scientist demonstrates life principles by examining drops of blood or infinitesi-mal particles of tissue." *Ibid.*, 292.

atlases were made possible by the biographical sketches paid for, of course, by "prominent men." They are generally found in the same places as county maps and should be used with due caution for dates and facts.

Gazetteers are of a different nature and are excellent sources of historical data. They were variously called emigrants' directories, companion handbooks of travel, emigrants' guides, pocket registers, geographies, "almanacks," and directories, but their collective name is gazetteers. Some appeared as early as 1775, but they seem to have reached their heyday in the generation which followed 1815. Those published for western states were intended as guides for travelers or immigrants. They were usually compiled by persons who had made the trip themselves and thus wrote from first hand experience. A number were written by Englishmen who failed to see the best side of their American cousins and who never could understand the lack of deference shown themselves. These gazetteers are becoming increasingly scarce and you will probably not be able to locate one except in the library of some large city, university, or state historical society. The Channing, Hart, and Turner *Guide* lists sixty of the best.

Gazetteers are of value in fixing local names and giving details of routes of travel, prices of commodities, rates of fare, lists of merchants, traveling accommodations, and similar information. If you are fortunate enough to live in a town which was located on one of the old trails leading west, such as the Santa Fé or the Oregon, you may find that your town in its infancy was quite accurately described in one of these old gazetteers.

Some state gazetteers have been published. The United States Geological Survey has issued in its *Bulletins*, gazetteers for the states of Colorado, Connecticut, Delaware, Oklahoma, Kansas, Maryland, Massachusetts, New Jersey, Rhode Island, Texas, Utah, Virginia, and West Virginia. These are compiled by Henry Gannett.

ACCOUNTS OF TRAVELERS

From the discovery of the New World to the present, men and women from Europe and from other parts of the world have visited our country and have written their impressions of it. If your community is off the beaten track, you may be inclined to believe that travelers rarely if ever came there. When you make an investigation, however, you will almost certainly find that at some time or other travelers, both foreign and American, have visited your locality and have published their impressions of it.

Descriptions of travelers vary widely in value. Some of them were well qualified to observe, while others were not; some honestly tried to present a fair picture, while others had a decided bias. Each was naturally conditioned by his own background, experience, and training, and would tend to see and record just those things he was looking for. Some of them liked what they saw; others received a definitely unfavorable impression.

Lists of travel accounts may be found in the bibliographies of general histories of the United States and in histories of the several states; in guides to American history such as that by Channing, Hart, and Turner; and in collections such as N. D. Mereness' edition of *Travels in the American Colonies* (New York, 1916). Your state library, the library of your state historical society, or state university, or some other large library can help you find such travel accounts.

ANNIVERSARY ADDRESSES AND SERMONS

You may also be able to locate anniversary addresses or sermons delivered long ago by a minister, lawyer, or other prominent citizen. Perhaps it was a Fourth-of-July oration in which the speaker with fiery patriotism not only "twisted the lion's tail," but told of the noble part his community had played in one or another of the wars of the country. Perhaps it was an anniversary commemorating the founding of the town, or a school, or a church, or a fraternal organization. Any of these occasions would give an opportunity for the introduction of some material on local history. Occasionally ministers of a generation or two ago wrote their sermons to be read later from their pulpits. Some of them used local illustrations to emphasize a lesson. If you can locate such a minister's "barrel" among any of his descendants, it may repay careful investigation to see what of historical interest it may yield. It may contain anniversary addresses, funeral orations of prominent citizens, or other items of interest. A few annivesay addresses may have been thought worthy of printing in the local newspaper, but the majority of them, if found at all, will probably be in manuscript form.

PHOTOGRAPHS AND PICTURES

Your research will not go on for long before you will begin to wish that you had not only maps but also pictures of some of the early residents, buildings, churches, and schools. Perhaps some individual organization has already made a collection of the period or some may even have been been published in the local newspaper. Old county histories abound in lithographic reproductions of "leading citizens" and their homes. Old county atlases and plat books often have them as well.

It is wise to find out from some of the oldest residents the names of the camera "fans" of a generation or two ago. In the attics of their descendants there may perhaps still be located the pictures of thirty, fifty, or even seventy years ago. The negatives of that time were on glass and may have been packed away in an old trunk, perhaps with the camera which took them. These negatives can still be used for printing new pictures. It is well to remember that photography was just beginning to come into use a century ago. Do not expect, therefore, to find any pictures earlier than about the middle of the last century or the time of the Civil War.

To secure illustrations of existing scenes you may be able to find some young man or woman who is experiencing the picture-taking urge, which seems to strike each of us at some time, and who, for a consideration, may be induced to take photographs of buildings which will not last many years longer, street scenes which will soon be changing, and other views which may occur to you. Perhaps your town or city has been photographed from the air. Such pictures are rather expensive to buy and to reproduce in a book, but they give an excellent bird's-eye view of the subject of your history. Old residents may have pictures of former persons of importance. It is a good idea to include some of these, especially of women, if for nothing else than to show the changing styles and to remind us that the earlier citizens, with all their good sense, nevertheless put up with hoop skirts, pantalettes, large and precariously-placed hats and hat-pins, and other such fol-de-rol.

You will want especially to include views of public buildings, churches, and schools which have long since been demolished or burned. Notice the landscape of some of these old pictures. Was the town of that period almost denuded of trees, due to its youth or the wood-burning stoves of our ancestors? Or were the streets overhung with maples, indicating the age of the town and the forethought and love of beauty of the earlier citizens? Notice the type and number of outhouses, barns, hog-pens, chicken-pens, wood-sheds, ice-houses, fruit-cellars, and summer kitchens. Also notice whether livestock wandered the streets at will, a common sight in many an American town and city up to the advent of the automobile. A historian of a central-western city wrote, as late as the year 1880, when this town's population was 132,000:

The old-fashioned Missouri hog, fitter for the race-track than for the pork-barrel . . . patrolled the streets and disputed the king's highway with the king and all his subjects. At night, when the hogs were off duty, a billion frogs in the green ponds at the bottom of the choicest unoccupied city lots told their troubles to the stars and saluted the rising sun with croaks of despair. In wet weather the town site was a sea of mud and in dry weather a desert of dust. There was no paving and the drainage was poor. A miserable breed of street cars, drawn by dissolute mules over a drunken track furnished the only means of street transportation by rail. The water supply made whiskey drinking a virtue and the gas was not of much better use than to be blown out. The population of the city included as fine a collection of ruffian brotherhood and sisterhood of the wild West as could well be imagined. Renegade Indians, demoralized soldiers, unreformed bush-whackers, and border ruffians, thieves, and thugs imported from anywhere, professional train-robbers of home growth, and all kinds of wrecks of the Civil War, gave the town something picturesquely harder to overcome than the hills and gulches of its topography.[30]

Pictures of your town of fifty years ago may reveal conditions as typical as the foregoing. On the Chinese theory that one picture is worth

---

[30] William Griffith, *History of Kansas City* (Kansas City, 1900) 106–107.

ten thousand words, you will want to include many pictures in your book. You will find the publishing of illustrations very expensive, however, unless a planograph method, to be explained later, is used to reproduce them.[31]

Finally, be sure to include a photograph of that pride of every ardent citizen's heart, the early fire engine and the volunteer fire company which operated it. While on this subject, let me remind you that a very interesting section of your book might be devoted to early fire engines and volunteer companies. Philadelphia had its first fire engine in 1718, New York City in 1730, St. Louis in 1822, Kansas City in 1867.

---

[31] See below, pages 155–156.

CHAPTER II

OTHER SOURCES OF INFORMATION—
OLD RESIDENTS, DIARIES, LETTERS, AND HEIRLOOMS

OLD RESIDENTS

BEFORE you have made much progress in your local history research you will be confronted by some would-be friend with the question, "Why are you reading all those books? Why don't you go to old Mr. Fenner or Grandma Stockwell? They know all about it." Well, these old residents don't know all about it, but they do know a great deal which can be of help to you. After all, octogenarians have memories rich in community lore. They themselves, or their fathers or grandfathers, were the settlers who shaped the patterns of community life. They have an inheritance of intimate knowledge and a fairly authentic eye for detail.

Some historians are quite skeptical about consulting old residents for information. One authority has observed: "The intelligence of the oldest inhabitant is not always as great as it should be, nor as it is alleged to be. No oldest inhabitant is ever as wise as he looks, nor as wise as he thinks he is."[1] Another notes that "experience has shown that each person usually knows accurately a small section over a brief period of time, and has vague but suggestive information concerning larger areas and extending over longer periods of time."[2] Still another has pointed out that "the typical town history is not of maximum usefulness, because it is based too exclusively upon data handed down by tradition."[3] It is this tradition—that unwritten information handed down to the old resident —that is the old resident's stock in trade.

Without the amusements and reading material that exist today, earlier generations used to sit around the hearth in the evenings and tell stories. They became skilled at making the most of the skeleton of their story, supplying and improvising such details, names, and even dates as were needed to produce the proper dramatic effect. As an experiment, a high school history class interviewed old residents and in some cases as many as eight versions of an Indian story were handed in by different students.[4]

---

[1] Humphreys, *How to Write a Village History*, 35.

[2] Vivien M. Palmer, *Field Studies in Sociology* (Chicago, 1928), 86.

[3] Joseph Schafer, *Wisconsin Domesday Book—Town Studies* (1924), I, 10.

[4] *Marion County in the Making*. This is a local history produced by the J. O. Watson Class of the Fairmont High School, West Virginia, in 1917. It is a notable book for several reasons: (1) It shows what a fine local history can be produced by students; (2) it is exceptionally well printed and illustrated; (3) the greater part of the material was gathered from the lips of old residents; and yet (4) "The Class . . . made every effort to present truth as truth, and legend as legend."

Yet tradition should neither be despised nor accepted literally. As historians realize, there is likely to be a germ of truth in every tradition. The germ may be misplaced as to time, place, or person, yet it furnishes a clue which may later lead to the truth itself. Old residents should, therefore, be questioned as to the source of what they tell; but an effort should be made to find out whether they saw the event happen, whether they experienced it themselves, or whether it is simply hearsay.

Good advice to the local historian is offered by a British writer on this subject who comments:

Very ancient traditions are liable to fluctuations and variations without end, being quite unconsciously played upon by the imaginations and tricks of memory of each recipient, yet in spite of the possibility of error there is much that is valuable in them for the very reason that from the beginning they have been in contact with living human minds, instead of having been crystallised in the dead, cold form of print.

But this is merely a warning by the way. All traditions and traditional information should as far as possible be collected, both those relating to the village, and the traditions of particular families. So long as they are frankly labelled as traditions no one will be misled and the grain can later by winnowed from the chaff.[5]

Yet how can the grain be winnowed from the chaff? An attempt may at least be made by remembering the axiom of history as stated by one historian: "When two or more contemporary witnesses independently of each other report the same event with numerous similar details . . . then the reports which thus agree, in so far as they do agree, must be true. . . ."[6] If, for example, you interview a half dozen or so old residents and hear from each a story of some important early event which he himself witnessed, you can perhaps accept as true those parts of the story which agree "in so far as they do agree." Even so, you should state it as mere tradition, and you should be sure that the stories do indeed come from independent sources. Often accounts by various persons, which at first appear to be entirely unconnected with each other, will all turn out to be based originally upon a single source. In such a case all the accounts will have to depend upon the reliability or unreliability of the first source.

Even if you have done your best to sift the grain from the chaff, the general historian may not place much reliance in what you consider the facts of the case. In speaking of traditions and legends, another historian states:

---

[5] Joan Wake, *How to Compile a History and Present Day Record of Village Life* (3rd ed., rev. and enlarged. Northampton, England, 1935), 23. This is the best of three books on local history in the English language; all three of which were written in England and are for the most part inapplicable to American conditions. See also *Suggestions to Local Historians, in Wisconsin,* 5.

[6] John M. Vincent, *Historical Research* (New York, 1911), 252.

25

The truth is that the historian can make nothing of them of any positive value, in the absence of corroboratory evidence of a documentary, archaeological or other kind, for the simple reason that they cannot be traced to their origins. And without a knowledge of origins the ordinary critical tests cannot be applied.[7]

Unknown to your old inhabitant you can often test his reliability by asking him to tell what he knows about a certain episode of community history the details of which he should know and with which you are already familiar. If his story is halting, or varies widely from what you know to be true, it would be well for you to question the dependability of his other stories. Try him on another, and still another, until you have noted his accounts of the past as being 50, 80, or 100 per cent dependable.

The human mind, especially that of an old person, is tricky. It has been observed that often, when questions are asked, an old person will say he does not remember, and perhaps he does not, at the time. If, however, you drop that particular enquiry and go on to another, the circumstances of which are related to the first, and then after a while, go back to the earlier question, you will find his memory "lured back by the train of thought evoked by the second question," and the whole subject will be spread clearly before you.[8]

Sometimes old residents are the best judges of other old inhabitants. After all, they should know their contemporaries with whom they have had many associations during the course of a lifetime. One may warn you, "Grandpa Crozier? Well, now, be careful about what he tells you. He ain't known for his accuracy any too well. I 'member way back when—" and he will launch off into a story to prove Grandpa Crozier's lack of veracity or accuracy. Then again, in a community which was rent by the bitterness of a factional struggle, you may find those who were on one side of an issue belittling the integrity of those on the other side.

Yet, if due allowance is made in each case, old residents will prove themselves a never-failing source of information. They can help you arrive at an interpretation of attitudes and issues, and will assist you in deciding the importance or relative strength of trends, movements, and sentiments. They can give you revealing character sketches of some of the community leaders of former days. Their memories retain vivid impressions of customs and habits to which the introduction of modern machinery, the railways, and the automobile have given the death blow. They can visualize the location of old mills, buildings, bridges, and other landmarks which have long since disappeared.

On this subject of interviews one writer points out that, if you are

---

[7] Homer C. Hockett, *Introduction to Research in American History* (New York, 1935), 90. This is an excellent book on its subject.

[8] Frank Allaben and Mabel Washburn, *How to Trace and Record Your Own Ancestry* (New York, 1932), 14.

trying to discover a particular bit of knowledge, "It is difficult to predict what type of person can give the desired information. Leaders of community life sometimes have surprisingly little intimate knowledge of the life of the area, while some inconspicuous person who has lived quietly and reflectively will have an amazing stock of knowledge."[9]

If your own family is one which has been long and favorably known in the community, you will experience little difficulty in approaching old residents. In your first visit lay your ground work carefully, mentioning and emphasizing any bonds which you and your prospect have in common. If you have never met him before, you might introduce yourself by saying: "Good morning. Are you Mr. Jones? Yes? Well, I've been wanting to meet you for some time. You may have heard that I am gathering material for a history of this community, and everywhere I have gone people have asked me, 'Have you seen Mr. Jones yet? He's one of the oldest residents around here and knows a lot of stories about the early years of the place.' You probably have heard of our family the Blanks? My grandparents moved here in 1866, but I understand that your family came here long before that. If you have a little time I'd like to talk to you." With that as a starter you will probably have an attentive response. You can emphasize the fact that there are only a few still living whose recollections run back so far as your host's, or that he knows more than anyone else on the subject, or even that he is the only person in a position to supply the desired information.

Above all, try to make the old resident feel easy in your presence. This can be done by stressing things held in common, by not seeming to pry into private affairs which do not concern you, by making him feel his aid is eagerly sought but not demanded, and by assuring him that any statements which he desires to have treated confidentially will be well guarded. The doubtful old resident must be transformed into the willing talker, confident of your good intentions, and subtly aroused so that he will relate his own knowledge of the past. When going to this interview avoid peculiarities of dress, manner, appearance, or speech which might distract or even irritate your timid and perhaps ungrammatical patriarch. Talk at his level and use simple language such as he is accustomed to use, but do not attempt to talk down to him. Draw out your informant by gestures, nods, and words of sympathy, understanding, surprise, or amusement as the case may require.

Good advice is to be found in the following:

It often serves the best purposes of the interview to ask as few questions as possible and as few leading questions as is consistent with the nature of the inquiry. Experience shows that when people are least interrupted, when they can

[9] Palmer, *Field Studies in Sociology*, 86. On pages 228–230 of her book are printed two interviews with old residents, showing exactly what kind of information on local history may be secured in this way.

tell their stories in their own way, when 'the interview is their moment,' they can react naturally and freely and express themselves fully. When unnecessary interruptions and leading questions are imposed upon them, either they tend to shrink and withdraw into their own habitual world, or they lose control of the situation and supply the answers which they think are expected of them.[10]

Allowing the old resident free rein may permit him to stray from his story as he thinks of interesting happenings associated with his main theme. The same writer observes: "Some interviewers find that when the story begins to drift, they must take a definite part in it, and try to steer it along channels in which they are interested: 'You know I was much interested in what you said a moment ago. That's very important. Could you tell me more about it?' And thus they can guide the conversation."[11] Still another method is to note questions which occur to you as the story is told and then ask these when the opportunity presents itself.

Be careful to take notes of your interviews. It is best to carry a small notebook and pencil inconspicuously when making your first contacts. Out of long experience an expert states:

The moment of first hearing the facts . . . is the psychological moment for making our notes. . . . As our informant begins his story, let us interrupt with the cry of the enthusiast, 'I must jot that down!' Out comes our notebook, conveying to our friend a very distinct impression of the importance of being accurate. He collects himself, and proceeds to give his facts and traditions with the greatest care.[12]

You will find old residents reacting differently to your note-taking. Some who have had unpleasant experiences of being quoted or signing their names to something may resent any recording. Others may be very glad to have you take as full notes as you can, and will slow down their own stories so you can keep pace with them. Others may be wary only when remarks about prominent families or people are concerned and may constantly be admonishing you, "Now, don't write down I said that." Or, "Better not write that down; they might not like it." In such a case, it is best to follow their wishes. The fact which they don't want written down will generally remain in your memory anyhow. You may later want to use the information, but you should not offend your informant by mentioning his name in connection with it.

At best, the most you can do in an interview is to jot down a few catchwords or as much as you would record if you were taking notes on the minutes of a formal business meeting. After you have left, at the first opportunity you have, write out the information in as full a manner

---

[10] Pauline V. Young, *Scientific Social Surveys and Research* (New York, 1939), 190. This excellent text devotes a chapter of twenty-five pages to the subject of interviewing.

[11] *Ibid.*, 191–192.

[12] Allaben, *Concerning Genealogies*, 23.

as you think necessary. Experience has shown that most people are able to reproduce an interview, of even an hour's duration, quite accurately without notes. With the use of a few catchwords, names, dates, and places, the task of reconstructing it should not be too hard.

Try to make the whole interview, from the time you enter to the moment you leave, a very pleasant affair. You may later want to return for further information. The second visit provides a good opportunity to take the draft of your first interview back and have it checked for accuracy of names, dates, places, events, statements, and shades of meaning. This can be done either at the beginning or end of your second visit. You may introduce the reading of your account with a statement like this: "Mr. Jones, you remember what you told me the last time? Well, I put it all down as carefully as I could when I got home so I wouldn't forget anything. If you don't mind I'll read it over to you slowly so you can tell me whether I got it straight. Just stop me if what I've written isn't just as you told me." Corrections and additions can be made as you read. Often you will find that the reading of the story will recall to the old resident other pertinent information.

On your written record of each interview indicate the informant's name, the time and place of the interview, and some explanatory remarks about the old resident's acquaintance with the facts of the story—whether he was a participant or an observer, or merely had the information from hearsay.

Most old people have certain characteristics in common. They are proud of their advanced age, as a rule, and may even pretend they are older than they are (this is especially true of men). They like to be appreciated and to feel that they are still of some use. They like to believe that they alone have information which can solve some of the community's riddles of bygone days, and they are often critical of stories told to you by other old residents. Some like a little flattery, tactfully applied. If you remember these points, you will find little difficulty in approaching the community's patriarchs and having them welcome you back on later visits.

Finally, it is well to remember that you can move too fast. Old people like to take their time and are uncomfortable under rapid fire questioning. It is better to let them ramble on and to have several short pleasant interviews rather than one long tiring session. Some things which cannot be remembered one day may be recalled at another time not as the result of a direct question but because of a casual suggestion.[13]

It may be that some individual well acquainted with the community's past lives too far away to be interviewed. The only recourse in such a case is to write to him. Since old people often find it difficult to answer letters, it may be best to address your letter to a younger member of the

[13] Doane, *Searching for Your Ancestors*, 32.

family with directions for him or her to ask the questions. These questions should be as specific and clear as possible. It is a good practice to number them and ask your correspondent to answer them under their appropriate numbers. It is also helpful to leave space enough after each question to allow your distant correspondent to insert the answer immediately after each question. Above all, remember to enclose a self-addressed, stamped envelope for your reply.

The old resident is not only a source of history and tradition, but also an almost inexhaustible source of local folklore. From him you can accumulate "a heap of miscellaneous items that are curious but possess points . . . worth preserving . . . cases of witchcraft, ghosts, charms, obsolete punishments, people put in the stocks, local sayings and ballads, beliefs about birth, weddings and funerals, details of fairs and revels, local sports and feasts, eccentric characters, dialect and word-lore peculiar to the neighborhood. All these items are . . . folk-lore."[14] If one purpose of history is to make us understand the past, certainly the recording of such material will help to make us realize that the early generations of the community were human beings, that they lived and breathed, had their joys and sorrows, their trials and victories.

If the dialect of your community is peculiar, note the main differences, indicating how these may have arisen. Similarly, if certain phrases are special to the locality, record these and tell their meaning. For example, near Kansas City the words "feist" and "feisty" are in common use. Upon inquiry it appears that these expressions are used here and there over a wide area of the Central West. A "feist" is a small dog, a pup; "feisty," therefore, means troublesome, impudent, annoying—all characteristics of a pup. These words appear in *Webster's International Dictionary* as localisms.

From an old resident you may often learn how the early settlers concocted their medicines and household remedies from flowers and herbs, and what they did to cure certain ailments of man and beast. Again, you may learn of early, highly esteemed foods and dishes, now long since out of fashion.

Nearly every community has its ghost houses, secret rooms and closets, hidden stairways, and false walls; its cranks, spies, and murderers; its railroads which went the wrong way and prevented a growth of metropolitan proportions; inventors whose machines wouldn't work, and new mineral deposits which didn't pan out. Such stories have a way of seldom being recorded, but the old resident is likely to know them. So long as they are labelled as folklore, no harm can be done in repeating them, and much interest will be added to the lighter side of your local history.

---

[14] Humphreys, *How to Write a Village History*, 33–34. See also Wake, *How to Compile a History*, 22, 53–54. Though this writer describes English conditions, much of what she mentions also applies to the older and more stable communities of the eastern part of the United States.

Perhaps the old resident can recall predictions in his boyhood of the great future your present, quite ordinary community would have. It has been said that every new crossroads village was, at one time or other, certain it would become the metropolis of the region or of the state. Were any such predictions made of your locality? Or were there predictions, perhaps, of its certain future insignificance? Arthur Lee, a Virginian who visited Pittsburgh in December, 1783, wrote of it:

Pittsburgh is inhabited almost entirely by Scots and Irish, who live in paltry log-houses. . . . There are in the town four attorneys, two doctors, and not a priest of any persuasion, nor church, nor chapel; so that they are likely to be damned without the benefit of clergy. *The place, I believe, will never be considerable.*[15]

Perhaps your community was really "first" in something at some time, and the old inhabitant tells you of that thing and time. A certain midwestern town in 1854 truthfully boasted that it had a new stone hotel, the largest and most commodious west of St. Louis." A county in the region laid claim to having produced more hemp than any other county in the United States. For one brief day your community may have "made" the headlines of the newspapers throughout the country. These items are of interest and of historical significance. Ferret them out and record them.

One small section of your book should be given over to local place-names. Some small towns and villages have forgotten even the origin of their names. A village near Chicago bears the name Halfday. Because it was a half-day's wagon journey from Chicago in the horse and buggy days, some present-day residents have imagined that it derived its name from this fact. It was, however, named after an Indian called Hafda. When the early residents sent the name Hafda to Washington to designate their village, an omniscient postal clerk, thinking the "folks out West there" were illiterate, changed the spelling to Halfday. The clerk's version, rather than the Indian's name and the residents' choice, has become the accepted form.

American place-names are perhaps more varied than those of most other countries. There are cities, counties, towns and villages, lakes and mountains, rivers and streams named for national heroes and their homes, local "founders," families, Indians, Old World towns, villages, and cities, natural and physical objects, hopes, disappointments, discoveries, misfortunes, virtues, directions, and what not. Look about you: do you find a Dead Man's Gulch, a Hell's Kitchen, a Lone Tree, a long Indian name, or an ideal? At a certain crossroads there is a sign pointing north reading "Independence, ten miles." Make the most of your picturesque designations and discover the derivation of others. Old residents should be able to help in this and they may know how certain fields, woods, streams, hills, houses, and streets got their names.

---

[15] Quoted by Luce, *Town and City Histories*, 315.

Occasionally you will find that the naming of your community had considerable drama connected with it. When Kansas City's early settlers met in the log-house and store of "One-eyed Ellis" to choose a town name, one Abraham Fonda wanted it called Port Fonda in his honor. Threats of law, fists, and buck-shot by one Henry Jobe prevented this immortalization of Fonda. The chronicler related:

The first suggestion having failed of approval, the perplexed promoters next procured a copy of Webster's spelling book, which contained a list of important towns and cities. None of the names contained therein seemed to suit the fancy of the grave assemblage. Squire Bowers, a droll old character who lived a mile or two down the bottom, suggested with mingled humor and sarcasm the name of 'Rabbitville' or 'Possum-trot.' His attempt at mirth met only with obvious contempt and withering silence. . . . Finally, after much dissent and disagreement, it was decided to name the new village the 'Town of Kansas,' after the Kansas (Kaw) River which empties into the Missouri at this point.[16]

Investigating the origin of each local name is interesting, and quite often the old resident may be the only source of this knowledge which he, perhaps, has obtained from a still earlier generation.

An adventuring pioneer may have seen your valleys in the mellow light of an October sun, loved them and remained to give them his name. Indians may have planted corn in your city park and liked the location so well that tribal history thereafter centered in that region, bequeathing to it a name long bright with savage glory.[17]

PRIVATE LETTERS

When interviewing old residents inquire whether they have any old letters, diaries, or account books, for these will be found an excellent source for local history material. Such old papers may be in almost anyone's attic or basement, or they may be deposited at the local or state historical society. If you can locate any of these old private letters and diaries—and what town does not have some?—and can persuade their owners that you are not trying to delve into their family secrets or disclose the proverbial skeleton in the family closet, you have a gold mine, the importance of which cannot be ignored. Old letters and diaries often give a more truthful and vivid picture of the past than any other kind of record. They are more likely to be accurate than recollections told or written long after the events recounted.

In your inquiries you may be informed that "Mrs. Crozier has a bundle of old letters which date back to the 1850's, written by her great grandmother to her grandfather who had gone away from home for several years and who, naturally, wanted to know all the home-town news." Search out these letters. Perhaps in another home you will find letters

---

16 Ellis, *Civic History of Kansas City*, 7–8. In 1889 the name was changed to Kansas City.

17 Henrietta Murdoch, "Giving the Past a Future," *Ladies Home Journal* (Philadelphia), vol. LIV, February, 1937, p. 99.

written by an early settler to a friend back East, urging him to try his fortune in the newer West, and describing the conditions he would meet in the new location. The Yankee friend may have heeded the call, "Go West, young man," and may have brought the letters with him, perhaps to verify the statements. Eventually these were consigned to an attic trunk, where they remained awaiting your eager eyes and itching fingers. Many attics throughout the country contain letters of this sort, and eastern attics, especially, are the unwitting depositories of great masses of letters written home by younger members of a family who have gone West.

Letters are of various sorts and often tell of many unexpected things. An occasional old letter, in dim handwriting and badly worn along its folds, may contain an important name, date, or event which cannot be found elsewhere. Then too, "old letters, faded and torn, may describe gay festivities of the olden times, in reading which we again breathe the perfume of our ancestresses' fans, flounce with them their brocaded draperies, and chuckle with them over their demure flirtations."[18] While old family letters will often yield valuable data, you may wonder as you read them just who Bob and Henry and Betty are, for the surnames are seldom mentioned, having been familiar to both the writer and receiver. This need not discourage you, however, for often you will not need to know, since you are interested primarily in events, not people. If you need the full name, no doubt the relative in whose hands the letters were found can supply you with it, or a careful reading of a number of epistles will furnish the missing information.

DIARIES

Diaries are perhaps more personal than letters and they are even more concerned with exact dates, names, and events. It is usually true that the better-educated people were inclined to keep diaries, so that your task of deciphering the handwriting will be less difficult than with letters. In your search someone may ask you: "Have you seen Mr. Patterson? You know, his grandfather was the first minister of the Presbyterian Church. Apparently he was a well educated man, opened a school here, and, what is most important for your purpose, he was in the habit of keeping a diary. Mr. Patterson has it now and, as I recall, he said it runs for about fifteen years and tells all about the early residents." Ministers sometimes kept private records of their parishioners and of domestic and social events occurring in the community. The discovery of such a diary is a veritable bonanza. What a wealth of local color, for example, is found in the following entry from an unpublished diary of a minister:

Child of J___ S___ died Sept. 24, 1773—their foolishness in making a great wedding ye night before. Both got Drunk ye father & mother. It is supposed they

---

[18] Allaben and Washburn, *How to Trace and Record Your Ancestry*, 44.

33

lay on it and killed it in their drunkenness. A numerous company of weddingers at night. but not one of ye whole company attended ye funeral. Shame.[19]

Diaries, like old letters, are of various sorts. They help establish dates, give character sketches of early residents, picture the early social, religious, and political life, and are much more to be relied upon than the memories of living residents. Some have been preserved in the collections of historical societies and others remain family possessions.

ACCOUNT BOOKS

Occasionally a diary may be also a business record like the one kept by a miller who set down day by day what work he had done and for whom he had done it.[20] It is to account books, however, rather than to diaries, that you will usually have to go to find out about the early business life of your community. If you can secure the records of the general merchants—and general stores were almost the rule in pioneer days—you can perhaps trace how the Indian trade died out as the trade of the white settlers increased. Prices of commodities will be given, and often other valuable data. Sometimes account books serve as practical censuses of small communities like one kept by a storekeeper in Dutchess County, New York. The opening and closing of accounts and changes in name gave approximate evidence of the time of marriages, deaths, and movings.[21] When an account of this sort was marked "Paid in Full" and the name dropped from the accounts, it is fairly certain that the community saw another family depart to seek its fortune in the newer West.

Within recent years state historical societies, libraries, and other agencies have made systematic efforts to collect and preserve important collections of private letters, diaries, account books, and other manuscript records, so that some of these materials relating to the history of your own locality are likely to be found in one or more of these central depositories. The *Historical Records Survey* has now published guides to manuscript depositories in a good many of the states, listing the various institutions and giving a brief description of the holdings of each. In addition, the Survey or its sponsors have published detailed guides to the materials in many individual depositories. For example, the *Guide to the Manuscript Collections in the Archives of the North Carolina Historical Commission* (Raleigh: North Carolina Historical Commission, 1942) describes the 815 private and unofficial collections (but not the official materials) in the custody of that agency. Most of these guides are well indexed, so that you can readily see what materials are available for the history of your own community. Certain historical agencies also have published calendars or catalogues of their holdings. Although new collec-

[19] Donald L. Jacobs, *Genealogy as Pastime and Profession* (New Haven, 1930), 13.
[20] Doane, *Searching for Your Ancestors*, 51.
[21] *Ibid.*, 56.

tions are being added daily and the listing of the old acquisitions is by no means complete, yet there has been an excellent beginning toward making such materials available to the historical researcher.

KEEPSAKES, HEIRLOOMS, AND RELICS

The thought of finding a source of local history in keepsakes, heirlooms, and relics may have never occurred to you. These cannot, as a rule, tell their stories, but their proud possessors generally can and probably will be glad to do so. Ask old residents to show you the heirlooms in their possession. A sympathetic and understanding attitude may win you a sight of the first piano ever brought to your community, the first kerosene lamp used, or a "Beecher Bible" brought overland in a covered wagon in the 1850's. Each heirloom will start a line of reminiscences and your alert ear should be set to guide the conversation into fruitful channels. Some keepsakes may in themselves be of such historic importance to warrant a description and paragraph, and perhaps a picture, in the local history.

An interesting observation is made by an English writer on the subject:

It is hard for some people to realise that the common events and objects of every-day life are worth attention, or that they will ever be interesting to future generations. Most things in this world go through three stages. When they are new they are exciting and interesting; when they become old-fashioned they are dull and there is a revulsion of feeling against them. If they manage to survive this dangerous period they become interesting again, even what is called romantic, and then humdrum details are treasured for the power they have to give us an insight into the lives of our ancestors.[22]

Having reached this last stage the old iron kettle, the fragile teacup, or the whatnot suddenly becomes an heirloom to be treasured. A keepsake may be almost anything—an old portrait, a quaint silhouette, furniture, books, laces, jewels, family Bibles, embroidery, samplers, grandfather clocks, water jugs, firearms, household equipment, personal articles, old china, pottery and glass, clothes, tools, and many other articles.

Sometimes these old things have not yet reached the stage where they are treasured, but nevertheless they have historical value. The writer of an editorial states:

Passing through the yard of the Rock Island arsenal the writer saw great heaps of old iron waste—'Gathered, sir, from New England cellars.' There were tons of pikes, boarding pikes, halberds; the iron work of home-made machinery, and carts, such as pioneers invented. It was a curious freak of social economics that dumped New England history in the Mid-West to be worked over into war material or to lie and rust in forgotten heaps.[23]

---

[22] Wake, *How to Compile a History*, 23.
[23] "Local History Clubs," *The Independent* (New York), LIII, 1901, p. 686.

Family Bibles may well be classed as heirlooms or keepsakes. A very few go back as far as 1650 in this country, but the genealogist, Doane who has examined many of them, finds that the larger number date no further back than the 1780's and 1790's. Many respectable families of the nineteenth century were accustomed to buying large Bibles to place in their parlors. In them they would record the vital records of the families. Old Bibles, therefore, may give the birth, marriage, and death records of some of the prominent early settlers, but this is about the extent of their value as a source of local history.

The museum of your state historical society or some other historical museum may possess relics from your own community. Even though this is not the case, such a museum will have articles of the type which were used in your community. For instance, in the fine collection of agricultural implements of various periods in the Ford museum at Dearborn Village, near Detroit, you may see some of the types of ploughs which were in use at different times in your local area. If practicable, visit one or more of the most up-to-date historical museums. Not only will the displays themselves be informative, but the way they are arranged and the story they tell will be suggestive both in gathering your materials and in writing your history. If you will tell those in charge of such an institution what you are doing, no doubt they will be glad to make suggestions and perhaps even to help you obtain illustrations for your book.

CHAPTER III

NEWSPAPERS AND PERIODICALS

THE importance of the newspaper as a source of information for local history is very great. The historian Goss goes so far as to say "The chief mine of information for writing local history is the files of old newspapers."[1] Not only will you find that newspapers mirror the daily life of the people of the community, but the older ones are "rich in accounts of travel, adventure, expansion, and festivity,[2] as well as in discussions of national and local politics, and in abstracts of speeches on all the great issues of the day. One writer remarks: "The value of the information which these papers contain can hardly be overestimated. They are a primary source for national and local history and for a study of the evolution of economic and political opinion . . . the record of our industrial and business history."[3]

In examining old local newspapers note, wherever it is possible, the political affiliations of the editor and publisher. This will enable you to make due allowance for the partisan character of many editorial pages, so that you can determine what is historically valuable.[4]

When examining old papers you will notice the difference between the early newspapers and those of the present, for the papers of bygone generations gave very little space to chronicling local events. Instead, as much as ninety per cent of the news space was devoted to contemporary politics, speeches, travel, and essays—or, to what is found today in a news weekly with national distribution.

Go to your local publisher and ask him what he knows of the early

---

[1] Goss, "Methods of Seeking Information," 56.

[2] Carl L. Weicht, "The Local Historian and the Newspaper," *Minnesota History* (St. Paul), XIII, 1932, p. 51.

[3] Winifred Gregory, ed., *American Newspapers, 1821–1936: A Union List of Files Available in the United States and Canada* (New York, 1937), introduction. This is the most complete index of newspapers. It lists all known newspapers for the period and tells what issues are still in existence and where they can be consulted. It does not have, however, a general index and the seeker must know the state and city where the paper was published in order to find his data. An older work on the earlier period is Clarence S. Brigham, *Bibliography of American Newspapers, 1690–1820, American Antiquarian Society Proceedings* (Worcester), XXIII–XXXVII, 1913–1928.

[4] There are several publications which treat of the newspaper as a source of historical data. The best is Lucy M. Salmon, *The Newspaper and the Historian* (New York, 1923). John M. Vincent, *Historical Research* (New York, 1911), devotes a chapter to "The Newspaper as a Source of History." Hockett, *Introduction to Research*, 87, gives space to the subject. See also James F. Rhodes, "Newspapers as Historical Sources," in *Historical Essays*, 81–97; Walter Spahr and Rinehart J. Swenson, *Methods and Status of Scientific Research; with Particular Application to the Social Sciences* (New York, 1930), 120–121, and note 6; and Weicht, "The Local Historian and the Newspaper."

newspapers of the community, and whether he has any on file. It may be that his paper is the successor to the earliest newspaper, in which case his office will probably have a complete file. Go also to the local library and ask what old newspapers are to be found there, and if they have any newspaper scrapbooks. Inquire, too, among old residents if they know of any one in the community who may have a file, or even a single copy, of an early newspaper. Often single copies have been kept because they tell of a marriage, or contain an obituary notice or some other item of sentimental value.

Even after you have exhausted all local possibilities, do not give up the search. Local newspapers used to be more common than they are today, and it is quite probable that your community had one or more of them as early as fifty, seventy-five, or a hundred years ago. Examining Miss Gregory's union list of newspapers you can easily discover if any early papers are listed for your locality, how long they existed, and what they were called. Next write to your state historical society, state library, or large university library and ask if they have any early newspapers published in your own or nearby towns, what years their files cover, the names, and the possibility and price of securing photostatic copies of the papers.

State historical societies and state libraries have been very assiduous in recent years in getting newspapers of every locality to send a copy of each issue to them for preservation. They have also secured all back issues of newspapers in case the local publisher did not care to bother keeping them. If your own state historical society library or state library does not have early local newspapers of your community, perhaps they can be found in the library of a nearby state, for newspapers have a way of wandering far from their point of origin. The Ohio State Archaeological and Historical Society, for example, has the largest collection of Ohio newspapers in the country, but also has on file a number of out of state papers. Probably the most important general collection of newspapers in this country is to be found in the Library of Congress at Washington.[5]

If you find a nearby state historical library which has even a few single issues of the early local newspapers, you will weigh the time and expense involved in getting access to them. If possible, by all means go directly to the newspaper files. The trip will serve a double purpose, for while you are there you can also consult the vast resources of the state historical society library and discover what it may have about your community. If the trip is impossible because of time or expense, you can still secure photostatic copies at no prohibitive cost. If you find the society's library has on file, let us say, your local newspaper from 1843 to 1877, it

[5] In 1901 was published the *Check-List of American Newspapers in the Library of Congress.* See also Brigham, *Bibliography of American Newspapers,* for years prior to 1821. A new edition of this work is in preparation. For the location of newspaper files, consult Gregory, *American Newspapers.*

would, of course, be out of the question financially to secure copies of all issues of those years by use of the photostat. Instead, you can secure a good picture of local community life by securing photostatic copies of single issues at intervals of five or ten years. Thus, you should ask for a copy of the first issue the library has for 1843, as well as single issues for 1848, 1853, 1858, 1863, 1868, 1873, and so on. You might want to designate that one be an issue published in the spring, one in July, one in the autumn, and another in the dead of winter. This would give you an idea of year-round activity over a long period of years. It may be that in your library reading you have learned that the local paper of July 17, 1863, contained a long article of reminiscences, over a period of fifty years, by an old resident of the vicinity. You would, of course, want to secure a copy of that issue. Perhaps your community went through some stirring events for a brief period in 1855. You would want contemporary accounts of that. Or again, suppose the grasshoppers ate everything in sight in the summer of 1875. A record of the local havoc at the time should prove quite enlightening.

The cost of photostatic copies of newspapers varies. The Newberry Library in Chicago has a minimum charge of fifty cents for a negative 11×14 inches. A negative is sufficient for your purpose, but if a positive is wanted, this library charges thirty-five cents extra. If a considerable number of photostats are ordered at one time the photostat prices are slightly reduced.[6] A large page of a newspaper can still be read when reduced to a photostatic copy of $8\frac{1}{2}$×11 inches or 11×14 inches. Old local newspapers usually have four pages. To secure photostatic copies of single issues of a local newspaper at intervals of five years from 1843 to 1877 would, therefore, cost anywhere from five to fifteen dollars.[7]

---

[6] Robert C. Binkley, *Manual of Methods of Reproducing Research Materials* (Ann Arbor, Mich., 1936), 67. Above prices as of 1944.

[7] Most libraries are not equipped to do photographic work, but they can always call to their aid, if they will, local firms. Maxwell H. Savelle writing in the *Library Journal* notes: "Today, only three or four libraries in this country have divisions of photography and photographic reproduction." He also says, "Some of the libraries in this country are now equipped . . . and it is possible for one to get photocopies from such libraries as Huntington Library and the Library of Congress with a minimum of effort, time and expense." Savelle, "History, Photography and the Library," *Library Journal* (Chicago), LX, Nov. 15, 1935 pp. 876, 877.
The Bibliofilm Service has been developed for the use of research workers. It draws on the vast resources of the Library of Congress and other large libraries throughout the country. It will make photoprints on paper 6×8 inches, legible without optical aid, at $.50 for each ten pages or fraction thereof. These are positives, that is, black letters on a white background. To photoprint a 20-page article would cost $2.20. This Bibliofilm Service is primarily interested in microphotography. A microfilm consists of a series of still images about one inch high on a strip or roll of 35 mm. standard safety photographic film. Any article from a single volume of a periodical can be copied for $.50. Portions of books and serial publications are copied at the rate of $.50 for fifty pages or fraction thereof. For information, address Bibliofilm Service, care of Library of U. S. Department of Agriculture, Washington, D. C.

During the advent of WPA, projects for the indexing of newspapers were undertaken in certain states, particularly in Ohio and Illinois. Some of these indexes are quite detailed and can actually be called abstracts. For the periods and papers covered, such indexes are highly useful even if they only enable you to determine which issues you wish to examine in greater detail.[8]

A copy of the *Parkville Industrial Luminary* for October 25, 1853, volume one, number 14, published on the Missouri River, in a small town facing Kansas, at the time the question was being raised as to whether Kansas would be a free or a slave state, is probably typical of small newspapers during the 1850's. Parkville, Missouri, at this time was a rapidly growing town of three hundred people, firmly attached to the idea that it was certain to become the metropolis of the heart of the nation. The paper's four pages are 25 by 18 inches in size, with six columns each. Under the large title caption these words appear in smaller type: "A Newspaper Published Weekly for the Farmer, Mechanic, Merchant, Politician, and the Family Circle." It appeared every Tuesday and sold for $2.00 a year.

On the first page is an address delivered by the president of the nearby Christian Female College "On the Education and Industrial Sphere of Women." In two columns of small type the speaker reached the conclusion that only when properly educated "will Woman become the glorious reality of man's fondest dream—then, and not till then, will the husband and father realize at home, that bliss, which she once dispensed in Eden."

One column is filled with six letters from a state senator to the postmaster of St. Louis. A quarter-column discusses "Courtesies of Life" and a full one is given to a story of a physician's experience. Then appears a short article on "Politeness" and numerous short articles of an educational and humorous nature, besides a poem entitled "Miss Low," whose "eyes stood out as visibly, As letters on a sign."

An editorial at the head of page two is on the "Union of the Anties of Missouri with the Freesoilers, against the Organization of Nebraska." The editors put up a spirited fight for the abolitionists and end with a bitter thrust at two newspapers of nearby towns with whose political views they did not agree: "O, slippery 'Platform'—O, rotten 'Argus'! ye are a nuisance in the realms of principle, the froth and scum of partisan warfare!'" In another news item farther down appears the following information: "'The Democratic Platform' is the title of a new paper just started at Liberty, Clay County, an old broken down nullifier, is the

---

[8] Indexes to Ohio newspapers, for certain periods, as well as translated digests of some foreign language papers, may be purchased for $1.00 per volume from the Library of the Ohio State Archaeological and Historical Society at Columbus. An index to the Ohio State Archaeological and Historical Society's file of the *Centinel of the Northwestern Territory* (the first paper published in Ohio) appeared in the July–September, 1943, issue of the *Ohio State Archaeological and Historical Quarterly*, LII, 217–247.

real editor, but the proprietors have persuaded a little fellow from this place—known as 'Weazel-faced Bob'—to take the responsibility."

Another editorial states the *Luminary's* political views and its determination never to support for a political office "an anti-Benton man." This is followed by a children's sermonette about some little boys who stole apples from a local orchard.

The newspaper then mentions the trip the junior editor took to Nebraska and promises to tell in the following issue what he saw and did. A half-column is given to an account of a local lecture on the history of music delivered by one of the two editors. The lecture had been interspersed with some vocal exercises "sung by the audience, demonstrating the proposition that with very few exceptions, all can sing and that 'reading music at sight' is not so exceedingly difficult as most people suppose."

The remainder of page two is filled with numerous short articles on various subjects, some of which have political bearing. Others tell of national events such as "The Peruvian Outrage" against some American seamen, the war raging in Europe, the settlement of Nebraska, and "Why Mr. Buchanan Never Married." Very little space is devoted to local affairs, and one can only conclude that the editors felt that these were already sufficiently well known to the citizens to preclude their publication in favor of less known national and political news.

Page three consists entirely of advertisements of local firms. About half of the fourth and last page is also of this sort, though more eastern firms appear in the list. *Scott's Weekly Paper, Harper's Magazine, Arthur's Home Gazette, The Flag of Our Union,* and *Graham's Magazine* each occupy from a sixth to two-thirds of a column to set forth their merits. Several administrators' notices are followed by a good-sized advertisement for Chinese Ague Killer, guaranteed to cure chills, fever, pains, cholera, gout, rheumatism, sore eyes, lame horses, and what have you, all for one dollar a bottle. The *Luminary* itself advertises that it had "just received from St. Louis a complete stock of Job Type," and was "now prepared to execute printing of any size, in a style unsurpassed in Upper Missouri." A short piece urging citizens to "Paint Your Houses" now that the "heat of summer is over" is followed by "An Excellent Washing Recipe." These are accompanied by two articles of interest to farmers, one on "The Grape Disease," the other an extract from a recent address before the State Agricultural Society.

The two editors took half a column to set forth the principles they intended to follow in their paper:

We shall give the general news of the day from all quarters, both in our own and foreign countries, and all political movements both at home and abroad. We shall notice Congressional and Legislative reports, proceedings of public meetings, and whatever may be of importance to the community. We shall endeavor from time to time to furnish leading articles upon all matters of importance to the dweller in the Missouri valley.

The Political principles will be Democratic.—The Editors hold to free and independent expression of opinion, tempered in all cases with reason, judgement and a decent respect for the opinions of others. We hope so to conduct our paper, that even those who differ from us in politics will take it on account of the other useful matter it contains. . . . Our object will be to enlighten and elevate public sentiment and to infuse into society purer principles of action. To discountenance interference with the local institutions of our country and to substitute reason and enlightened, liberal and candid judgement for prejudice and personal detraction in all our discussions. We shall not confine our Patriotism to sectional limits but inculcate the purest devotion to the American Union. Situated on the Western Borders of Missouri, looking out upon the beautiful Groves and Prairies. . . . Now inviting the hand of civilization, we shall keep our readers informed of all matters of interest there, as the country opens for settlers. It is hardly realized that half of the American Territory lies West of us and is opening to American Citizens. . . .

The current literature of the day will not be neglected. Liberal extracts will be made from our best reviews and Magazines, keeping in mind a high moral tone. New works, and the new inventions will be noticed. . . .

Subjects connected with scientific and practical agriculture, manufactures, mechanics, farm buildings, cottages, fruit trees, flowers, landscape and kitchen gardening, and the rearing of stock, will constitute a leading feature in the columns of our paper. . . .

Occasionally a column or more of the paper will be given to an extensive review of the markets, the present and probable prices of produce. . . . Communications from practical business men are solicited, and if we can enlist an able corps of correspondents united with untiring industry on our part, we shall be able to keep pace with American progress to open to view the vast resources of Upper Missouri and make our paper truly an Industrial Luminary.[9]

The advertisements of local business men in the *Luminary* provide better revelations of the economic, industrial, and social life of Parkville than does the local news. The business cards and advertisements throw much light on how early business was conducted, the trade ethics of the time, barter, the source of goods, and their variety. It was just at this time that the merchants of Parkville and other western towns were beginning to shift their buying from New York, Philadelphia, Baltimore, and other eastern cities to St. Louis, with its rapidly increasing population of over 100,000. A number of merchants mention this fact. One such notice reads:

Our goods were bought in the St. Louis Market, in advance of the late rise on staple articles, and purchased on terms unequaled by any dealer in this county, and that long song and old story of buying in Philadelphia and New York which some of our merchants preach up is now found to be all humbug, as more than half the merchants who bought East this fall say the expense of getting goods here over run the profit.

---

[9] The *Parkville Industrial Luminary* was destined to live but a year and a half after the foregoing was written. The editors opposed the extension of slavery into Kansas. Their paper was raided on April 14, 1855, by a mob of pro-slavery men, the editors were threatened, and the type and press thrown into the Missouri River.

Another is as follows:

We need not say we have the largest stock in town, for others have said they have, and it would not look well in us to say so, though our stock is large. Neither will we say they were purchased in Philadelphia, New York and Boston, and that consequently we can sell them lower than anyone else. But this we do say, that we intend to sell as low as the lowest. . . .

Almost without exception the advertisements of each merchant claimed that his goods were sold at the lowest prices in town. It was a day when general merchants flourished. One of these advertised:

We will always have on hand a large and well selected stock of the most fashionable Dry Goods, Boots, Shoes, Hardware, Tin Wear, Groceries, Saddlery, Bonnets, Hats and Caps, And every and anything else usually kept in a country store, which we promise shall be of the best quality and at the lowest prices.

Another offered the same line of goods "for sale at the lowest market price for cash, or on time to punctual men." Still another merchant clinched his ad with the following:

Our extensive acquaintance with the citizens of Platte and Clay Counties forbid an effort, on our part, of trying to humbug them, as do some of our neighbors, by telling them that we can sell goods twenty-five per cent cheaper than any other house in Parkville, which every man will admit is nothing but humbugery of the deepest cast. We can sell goods without resorting to anything of the kind. Just call, examine our stock before purchasing and if we fail to sell you it will all be O. K.

One merchant advertised that he had "35 cases boots and Shoes that will fit every thing from a 7 foot Hoosier down to the smallest size . . . for sale low." Another advertised that his clothing would "suit any one wanting to purchase ready made Clothing from the size of a Tom Thumb, to that of a Kentucky Porter."

Two merchants waxed poetic. "B. F. Nickolson, he does repeat, At No. 9 on Old Main Street, His Saddlery you cannot beat, Either on Main or Water street." M. T. Summers advertised:

Coffee, molasses, mackerel and tars; Teas, rice, and honey in jars; Spices, glassware and nails; Tobacco, crackers and pails; Knives, forks, files and latches; Door-locks, augers, screws and matches; Domestics, silks, and laces; Log-chains, hose, and traces; Sugar—clarified, crushed and brown—Truly the cheapest and best in town; With saddles, blankets, harness and collars, For all of which we want the dollars.

A few merchants specialized. One had a grocery, another a drug and book store, still another a lumber yard. There were also a furniture store, a mill, and, temporarily at least, a daguerreotype shop "prepared to take the best of pictures." Miscellaneous advertisements show that there were houses for rent or sale, and even a hotel, "the largest and most commodious Hotel West of St. Louis." Oxen strayed and books were borrowed without being returned. One doctor and several lawyers advertised their professional services. Two school teachers praised their rival schools.

The contents of a single number of this four-page issue of the *Parkville Industrial Luminary* have been given rather fully to demonstrate what almost any copy of a newspaper of the period is likely to contain. Perhaps you will agree with a writer who says, "The chief mine of information for writing local history is the files of old newspapers." In the newspaper you can see mirrored the daily life of the people—merchants competing with one another, citizens gathering on the streets to discuss politics, prices, last night's lecture on the history of music, or even the relative merits of the two school teachers.[10]

The newspaper is one of the most important sources for discovering popular attitudes, not only in the editorials but more particularly in letters to the editor which may be printed in these sheets. One should be careful to probe deeply to learn the interests of the persons writing such letters and learn, if possible their status in the community. Is the attitude typical, or may it be that the writer has some specifically personal axe to grind? For example, a farmer or townsman with no children is often more likely to resent school taxes or the construction of a playground than one who is worried about the education and leisure time activities of his own children.

The newspaper, too, may be a source of information relating to early transportation and communication. Such data sometimes appear in news articles, but oftener, perhaps, in advertisements. The *Luminary*, for example, carried the following item:

New Ferry. The subscriber having received license, and established a Ferry between Parkville and Nebraska Territory[11] is now prepared, and will be at all reasonable hours ready to accomodate [sic] those who may wish to cross. His Boat is new and safe, under the charge of experienced Ferrymen, of sufficient capacity to take Waggons and stock of all kinds.

Persons wishing to cross the Missouri River will find it decidedly advantageous to make this their point.

It is the best point to cross and go down by Wyandott, Kansas, Westport to Independence. Travellers from the North and East going into the heart of Nebraska, or to the Southwest part of this State or to Texas, will cross here and take the Military road south. They will find this the most direct road connecting the Northwest portions of the Mississippi Valley with the great South West. And it is the most eligible point to cross and take the Military road westward for those going to Sante Fe, Salt Lake, California and Oregon, and for those below, going to and from Fort Leavenworth and the new Fort on Kansas river.

JAMES M. KUYKENDAL.

---

[10] For an analysis of the newspapers of one colony (state), see Charles Crittenden, *North Carolina Newspapers before 1790, The James Sprunt Historical Studies* (Chapel Hill), XX (1928), No. 1.

[11] Nebraska Territory then included what is now Kansas and Nebraska.

Notices in old newspapers also generally carried information about stage lines and posts and about steamboat schedules. Negroes were often advertised for sale in the southern states. Newspapers frequently printed news of elections and other legal announcements. Public documents and city ordinances were frequently published. Other miscellaneous information of various sorts was printed from time to time. One editor even tried to take revenge upon an absconding subscriber by publishing the following: "John Hoffman, who lived near Ice's Ferry, Monongahela County, Virginia, has left without paying, as far as we know, his subscription to this paper. We understand he has gone to Baltimore. Will the papers there please copy this?"

Not only newspapers, but magazines and periodicals published in the early days or dealing with articles about early history will prove of considerable value to the local historian. The first magazines in this country printed articles dealing with eclecticism, essays, fiction and verse, but they also devoted space to political writing, literary and dramatic criticism, religious discussions, comment on social customs, economic questions, educational questions, and the place of women.[12]

The city of Cincinnati, for example, in 1831 had six weeklies, two semi-monthlies, one monthly and one quarterly publication. Seventeen years later it had twenty-five weekly and six monthlies.[13] An early number of one of these Cincinnati periodicals surveyed western culture, pointed out that there were several colleges and fifty common schools in Ohio at that time (1827), that Cincinnati itself had two paper mills, a type foundry, and an extensive printing industry. The same article then went on to say that "perhaps there is no town in the United States, where, among an equal number of people, so many will be found, able, and disposed to join in a literary conversation, as in Lexington [Kentucky]."[14] It is such statements, if you can find them about your local community, that will reveal much of contemporary opinion and point of view not to be found in other sources.

---

[12] Frank L. Mott, *A History of American Magazines, 1741–1850* (New York, 1930), I, 39–67. Benjamin Mecom's quaint *New England Magazine of Knowledge and Pleasure* (1758) advertised its three numbers in the following verses:

> "Old-fashioned writings, and Select Essays,
> Queer Notions, Useful Hints, Extracts from Plays;
> Relations Wonderful, and Psalm and Song,
> Good Sense, Wit, Humour, Morals, all *ding dong;*
> Poems and Speeches, Politics and News
> What *Some* will like, and other *Some* refuse;
> Births, Deaths, and Dreams, and Apparitions too;
> With something suited to each different Gen,
> To Humour *Him* and *Her,* and *Me,* and *You."*
> *Ibid.,* 41.

[13] *Ibid.,* 387.

[14] *Western Monthly Review* (Cincinnati), I, May, 1827, pp. 62–63, cited in Mott, *History of American Magazines,* I, 206–207.

The mere fact that western magazines were limited in circulation to local communities,[15] makes them better reflectors of the mores and special qualities of the community in which they were printed. The first magazine west of Pittsburgh was the Lexington *Medley or Monthly Miscellany*, published in 1803. Cincinnati did not have much to show in the way of periodical publication until 1825. About that time, however, the *Cincinnati Literary Gazette*, "itself a local-pride weekly" called on the Muse to chronicle the multiplicity of local periodicals:

> This is the Age of Magazines—
> Even skeptics must confess it:
> Where is the town of much renown
> That has not one to bless it?
>
> . . . .
>
> Museums, Mirrors, Monthlies strike
> Our view in crowds and dozens:
> And so much do they look alike
> We see they all are cousins.
> Their phizzes seem so thin and wan,
> So hopeless their conditions
> They all must go to shades below
> In spite of their physicians.[16]

Indeed, there were an abundant number of periodicals and these were of all types, scientific journals, medical magazines, agricultural papers, legal publications, anti-slavery and other reform tracts, theatrical reviews, comic periodicals, as well as art, fiction, biography, travel, and poetry publications. The *American Journal of Science*, begun in 1818, at New Haven, Connecticut, by Benjamin Silliman, was read in Ohio and other parts of the Old Northwest; the short-lived *Agricultural Museum* of Georgetown, D. C., began in 1810 and lasted until 1812, and the *American Farmer* (Baltimore) which started in 1819 continued until 1897. Ohio, a hot-bed of anti-slavery sentiment, had Elisha Bates's *Philanthropist* (Mt. Pleasant, Ohio, 1818–1822) and Benjamin Lundy's *Genius of Universal Emancipation* (Mt. Pleasant, 1821–1839), while other Quaker antislavery leaders were responsible for the *Manumission Intelligencer* (Charles Osborn) and the *Emancipator* (Elijah Embrie, 1834–1850).[17] During the period from 1830–1850, Louisville, Kentucky, Columbus, Ohio, and St. Louis, Missouri, were the leaders in magazine publication but Cincinnati with its publication of the *Ladies Repository* (1841–1876), its children's publication of *Golden Hours*, and for a brief period, William T. Coggeshall's *Genius of the West* (1853–1856), continued to be an important literary center.[18] From such periodicals and from any

---

[15] It took 19 days from Philadelphia to Lexington for mail in the early 1800's, and sometimes it took a full month.

[16] Mott, *History of American Magazines*, I, 126, 206–207.

[17] *Ibid.*, 149–170.

[18] Some of the editorial problems and correspondence of the *Christian Advocate, Golden*

corroborative correspondence one may be able to find about the editors and publishers of these early magazines, the writer of local history will be able to uncover a rich storehouse of material about the locale of his community.

In addition to the contemporary periodicals, the files of historical and genealogical publications should not be overlooked in a search for local material. Not only the general historical quarterlies such as the *American Historical Review* (New York, 1895–), the *Annual Reports of the American Historical Association* (New York, 1884–), the *Mississippi Valley Historical Review* (Cedar Rapids, 1914–), and the *Proceedings* (1907–) may offer helpful data but there are also state and regional periodicals and published collections which should be very useful to you in your quest. For the Eastern states, the *Collections* and *Proceedings of the Massachusetts Historical Society* date back as far as the last decade of the eighteenth century, while the *New England Historical and Genealogical Register* began in 1847 at Boston. There is, likewise, the *Pennsylvania Magazine of History and Biography* (Philadelphia, 1877–). Middle-western publications are of a later vintage, such as the *Old Northwest Genealogical Quarterly* (Columbus, 1898–1912) and the *Ohio State Archaeological and Historical Quarterly* (Columbus, 1887–), the *Collections of the Michigan Pioneer and Historical Society* (Lansing, 1874–1915), the *Journal of the Illinois State Historical Society* (1908–), the *Wisconsin Magazine of History* (Madison, 1917–) and the publications of the state of Iowa, *Palimpsest*, 1920– and the *Iowa Journal of History and Politics*, 1903–, as well as the *Annals of Iowa* (Des Moines, 1863–). Those of the Pacific Coast are of a still later date, i.e. *Huntington Library Quarterly*, San Marino, California, 1937–. For the South there is the *Journal of Southern History* (Baton Rouge, 1935), the *North Carolina Historical Review* (Raleigh, 1924–), the *Louisiana Historical Quarterly* (New Orleans, 1917–), and the *Filson Club Publications* (Louisville, 1884–).

These are but a few periodicals and annals named at random from a host of half-a-hundred or more historical publications still in existence or at one time published in this country. The *Union List of Serials in Libraries of the United States and Canada* (New York, 1927 and supplements) will help you find the particular publications for your locality and tell you which libraries have files for the period you wish to study.

Periodicals, thus, will be useful to you not only for the contemporary life they will mirror but also for the historical or genealogical articles you may find in them about life in an earlier period. Newspapers, on the other hand, are most useful for the contemporary picture they present. The files of both are important to you, however, in your search for the local history of your community.

Hours, and the *Ladies Repository* may be found in the Williams MS. Collection in the Documents Department of the Ohio State Archaeological and Historical Society Library. Some of the letters of Coggeshall are also in this same library, in the Coggeshall Collection.

CHAPTER IV

PUBLIC RECORDS

CENSUS REPORTS

CENSUS reports, rightly used, are a revealing source of information on many aspects of local community life. The Federal Government, beginning in 1790, has taken the census at ten-year intervals. The first one was confined to the states of Connecticut, Delaware, Georgia, Kentucky, Maine, Maryland, Massachusetts, New Hampshire, New Jersey, New York, North Carolina, Pennsylvania, Rhode Island, South Carolina, Tennessee, Vermont, and Virginia. Census schedules were sent to the State Department, but those for Delaware, Georgia, Kentucky, New Jersey, Tennessee, and Virginia were destroyed when the British burned the Capitol at Washington in the War of 1812. The remaining schedules were published by the Bureau of the Census in 1909 in twelve volumes and are known as the 1790 Census.[1]

This census record has been widely distributed among libraries and should be easily found in most larger ones. Though the work of preparing the 1790 schedules for publication was very carefully done, many mistakes in reading names crept in. Nevertheless, it is "one of the most useful source materials to be found in print, as it definitely locates each male head of a household in a definite town, and shows the general distribution of surnames."[2] The 1790 census gives the full name of each male head of a household, the number of free white males sixteen years and upward, and the same information for those under sixteen. It also gives the number of free white females including heads of families, the number of all other free persons, and the number of slaves.

The 1800 census was taken in all the states previously mentioned as well as in Indiana, Mississippi, Ohio, and the District of Columbia. None of the schedules for any of the early censuses after 1790 have been printed by the government, although they are all to be found in Washington—except a few which have been lost, notably the Alabama census for 1800. Referring to the 1800 census, it may be noted that

the information gathered was the names of heads of families, and the number of free white males and free white females in five sections, under 10 years of age, of 10 and under 16, of 16 and under 26, of 26 and under 45, and of 45 years and upward; the number of all other free persons, except Indians not taxed, and the number of slaves.[3]

---

[1] This includes Virginia, whose volume is based on the state's own enumerations, or tax lists, of the years from 1782 to 1785.

[2] Jacobus, *Genealogy as Pastime and Profession*, 70.

[3] *Heads of Families . . . 1800—Vermont* (Montpelier, Vt., 1938).

Each decade those states admitted to the Union since the last census were added to the steadily increasing list. From the date of statehood, it is relatively easy to discover when the census schedules for your state begin.[4]

In the first six censuses, 1790 to 1840, only the name of the head of the family is given in full, but, beginning with the census of 1850 each individual member of the family or household was listed by name. The age in years, the occupation, the place of birth (that is, the state or the country), and the value of the real estate of each was given. This census also included for the first time the nationalities of the population. The records contained in the 1860, 1870, and 1880 censuses are open for examination in Washington, but those in the later censuses, taken within the last fifty years, are sealed to public use.[5]

Some states, such as New York State, for example, have taken censuses midway between the periods of the federal censuses. Others occasionally took a census for some special purpose.[6] In addition to the formal censuses there are tax lists, which, according to one writer, provide a sort of census of the town, in that all taxpayers are listed. As the federal census it taken every ten years only, these tax lists frequently serve as an intermediate census, and from them you can determine just when your people moved away from town, or ceased to pay taxes, at least. You can figure out the size of their farms or how much land they owned and the value of it.[7]

Considering the census as a source of information, the historian, Joseph Schafer, recounts the story of the search made by a writer for the early boyhood environment of a prominent man whose biography he was writing. Nothing was known of the man's parentage until his name was looked up in the 1860 census. There, under the proper town, county, and state, one found:

Thomas Anderson was described as 41 years of age, farmer, with $3,000 real estate and $800 personality, born in Norway. His wife, also born in Norway, was thirty-five. All of his six children, the eldest, Anders, being eleven, were born in Wisconsin. . . .

Turning now to the Census of Agricultural Productions for the same town, the farm of Thomas Anderson was described as containing eighty acres of improved land, eight acres unimproved, total value $3,000. He had "implements and machines" worth $100; also three horses, two working oxen, five milch cows, four "other cattle," eighteen sheep, five swine. Total value of livestock, $500.

---

[4] Doane, *Searching for Your Ancestors*, 232–235, gives in detail the list of states represented in the censuses of 1800, 1810, and 1820, together with a list of all missing schedules of these censuses as well as for the 1790 census. Consultation of this book, if available, may save time and postage in writing to Washington.

[5] *Ibid.*, 154, 155.

[6] *The 1864 Census of the Territory of Arizona* was published in mimeograph form in 1938 by the Historical Records Survey.

[7] Doane, *Searching for Your Ancestors*, 91–92.

The crop in 1859 included one hundred bushels of wheat, one hundred bushels of oats, ten bushels of peas, four bushels of grass seed, sixty bushels of potatoes, twenty pounds of wool, seven hundred pounds of butter, eight tons of hay; and he slaughtered animals valued at $50.

The census schedules enable us to affirm that this Norwegian family must have lived in the state at least since 1849, and probably longer, that it ranked well in the social group to which it belonged, owning a relatively prosperous pioneer farm, and that the presence in it of three boys, two of them already old enough to perform farm work, prophesied greater prosperity in the future. The information was not extensive, and to cold imagination it may not reveal very much. But what there was of it was concrete, definite, and dependable. Many a novelist would rejoice to find so much about his hero's boyhood. And the delectable quality about the source from which that knowledge comes is the fact that it would yield similar information about every person living on a Wisconsin farm in 1860.[8]

The fullness of information about this forgotten pioneer of the Central West is truly surprising. Even though you would not want to give so detailed an account of every one of your early settlers, yet to have information of this sort available for the first census taken in your community would be of inestimable worth in drawing an accurate picture of the times, the state of development, population, and economic conditions. Depending upon the particular census, you should be able to find the heads of families for each decade, the approximate age of minors for the decades from 1790 to 1840, and the real age as well as the full name of all persons beginning with 1850. After 1850, too, you should be able to find the state or country in which each one of the community's individuals was born. The 1850 census, therefore, for the first time might inform you of the birthplace of settlers who came into the locality thirty, fifty, or even seventy years before 1850.

Another historical writer obtained the 1860 census report for Craighead County, Arkansas, when he was writing his local history. This report shows the number of dwellings in the county, the number of families, the name of every person in the family plus the farm laborers, the occupation of the head of each family, the value of the real estate and personal estate, the place of birth of each individual, the names of those married within the year, those who were attending school that year, the number of persons over twenty years of age who could not read and write, those deaf, dumb, blind or insane, and the age, sex, and color of each person enumerated.[9] The census reports for other counties would reveal similar data.

You may say, "Fine, now where do I get hold of the earliest census of my community?" The original census population schedules for the years 1790–1870 are in the National Archives. There are some gaps in the

---

[8] Schafer, *Trans-Mississippi West*, 298–299.
[9] Harry L. Williams, *History of Craighead County, Arkansas* (Author, c. 1930).

returns, however, and the schedules are missing, in whole or in part, for some of the states, particularly for the period prior to 1830. Requests for information concerning an individual should include the name of the head of the family with whom he resided, the town or township, county, and state, as well as the census year. Prior to 1850 the census schedules contain only the names of the heads of families and not the names of all the individual members of the families. For the duration of the war the National Archives can supply information from the census schedules only for legal or war-related purposes. Upon request it will, however, furnish a list of experienced private searchers who have indicated willingness to undertake investigations for a fee. Photostatic copies can be made of single pages showing the entries covering one or more families or of the pages covering an entire township or county. The cost will be determined by the number of pages to be photostated.[10] Inquiries concerning census population schedules prior to 1880 should be directed to the Chief, General Reference Division, National Archives, Washington 25, D. C.

ABSTRACTS OF TITLE AND TITLE DEEDS

Abstracts of title and title deeds are unquestioned local history sources. The smaller the area included in your local history, the more important these become. In fact, in such a very limited area such as a village, town, or city, the township plat of land grantees is a good starting point for the local history.

If you happen to own land, you know the importance of an abstract in establishing ownership of real estate. You probably know, too, upon examination of your abstract, that all the original land belonged to the states, to the United States—or, in the East, to personal or corporate proprietors like the Penn family or the Massachusetts Bay Company. When the country was opened for settlement, the government or the proprietors sold the land to the settler, who was variously called the pre-emptor, the original entryman, or the original grantee. Whenever this man in turn sold his land or part of it to another, a record or abstract of title was drawn up and duly certified and filed by an abstractor. Suppose, for example, that a town has grown up squarely in the center of a tract of land which was originally granted by the government years ago to one Thomas Fenner. The town has now many individual property owners, each of whom has an abstract showing his right to his property. Just as a

---

[10] See above, pages 39–40, for the prices of photostatic copies, photoprints, and microfilm. It is possible that a prominent lawyer or abstractor in your locality may already have secured a photostatic copy of the earliest census or of a later one. If not, perhaps he, the local newspaper editor, the head of the local history society, or the librarian might be willing to share in the expense for the sake of having a permanent record of the earliest settlers at hand and readily available in the community. It should be remembered that the 1790 census is published as well as the 1800 census for Vermont. These may be consulted in large libraries throughout the country. The 1850 census has been copied and may be found in many state historical societies.

family tree leads back to a common ancestor, so all these abstracts lead back through the various divisions to the original tract granted to Thomas Fenner by the government.

Often a prominent lawyer of your community will be able to show you abstracts which will give you the necessary information regarding the time and details of the original grant and the one to whom it was granted, together with the dates of all the subsequent early purchases of subdivisions etc. The lawyer should make no charge for this and will usually be glad to cooperate when he learns your purpose.

If a lawyer or a banker does not have what you want, you will have to go to the abstractor, usually located at the county seat, or—as in New England—in the local town. Joseph Schafer describes the situation in the Middle West as follows:

> Now, the professional abstractors of every county are the historians of land ownership for their appropriate constituency. At much labor and expense they have compiled a title index covering every forty acre tract of land in the county. This index gives the name of the original entryman, with date of entry, and similar data for each transfer following. Ordinarily, this information is marketed in the form of abstracts of title. But the public spirited abstractor will be disposed to aid historians by permitting them to take necessary items from his title index, or by supplying desired information at the actual cost for clerk hire.[11]

SURVEYORS' NOTES

Perhaps you will think that, having gotten as far back as the original grant, you can go no farther, yet there is one step more, and that a very worthwhile one. Having bought the land from the Indians, the government or the proprietor wanted it surveyed, so that it could be opened up for settlement in an orderly manner. In the case of government lands, the Deputy United States Surveyor General commissioned a surveyor of the locality to establish the base lines and principal meridians, then to lay out the ranges of townships north or south of the base line and east or west of the meridians, and finally to divide the townships into sections.

Schafer has aptly described the activities of this early visitor to western communities:

> With his chainmen and axemen, the surveyor pitched tent in some sheltering grove, by creek or riverside, unlimbered his instruments, and began running lines. He might be a man of wide experience who had inspected many diverse types of widely separated regions, or he might be a recent college graduate altogether wanting in the landlooker's guile. In either case, the new field of his labors was to him interesting in itself and besides he was instructed to record concerning every part of it covered by his survey certain definite observations.
>
> If the outer boundaries of townships had not been established, his first problem was to run these. Then, beginning at a point one mile west of the southeast corner he ran one mile north, and closed section 36 by running to the east boundary one mile. Another mile north, with a right line east set off section 25. So he continued till the range of sections was outlined from 36 to 1, when he proceeded

[11] Schafer, *Trans-Mississippi West*, 296–297.

to the next range, and the next, until the township had been divided into thirty-six numbered sections.

In accomplishing the work he had, of course, to walk all around each square mile of territory and, unless the land was either densely wooded or excessively broken, he was sure to have seen nearly every part of every section.

And what the surveyor saw he described according to formulas for that purpose made and provided. He exhibited on his township plat the courses and junctions of streams, the direction of trails or roads, the location of mineral outcrops; also such human signs as Indian villages, battle fields, earthworks and squatters' cabins. Above all, however, he described the land, using simple designation like first class, second class, and third class to indicate how relatively desirable it would be to future cultivators; and he also called attention to its broken, rocky, swampy, or hilly character.

This information is historically valuable; yet wherever in our state the federal and state *soil survey* has been completed, the description of the land given therein supersedes the surveyor's description because it is vastly more detailed and more scientific. But there is one feature of the surveyor's notes for which no substitute can be found, namely, the record of the nature of the original covering of the land. The surveyor was inevitably impressed by facts about the timber and the underbrush, for these would have a decisive bearing upon the desirability of the lands for agriculture and his notes were designed to be useful as an aid in land selection. Prudent landlookers habitually provided themselves at the land office with transcripts in which they hoped to locate and the evidence these notes furnished about the land being 'prairie,' or 'lightly timbered,' or 'free from underbrush' was usually the determining point affecting its selection, soil conditions being equal to those of competing areas. Everybody, native and foreign, preferred open land.

By studying the record left by the surveyor of a given township, which may have been settled ninety or one hundred years ago, the student of today can imaginatively enter into the human motives governing the process of settlement and farm making. With the immigrant, who has visited the land office and brought away plat and notes, he can penetrate the heavy woods of section 12, or follow a trail through the brush-free oak opening in section 30. He can see that the long swale lying athwart sections 23 and 31 prevented the early occupation of section 24 by cutting that part of the township off from a practicable road to market; and the early purchase of the lands in sections 9 and 16 is explained to him by the fact that here a combination of high prairie, woodland, and low prairie or meadow gave opportunity for ideal farm locations.[12]

The surveyors penciled their notes in thin hip-pocket books. The same writer observes that "the plats and notes of the original survey were usually executed in triplicate. One was sent to the General Land Office in Washington, one to the local land office in the given land district, and one to the Surveyor General's office.[13]

[12] *Ibid.*, 293–295.

[13] *Ibid.*, 295. Some of these note books as well as surveying records and interesting correspondence may be found in the extensive Samuel Williams MS. Collection recently acquired by the library of the Ohio State Archaeological and Historical Society at Columbus. Williams was the chief clerk in the office of the Surveyor General at Cincinnati, Ohio, during many political administrations in the first part of the nineteenth century.

When three copies of a surveyor's notes were made, it seems impossible that they all should entirely disappear. If they cannot be located in one of the three offices mentioned, they will probably show up in another. Photostatic copies can always be procured from the General Land Office in Washington.

PUBLIC SCHOOL RECORDS

Your local superintendent of public schools can be depended upon to inform you of the way the schools are organized and where the local records are most likely to be found. The minutes of the local board of education, if available, should give much important data regarding the schools. Many states give state funds for the use of local schools. If this sum is larger than that given by the local taxpayers, the records have a tendency to be filed in the state capital. Otherwise they should be found in the county courthouse or in the office of the county superintendent of schools. Records should be found there for each school district organization, giving the financial statement, the teachers' names and the pupil attendance, information about the buildings, especially about the erection and repair of school buildings, the number of grades taught, and other data. Be on the lookout for school censuses taken in some localities in the decade of the 1870's. In the absence of vital records these censuses tell much, particularly regarding ages and places of residence.[14]

Occasional teachers' registers or classbooks as well as other school records have been acquired by historical society libraries, often along with other collections. It is, therefore, wise to inquire at such a library for the scattered school records which they might have for your locality.

OTHER PUBLIC RECORDS

The local archives containing the public records of the counties, cities, towns, villages, and countryside are probably in a worse condition than other public archives in the United States. Even the state records have not had adequate housing or servicing in many states and only the awakening of an enlightened public to this sad neglect will remedy the situation. Hardly any two of the 3,066 counties of the country preserve the public records in exactly the same way. When to these 3,066 units are added the thousands of towns, cities, and villages, each with its particular public records, one can easily see how heterogeneous are the methods and means for caring for the records upon which these units must ultimately depend for the writing of their local history.

Dr. Luther H. Evans has stated it well when he said, in referring to the local archives of the country:

We may safely say that the vast majority of these records and papers are unorganized, that they have no titles which can be used for purposes of citation, and

---

[14] Doane, *Searching for Your Ancestors*, 92.

that their contents are known in each case only to the person immediately in charge, and, in most cases, not even to him. In other words, we have to deal with mountainous heaps, indeed thousands of tons, of unassorted and unknown documents, some of which are priceless and some of which are plain rubbish.[15]

Within recent years the condition of the local records has been improved and their use has been facilitated to some extent by the work of the WPA Historical Records Survey, which was conducted from 1936 to 1942 for the "discovery, preservation and listing of basic materials for research in the history of the United States." Throughout the country, workers of the Survey proceeded to arrange, classify, and inventory the official records of towns, cities, counties, states, and the federal government, as well as the records of churches and collections of manuscripts in public depositories. By the end of June, 1942, when the Survey was terminated, there had been published more than 700 inventories of county archives, over 200 inventories of the archives of municipalities (including the New England towns), over 100 volumes of inventories of public manuscript collections, nearly 200 volumes of inventories of church archives and directories of religious bodies, over 600 volumes of inventories of federal archives, and more than 250 other publications—a total of over 2,000 inventories. Sets of these have been placed in a selected list of libraries throughout the nation, and in every case copies of an inventory have been supplied to the agency whose records were covered in that particular volume. Each inventory contains an historical sketch of the locality and of the agency, together with other useful information. Be sure to see whether such a publication has been issued for the local area in which you are especially interested.[16] The job was, of course, not completed, and there are still not only numerous areas but long periods which remain entirely unrecorded. Some day, it is hoped, that communities will become conscious enough of local pride to apply sufficient pressure upon their political leaders for the preservation of these valuable materials.[17]

COUNTY ARCHIVES

When you come to use county records, you may not find the same kind of reception in the courthouse that you are accustomed to receive in a public library. Both are public buildings and, for your purpose, both are depositories of information, but that is about as far as the comparison will carry. There is no fee in American public offices for examination of records. The hours are usually from about nine to twelve and from one to four, so you should plan to do your work during the day time. County

---

[15] Luther H. Evans, *The Historical Records Survey* (Washington, 1938), 4–5.

[16] All research projects of the WPA are listed in "Bibliography of Research Projects Reports" published in mimeograph form from time to time, beginning with Feb. 2, 1940. Four were issued in 1940; the fifth on Sept. 24, 1941.

[17] C. Kenneth Blood and Margaret C. Norton, "Some Problems in the Administration of County Records," *Illinois Libraries* (Springfield), XXV, 1943, pp. 137–142.

and town officials have many duties and do not expect to wait on those who wish to consult their records, but as a rule they are courteous in giving information about the material in their custody. Generally the volumes are large and bulky and, if you aren't a Hercules or have that helpless look, the public official may take pity on you and assist you in lifting the numerous tomes from his top shelves. Nevertheless, you should have consideration for the official, since, as one writer reminds us, "Clerks of towns and municipalities, registrars and court officials are busy people. If they were to spend the time to do all that seekers for information ask of them they would often have little time left for their regular work."[18]

Some people become timid, even panicky, when they come into contact with a public official. If you are of this sort, just pluck up your courage, and remember that officials are public servants, eager to please—especially just before election time. Local officials are human and some of them may enjoy seeming annoyed and look upon it as a prerogative of their dignity. You will probably get more by tact than by insisting upon your rights as a citizen. If they find you appreciate what they are doing for you they will often be of great help when the ice has been broken.[19]

It may be that you have no personal acquaintance with the county officials. In such a case you may find it advantageous to secure a "To Whom It May Concern" letter of introduction from some prominent man in the county. You can draft the letter yourself, suggesting what you want it to say, and ask the leading citizen to include that information in what he writes. Such a letter should state your purpose, and if the writer can properly emphasize the contribution to the community your local history will make, you will find little or no difficulty in securing access to all the records of the county.

It is wise to have a talk with each of the more important county officials. In this conversation state your purpose and ask what he thinks his records, past and present, can contribute in the way of material for a local history. If he is intelligent and alert he may be able to suggest data which would never have occurred to you. If, however, he knows little of how material is gathered, he may be unimaginative enough to believe that his records contain nothing of historical value. The duties and abilities of public officials differ so much from one state to another that it is impossible to say that all officials bearing the same title will have the same records.

It is hoped that for your particular county and period the inventory of your county records may have been printed. Inquiry there will reveal whether this is the case. If it has not been published, you will have to start in without this great aid.

---

[18] Stetson, *Art of Ancestor Hunting*, 71.
[19] Doane, *Searching for Your Ancestors*, 80–81, 95.

In such an inventory you will find a general table of contents as well as a valuable index with ample cross references. These will refer you to the entries pertaining to the subjects on which you are seeking information. Suppose you are gathering material for a history of Lebanon, Indiana, or for Boone County in which the town is located. You would like to know something about the family affairs of the "founder" or of some other prominent individual whom you have run across. Evans explains what you, or any student of local history, inventory in hand, would do.

He would probably be first interested in examining the birth records of his family members so that he may gain the earliest accurate chronological data about their lives. In this instance he is told to consult entry 543, titled, 'Records of Births,' which is located in the vital statistics division of records kept by the health commissioner.

By reading the . . . description of the duties of the health officer and . . . the history of this local office, the student will learn that the health officer first became a part of the Boone County government in 1881. In the following year the regular keeping of birth records was initiated. At the same time the health commissioner began to keep records of marriages, deaths, and dangerous diseases. . . . The entry will further inform the student that these records are contained in 19 volumes and are complete with the exception of the records for December 26, 1906, to October 1, 1907, which are reported as missing. He will also learn that 13 volumes which cover the years 1882 to December 26, 1910, are located in the recorder's record room in the county courthouse, and that since that date, records have been kept in the office of Dr. O. C. Higgins, the present health commissioner, in the Pioneer Equitable Building, at Lebanon. Aside from learning of the exact location of these records, the student will be further informed of the specific details contained in the original records. He will be told that the birth records bear dates, and tell the sex, race, and name of the newly born; the names, ages, residence, and number of children of parents; and the date of the filing of the health record. He will also be aided in his study by learning that the records volumes are indexed alphabetically by names of children.

. . . the student . . . must not ignore the marriage records. By following his cross references, he will be referred to entries 66 to 69 . . . that marriage records have been kept by one or another official in Boone County since 1831.

Upon consulting entries to deeds and tax records he may note that these have been kept for approximately a century. This observation should cause the student to wonder why these important public records were not kept earlier in Boone County. If he consults the historical sketch contained in the front of this volume he will . . . learn that the county was not formally organized until January 29, 1830, and hence no county records existed prior to this date. . . . If the student is eager to gain more detailed information concerning the history of the locality he will be able to do so by use of the select bibliographical list which follows the historical sketch. . . . One of the features in this sketch is the short account of the courthouses and other structures in which public records have been kept since the creation of Boone County.

The story of the courthouse changes should give the student a conception of the growth and importance of the county as a governmental unit of the national structure. The present Boone County limestone courthouse built in 1912, four stories in height, is the fourth structure to house the county offices and their records. This building, he will realize, is far more impressive than the original courthouse, a hewed log cabin, built in Lebanon in the autumn of 1833.[20]

The following items from a county inventory should supply some idea of the sort of records that are kept by each county official:

I. *County Court and Clerk.*

Proceedings; commissions; oaths and bonds. Bond issues. School: reports, apportionments, accounts, land sales, surety bonds. Roads and bridges; drainage ditches. Taxation and revenue: petitions; judgments and sales, pool tax assessments. Social Welfare: insane and indigent; children, public health. Accounts: claims, settlements, reports, statements, receipts. Certificates and licenses: professional, dealers, game and fish. Disbursements. Jurors. Fees and costs. Elections. Vital statistics: births, deaths. Inquests. Animals: livestock, bounties. Agriculture. Military. Management of county property. Miscellaneous.

II. *Recorder of Deeds.*

Real property: register, deeds, mortgages, levies, surveys, sales. Personal property. Vital statistics. Commissions, bonds, and affidavits. Military. Claims.

III. *Circuit Court and Clerk.*

Proceedings. Minutes, case records, juvenile division, dockets, divorce records, back tax suits, criminal, naturalization. Executions. Judgments. Jurors. Orders of publication. Office accounts: fees, cost bills. Licenses and permits: firearms, professional, liens, appointments, transcripts.

IV. *Probate Court.*

Proceedings. Minutes, case records. Executors and administrators: wills, dockets, bonds and letters, applications, inventories and appraisals, settlements, claims and allowances. Guardians and curators: bonds, settlements. Fees. Inheritance tax. Notices.

V. *Public Administrator.*

VI. *Justice of Peace.*

VII. *Coroner.*

VIII. *Sheriff.*

IX. *Prosecuting attorney.*

X. *Assessor.*

Assessments: real and personal property, income, commercial, utilities. School estimates.

XI. *Board of Equalization.*

XII. *Collector.*

Collections: general, real estate, personal property, drainage ditches, school, commercial, utilities. Delinquent taxes: real and personal tax sales, receipts.

---

[20] Luther H. Evans, "Archives as Materials for the Teaching of History," *Indiana History Bulletin* (Indianapolis), XV, 1938, pp. 150–152.

XIII. *Treasurer.*
Accounts: general, school funds, surety bonds, receipts, disbursements.
XIV. *Superintendent of Schools.*
XV. *Deputy State Commissioner of Health.*
XVI. *Social Security Commission.*
XVII. *Surveyor.*
XVIII. *Highway Commission.*
XIX. *Highway Engineer.*
XX. *Farm Bureau.*

The Historical Records Survey states that the following standard records should prove valuable sources of historical information in any county:

Minutes and Enrollment Dockets of the County (Quarterly and Probate), Circuit, and Chancery Courts, Appropriation Dockets, Cash Books, Revenue Dockets, Birth and Death Records, Marriage Records, Deed Books, Entry-Taker's Book, AAA Contracts, Juvenile Dockets, Reports to the Quarterly Court, Scholastic Census Records, Superintendent's Annual Statistical Reports, Tax Books and Records of all descriptions, Audit Reports, Trustee's Reports, Poll Tax Receipts, Automobile Registers, Vital Statistics Records, Professional Registrations, Privilege License Duplicates, and Poll Tax Receipts. . . .

The minute books should prove to be the most prolific source. The reports to the quarterly county court (or court of pleas and quarter sessions or county court) should supply much information on the finances of the county, and on roads, education, health, and agriculture—subjects in which we are deeply interested. The trustee's records will give a further insight into the receipts and expenditures of the county. Likewise, the records of the road commission, superintendent of schools, health department, and farm agent should supplement material obtained from the quarterly minutes. If one record is not available, try another record. The quarterly minutes, for example, will mention the poor commission and we may gain some insight into the administration of poor relief. . . . A deed book might give the first register's name and could be cited, instead of allowing the question to go by in the absence of the first minutes of the quarterly court.[21]

Prior to 1917 partial surveys of the county and other local archives were made in a number of the states. Franklin F. Holbrook, writing of these surveys, states:

The inventories reveal the existence of material containing a wealth of information, much of which has not yet found its way into histories. The character of this material may be indicated by an enumeration of a few of the more important groups of records which relate to the life of a whole community, and cover, more or less completely, the period of its political existence. Of these the county commissioners' records constitute the nearest approach to a connected and inclusive account of a county's past, but an amazing amount of instructive detail may be

---

[21] *Instructions for Using the County Records as Source Material* (2nd ed. Nashville, 1939), 4–5. This is a small mimeographed manual of instructions issued for the use of workers employed by the Survey.

derived from such series as registers of births, deaths, and marriages, probate records, naturalization papers, census schedules, election material, agricultural statistics, abstracts of original entries of government land, assessment rolls, and tax lists. One cannot go through these records, even in the cursory manner which suffices for an inventory, without noting numerous separate documents or items of historical and of human interest.[22]

Wills and probate records, to be found in the probate office or probate court (called the surrogate's court in New York), are fruitful sources of information regarding blood relationships, divisions of property, marriages, and vital statistics, though probate laws differ greatly from one state to another. Other documents supplying much the same information are those dealing with the distribution of an estate. Occasionally guardianship papers contain data of this nature. Wills usually give the names of the testator's children and the name of the surviving husband or wife. Administrations customarily give the heirs at law and the next of kin to the deceased. Land records will also furnish the given name of the spouse, for when land is sold by a married person the husband or wife is obliged to sign away his or her courtesy or dower rights in order to convey good title.

Records relating to the buying and selling of land will yield their bits of historical data. The Recorder of Deeds will have indexes, the grantor and grantee index, which list the conveyances of land under the names of the persons conveying the land and those to whom it was conveyed. Usually records of deeds are very long, but a brief abstract of the essential part can be made. Deeds usually give the names, dates, occupations of persons concerned, relationships, prices paid, and a rather detailed description of the land conveyed.

For the very earliest land records, the following information may aid you:

When a man began the process of securing a Grant of Land from the Colony Government, he first made a formal application for it. These applications are not always to be found now, unfortunately. Sometimes they give the applicant's former residence; sometimes the length of his actual dwelling on the land (perhaps then a wilderness in which a few settlers had built cabins, without any legal ownership of the ground); sometimes the depositions of neighbors who relate what they know of the applicant's history. The next step in procedure was the issuance of Warrants to survey the land. These Warrants, as now preserved, often have the surveys themselves,—maps of the tracts. After the Warrant, came the Patent, or Grant, from the Colonial Government to the Warrantee. Of course, after our National Government was established, similar Grants were made by the several States. Sometimes a Warrantee sold his rights, and then, the Patent would be indexed under the name of the purchaser of such, provided the latter proceeded to take out the Patent.[23]

---

[22] Holbrook, "Some Possibilities of Historical Field Work," 72–73.
[23] Allaben and Washburn, *How to Trace and Record Your Ancestry*, 31–32.

Land grants and early warrants for the survey of lands, however, are usually found at the state capital rather than in the local county. Land records in many states are kept at the county seats, but in Connecticut and Vermont, in each separate town. While on the subject, it is well to remember that

the land office documents include, in addition to the plats and notes, the *Tract Books* in which are recorded the names of persons who became purchasers or pre-emptors of the government lands, with dates of entry. These might be used in telling the story of the absorption of the lands by private persons, the beginnings of settlement, the relative desirability of the general types of land as judged from the order in which they were taken up. However, the *Tract Books* are awkward to use on account of the interlineations and erasures which they bear.[24]

Since you will be consulting many indexes, the advice of Allaben and Washburn might be useful:

Indexes are differently arranged, some of them being more-or-less alphabetical, irrespective of the dates of the documents which they list. Other indexes are arranged according to dates, and these may be—usually are—alphabetical to some extent, within given periods. Few indexes in record offices are strictly alphabetical, either as to surname or Christian names.[25]

In dealing with the very early years of your county or any town within it, or with the years immediately before the county came into existence, it is well to remember that county and town boundaries were changed many times during the colonial and early state periods. For example, perhaps an extreme one, Russell County, Virginia, was formed in 1786 from Washington County, Washington from Fincastle in 1777, Fincastle from Botetourt in 1772, Botetourt from Augusta in 1770, Augusta from Orange in 1745, Orange from Spotsylvania in 1734, and Spotsylvania from Essex, King William, and King and Queen counties in 1721. These three in turn were formed from still older counties.[26] It might be that for some elusive bits of information the county seats of each of these counties might have to be visited.

Perhaps the published inventory of your county archives in its historical sketch will give information about the manner in which your county was formed or whether it was ever a part of a nearby county. A certain census publication may also be called to your aid, for it contains a series of maps depicting how the country expanded from 1790 to 1900. These maps also indicate the boundary lines of the various counties of the states and the changes which have occurred in them from time to time.[27]

---

[24] Schafer, *Trans-Mississippi West*, 296.

[25] *How to Trace and Record Your Ancestry*, 26. The index will often use the terms Liber and Folio, meaning volume and page. *Ibid.*, 27.

[26] *Ibid.*, 25.

[27] *A Century of Population Growth from the First Census of the United States to the Twelfth* is the work referred to; it was published in 1909 by the Bureau of the Census.

Again, you may find that your own county is the "ancestor" of a nearby county. If you learn that the population of your county in 1820 was, say, 6,543, and in 1830 was only 4,321, you might assume either that the figures were incorrect or that there had been a great exodus during the preceding decade. The true explanation might be that your county in 1820 included all of that is now an adjoining county, which was set off at some time between 1820 and 1830.

Remember that no hard and fast rules can be laid down for the searching of public records. Nearly every state and every county has its own sources, its own method or lack of method of keeping and indexing its public records.

TOWN RECORDS

In the United States there are approximately 16,600 cities, towns, and villages.[28] Very few town records have been published, except in New England, where the vital records, pertaining to births, deaths, and marriages have often been put into printed form. In Massachusetts there has been a great vogue of printing vital records down to 1850. You will find them for many towns. Connecticut and Maine have followed at a very much slower pace. You never know when you will find the vital records of some town printed in magazines or local histories.[29]

The keeping of vital records has gone through three stages. About the first stage a writer remarks: "In the earliest days of our country provision was made by local laws and ordinances for the preservation of records of births, marriages, and deaths. These records were not kept accurately nor fully, and probably in a majority of cases they have not been preserved."[30] When laws were finally passed requiring the recording of vital statistics they were often carelessly kept or not at all obeyed. Therefore in the late nineteenth century there are many blanks.[31] Fortunately the twentieth century has brought a new sense of recording and elaborate records are now kept. You are referred to the *New England Historical and Genealogical Register* (Boston), XC, 1936, pp. 9–31 for a description of state practice regarding vital records.[32]

---

[28] The 1930 census showed 1,833 cities of more than 5,000 population; 1,332 towns between 2,500 and 5,000; 3,087 places between 1,000 and 2,500; and 10,346 towns and villages with less than 1,000 population.

[29] Doane, *Searching for Your Ancestors*, 90–91.

[30] William Nelson, "Church Records in New Jersey," *Journal of the Presbyterian Historical Society*, March and June, 1904, p. 1.

[31] Doane, *Searching for Your Ancestors*, 83.

[32] *Ibid.*, 89–90. In Appendix B, referred to above, are listed only eastern states, plus Iowa, Louisiana, Michigan and Virginia. Harold Clarke Durrell's article of January, 1936, should be referred to for full information about the activities of the vital statistics offices in all the forty-eight states. Doane notes (p. 229): "In many of the more recently established states the county clerk seems to be the repository for marriage records, and in some case for birth and death records." The Historical Records Survey has now published guides to the vital statistics records of most of the states.

Town public records do not consist of vital statistics alone. In the New England town clerk's offices will also be found the town meeting records, chronicling the local governmental affairs. In other parts of the country a different system of town and city government may prevail, but the records which are kept deal with the governmental affairs of the locality.

Such town records, if complete, should go back to the beginning of the political organization of the community. The mayor or town clerk should know where they are kept. A village of from 500 to 1,000 population should not have more than half a dozen large record books. From them you should be able to secure a list of all town officers from the beginning to the present. They should tell of the boundaries of the town and of any extensions that may have been made. They should give in detail the limits of the various wards and give the names of the council members or alderman of each.

The debates of town meetings are not recorded or published but decisions reached are printed. The motives behind these actions should be studied. How did the people arrive at these agreements? Every town has its interest groups. On what are these interests based? Who was the leader of the group that won? Who was the leader of the group that lost? What was the role played by such leaders and groups in the town's day to day activities? What attributes of leadership were possessed by the organizer of each group? Was there a half a loaf philosophy, or a quid pro quo? For example, in the New England town meeting the warrant calls for an extension of the sidewalk on Main Street for an additional one-third of a mile. The warrant also calls for an extension of electric lights by 25 poles on Christian Hill. Main street was awarded one-fourth of a mile of sidewalk, while Christian Hill was granted 12 electric lights. What was the process behind this compromise which granted part to each group but not all to both? In the study of attitudes, in the absence of recorded opinions or statements the local historian must infer the role played by status, prestige, interest, and even isolation as factors making for or militating against decisions and actions.

The city or town ordinances will be found to yield information on many phases of community life. For example, you can read in the ordinances of Parkville, Missouri, whose population has varied from 300 to 650 during the past ninety years, that "no circus or menagerie or combination thereof shall be permitted to perform without first obtaining a license," and that "no theatrical or other exhibition or place of amusement . . . shall be permitted to exhibit without license, nor shall organ grinders, dancing or tamborin girls, or any thing of kindred character be permitted to wander about the streets" without a license. Since these ordinances were drawn up about 1855, you can imagine some of the amusements of the people at the time. If the accounts of receipts and disbursement have been accurately kept, you may even be able to find out what, and how frequently, circuses, menageries, organ grinders, dancing and tamborin girls, and ventriloquists paid visits to your community after, incidentally, having paid their $5 to $30 to obtain a license. The river port of Parkville, Missouri, for example, had a ventriloquist visit it on May 18, 1858. Ten days later a circus with two side shows arrived. Two months later came another performance as well as a "Thespian Show." Two days later still another exhibition was given. The following year an equal number and variety of attractions was afforded the residents of the community and countryside, including a panorama and a minstrel show. A decade later the amusement business was about as active as usual, if one is to judge by the number of licenses issued. It was the day of the showboat and probably any river port of the period would offer like amusements. From these same records one can learn that from 1858 to 1862 only four peddlers visited the town, though as many as three came in the one year of 1870.

Do not jump to hasty conclusions, but analyze before deciding. When you find an ordinance like the following in Parkville's records for the 1860's, you might think that the early citizens were a pretty rowdy group, or you could merely conclude that they were being given a warning of what would happen if they became rowdy:

Whoever shall in this city willfully disturb the peace of others by violent, tumultuous, offensive, or obstreperous conduct or carriage, or by loud and unusual noises, or by unseemly, profane, obscene, or offensive language calculated to provoke a breach of the peace or by assaulting, striking, or fighting another . . . shall be deemed guilty of a misdemeanor.

To help you arrive at a correct conclusion it would be well to remember that usually such ordinances are made after it was shown that they were necessary.

What was the public attitude toward religion when it was thought fit to pass an ordinance punishing anyone who should "disquiet or disturb any congregation or assembly met for religious worship by making a noise or by rude and indecent behavior or profane discourse within their place of worship, or so near the same as to disturb the order or the solemnity of the meeting?" It was a day of few bathtubs and bathing suits that prompted the town to protect its public morals with an ordinance like the following:

Whoever shall bathe, wade, or swim in the Missouri river or in any other water course, pond, or pool within three hundred yards of the city limits, within one hour before sunrise and one hour after sunset, being naked or insufficiently clad to prevent improper exposure of the person shall be deemed guilty of a misdemeanor.

The attitude toward Sabbath observance appears in an ordinance forbidding in this city "play on Sunday at billiards, ten pins, or other games of amusement . . . in any highway, thoroughfare, or other public place . . . ." Moreover, one can imagine that the citizens of 1858 were a modest group since they were not permitted even to "exhibit or show any stallion, jack, or bull in the street or any other public place in said city."

The ordinances also reveal the precautions the early city fathers took for preventing communicable diseases, fires, and even speed demons. A Parkville ordinance of 1858 forbade any person to

ride or drive any horse, mule, gelding, or other animal . . . attached to any sleigh, carriage, waggon, or dray, or other vehicle in or upon any street, alley, avenue, or public square within the city faster than a moderate trot or pace (unless in case of urgent necessity).

When a few years later the railroad came to the town an ordinance prohibited trains to pass through the streets faster than four miles an hour! Other ordinances discouraged vagrancy, gambling, burglary, and other vices. Also, "the Marshall as keeper of the Calaboose" was "to be allowed forty cents a day for every prisoner in the Calaboose and seventy-five cents as turnkey's fees for putting in and taking out the prisoner in addition to his fees as Marshall."

What was the attitude of your community toward the first automobiles? Turn to the appropriate year and you may find, as in Lake Forest, Illinois, that it was unlawful for an automobile to proceed through your quiet streets unless preceded by a man on a bicycle carrying a light at night or ringing a bell or blowing a horn by day. Such provisions often survive unrepealed after the need has passed and cartoons in recent issues of the *American Magazine* inform us, for example, that sheepherders are forbidden to wear false faces while driving their charges through Trenton, N. J.; that in Kentucky the law holds you negligent if you walk behind a mule without speaking to the animal; that Tulsa, Okla., has an ordinance putting a time limit of three minutes on kisses enjoyed in public; that in Ohio it is prohibited for dogs to worry anyone; and that in Idaho it is unlawful for any person to participate in a dogfight.

STATE PUBLIC RECORDS

In an earlier section of this chapter mention was made of inventories of public papers in state archives by the Historical Records Survey. There are, however, many other aids to the location of historical material. Most of these will be found in the state historical society library or state library, or in other large city and university libraries.

A number of bibliographies and guides were mentioned in chapter one. To these should be added others.[33] Hockett lists a number of guides to

---

[33] These are: (1) Richard R. Bowker, *State Publications*, 4 vols. (New York, 1899–1909). (2) Thomas L. Bradford, *Bibliographer's Manual of American History*. Edited and revised by S. V. Henkels, 5 vols. (Philadelphia, 1907–1910). (3) James B. Childs, *An Account of Government Document Bibliography in the United States and Elsewhere* (Washington, 1927). (4) Adelaide R. Hasse, *Index of Economic Material in Documents of the States of the United States*. 13 vols. (Washington, 1907–1922). (5) *Handbook of Learned Societies and Institutions: American* (Washington, 1908). (6) Library of Congress, Division of Documents, *Monthly Check List of State Publications* (Washington, 1910–).

historical documents for each of the states, for the South, for the Pacific Coast, for the Mississippi Valley, and for the original thirteen states.[34] Channing, Hart, and Turner's *Guide* gives an even longer list for each state and for Canada.

Many of the older states have printed their colonial and early state documents. These are vast storehouses of information for nearly every phase of the life of the period they cover. One writer on this subject informs us:

State Records, that is, the collections of original documents and papers usually to be found in the office of the Secretary of State of our older States—and which are easily accessible to inspection—furnish material of the greatest value . . . and should always be examined. These documents consist of petitions, affidavits, charges, and counter-charges, records of special court cases, commissions, etc.; bills of lading and commmercial papers, military rosters and report, surveys, etc., etc., which at one time or another have demanded the attention of the legislative or executive branch of the State's or colony's government and which will generally be found arranged and bound in order of years, and labelled Military, Ecclesiastical, Societies, Travel, etc., etc. Many of the States have already printed these documents.[35]

Some further idea of the historical data in the state documents is given by the following:

The records of the State . . . including the printed statutes and legislative journals, and reports of State officers and bureaus, should also be examined, to ascertain the relations between the State and the political section (county, town, village, or city) which is to be the subject of the contemplated history. For instance: The creation of the county, with its original boundaries, will be found in some statute; other statutes will describe the boundary changes, if there have been any, and any other legislation specifically affecting the county. Even petitions to the legislature, emanating from the county, may have bearing on local affairs. The reports of State officers, commissions or bureaus, may contain important matter of local interest,—affecting, for example, the manufactures, fish and game, agriculture, the schools, public libraries, or charitable and penal institutions. In short, the official records, properly utilized, will prove to be a mine of reliable information.[36]

In an earlier section it has been mentioned that land grants, early warrants for the survey of lands, military lists, and state census schedules are usually to be found at the state capital. To the office of the adjutant general of the state you may look for military records of service in domestic and foreign wars from Indian times until the present.

---

[34] Hockett, *Introduction to American History*, 149–156; see also pp. 42–45.

[35] *Guide to the Study and Reading of American History*, 132–150.

[36] Henry R. Stiles, *A Handbook of Practical Suggestions for the Use of Students in Genealogy* (Albany, 1899), 25. *Suggestions to Local Historians, in Wisconsin*, 3. Some day, it is hoped that every state will have an adequate State Archives such as that in the State of Illinois or the Hall of Records at Annapolis, Maryland, where state records may be properly preserved and accessible to qualified users.

The Pension Bureau at Washington has records of the soldiers of the Revolution and all subsequent wars who have drawn pensions. The bureau can furnish a transcript of any application which was made for a pension. These may be of value in gathering biographical data about early settlers or other prominent men, for the applications give the soldier's own statement, made under oath, regarding his military services. Doane states:

To secure a pension, an ex-soldier of the Revolution had to submit to the authorities in Washington proof of his service and his eligibility for a pension. Consequently, the papers which he submitted to the Pension Bureau contained statements, signed and sworn to, that he had served in a specified organization and had taken part in certain expeditions, campaigns, battles, or marches, and that he was identical with the soldier named in the rolls of the company or companies in which he claimed to have served. Moreover, he had to prove that he was 'indigent' and needed assistance. Therefore, he had to file not only his own sworn statement, but also affidavits from other soldiers who served with him or knew of his service, and affidavits certifying his financial condition at the time of the claim. In some cases these papers were unusually full and contained statements regarding birth and parentage, marriage, and migrations from place to place. Sometimes the information which they supply is disappointingly meager. If the claimant was a widow of the soldier, she had to submit evidence of her marriage to the soldier on whose service she was basing her claim and, in many cases, a list of the children she had borne to him.[37]

If you write for the records of some ex-soldiers, you should address your letter to the Pension Department, Veterans' Administration, Washington, D. C. You should ask if the department has on file the records showing that pensions had ever been granted to the ex-soldiers. You should include all the essential information about the men which would aid the department in identifying them, such as dates of birth, marriage, and death, the various residences at the time of military service and afterward. The War Department in Washington often has the military records of men who for one reason or other did not receive a pension. In an earlier section mention was made of various non-federal sources of information about former soldiers.

Though the various and numerous publications of the federal government are drawn upon for a great deal of the data used by historians in the general history field, they will not prove of great value to the local historian. Occasional printed reports, however, may touch on local subjects in which your community is greatly concerned or may even have been a "case study." Such reports are those on child labor, colonization, conservation, immigration, labor, Negroes, and various agricultural or mining reports. But unless you suspect the existence of these, or they come by accident to your attention, it is perhaps not worth the effort

---

[37] Doane, *Searching for Your Ancestors*, 166–167.

expended in trying to find out about them. The *Readers' Guide to Periodical Literature* and other indexes put out by the H. W. Wilson Company may help to locate such material quickly. The *Monthly Checklist of State Publications*, already mentioned, may also be used as well as the *Monthly Catalogue of United States Public Documents.*[38]

NEW PLANNING AGENCIES: NATIONAL AND STATE

The reports of the State Planning Boards of the various states should be consulted. These often deal with the background information needed in discussing and setting forth the geographical conditions of a locality and their significance in its past and present history. These publications deal with rivers, springs, caves, mineral resources, roads, transportation, utilities, etc.

What has just been noted regarding the states is true also of the cities. Their planning boards have gone into the same fields on a local basis. In fact, their publications should be of more value to the student of local history than the publications of state boards. Such publications deal with housing surveys, slum clearance, park and landscape development, residential areas, density of population, public utilities, incidence of diseases, crimes, relief cases, land uses, etc. Usually, such publications are profusely illustrated with city, ward, and district maps illustrating the various types of information dealt with in the text. These publications often give data on the distribution of various racial and language groups. Often the subjects are dealt with from a historical standpoint with maps and graphs illustrating developments by periods. It is possible that the cuts for some of the maps and illustrations may be available, since many of the publications are of recent date.

The publications of the various planning boards, state, regional, and city may prove to be a fruitful source of information for the local historian. In the regional field, the publications may overlap city, county, and state boundaries. The cooperating committees often include those dealing with government, highways, history, housing, industrial trends, land use, public works program, parks and recreation, population, sewerage and water, transit, and transportation.

The National Resources Committee in 1936 published *Regional Planning; Part II—St. Louis Region* and *Regional Planning; Part III—New England*. They contain 68 and 101 pages respectively and cost 25¢ and 30¢ from the Superintendent of Documents. In 1937, Part IV—Baltimore-Washington-Annapolis Area was published, 65 pages in length and costing 40¢.

Up to July, 1936, no less than 207 municipal planning boards had been formed in New England, 22 of which were unofficial. This represented an

---

[38] Hockett, *Introduction to American History*, 33–42, 147–148, mentions other indexes of federal publications which may be used.

increase of 36 over the total of 171 boards in existence in January, 1934. (See page 97 of Part III of the report.) This is a great growth since the first board was established in 1907. During 1935 state planning boards were established in all six of the New England states. Page 101 contains a list of the 15 publications of the National Resources Committee dealing with New England.

From 1910 to 1936 the City Plan Commission of St. Louis, Missouri, had published 55 reports dealing with such varied subjects as parks and parkways, riverfront, municipal institutions, districting, river development, plans, road planning, recreation, zoning, the housing problem, transit system, land subdivisions, ordinances, slum clearance, etc. From 1930 to 1938 the City Plan Commission of St. Louis made 134 studies of a social and economic nature dealing with its population, its various races, nationalities, language groups, rentals, workers, delinquency, crime, sick, relief, suicides, diseases, illiterates, home ownership, age groups, property use, location of industrial workers in various trades and industries, marital conditions, families owning telephones, automobiles, etc.

By January, 1939, State Planning Boards were organized and in operation for 45 of the 48 states. Regional planning boards had been set up in the Pacific Northwest, New England, Ohio Valley, and Great Plains. Metropolitan planning deals with the questions of urban population, congestion, housing, recreation, transportation, location of industry, education, delinquency, and crime. By January, 1939, over 1,700 towns and cities had developed some form of planning or zoning, while some 1,200 had continuing planning boards for making necessary adjustments in their zoning and community development.

The planning movement has even spread to our rural areas. Up to January, 1939, more than 400 county planning boards had come into existence, particularly in the Northwestern States and California. Regional history might be divided along with the natural drainage basins of the country, which are set forth in various publications of the National Resources Committee, North Interior Department Building, Washington, D. C.

CHAPTER V

BUSINESS RECORDS

MUCH local history can be found in business records. It has become more and more evident that the kind of human activity which we lump under the term "business" is of increasing importance in American life. Great business enterprises, employing thousands, sometimes hundreds of thousands of workers, selling their products to other hundreds of thousands, and using the savings of still other hundreds of thousands, have dominated the American scene in the not too distant past. The relations of these economic empires with the government, with each other, and with their myriads of owners, workers and customers, cannot be ignored.

Not all business enterprises are, however, giants. Scattered over the face of an increasingly urban nation are many small firms whose total efforts are greater than those of the giants. They, too, represent an important part of American economic life. When we speak of business records, then, we mean the records of any business, large or small, steel mill or corner grocery store. As we shall see later, the records of the small firm may be just as valuable in indicating a trend in business as those of the industrial giant.

Not only do business records show the local historian what has taken place, but through the use of such records he can follow the relations of business and government; trace the rise of credit institutions; watch the elaboration of the mechanism of distribution and exchange; and give the history of labor, not only from the standpoint of the trade union, but also from that of management. The growth of the size of the business unit from the clanging hammer in the village smithy to the mighty clamor of a steel mill can be traced. The increase in the tempo of business life can be measured. Through such media as mail order house catalogues the saga of clothing fashions can be followed; the replacement of the buggy by the automobile can be studied; and the substitution of the radio for the piano may be observed. Through business records the effects of competition and of business wars can be noted; the impact of the invention of machinery, or of the discovery of new processes upon old methods, may be felt; and the slow attrition of some lines of endeavor, owing to changed freight rates or the exhaustion of raw materials, can be followed.

Record keeping in American business firms is a subject which needs to be studied carefully so that the local historian can get the most from these sources. This includes an insight into methods of bookkeeping and accounting. In the old days, bound order books and letter press invoice books were used. Beginning with the nineties, the use of carbon copies, vertical filing, and card indexing caused a veritable revolution in business administration. The genesis, events, and effects of this revolution need to be traced. Perhaps, business records may even reveal the social revolution caused by the advent of office machinery: that the typewriter was an entering wedge for the introduction of women into this level of business is already well known; further research may disclose equally interesting developments. Finally, to the local historian, business records will not only show the threads in the increasingly complex pattern of American economic life, but may also permit the unraveling of some of the causes of periods of depression and prosperity.

The local historian can illustrate how acquaintance with business history can be of use to business men, and thus enlist their greater cooperation. Nearly every firm would profit from a knowledge of its past. Its history not only furnishes a useful perspective, but it may also answer questions and set examples to guide present and future conduct. Some firms have made use of their past history to supply them with useful illustrations for advertisements, but the complete records of a firm should show to its officers: (1) any gradual changes in the organization of the business or in the practices of the management; (2) changes in the sources of supplies, in the practices of rivals, in consumer demand, and in the attitude of their employees or the public; (3) the different problems which arise during the various phases of the business cycle; (4) any events the importance of which ought to be remembered. A number of firms have compiled their own histories for the use of their executives. The Dennison Company at Framingham, Massachusetts, which has been in existence since 1845, found, for example, that a knowledge of their firm's past was of great value in the solution of similar, present-day problems of general policy.

The local historian needs business records—records of factories, railroads, mills, general stores, sales agencies, cotton brokers, shipping lines, canneries, cooperatives—in short, concerns of every description. The treasure hunt for business records entails problems peculiar, to a certain degree, only to this type of historical research. Very often firms destroy all records, and in most cases it is difficult to get complete and unbroken files. Records of dead businesses are apt to vanish quickly, while those of live firms tend to stay in the hands of their owners. Businessmen, fearful of rivals or of muckrakers, may refuse to give up materials which, though useless to them are of great value to the historian.

The storaging of business records presents a practical problem. Such records accumulate rapidly, and even those of a medium-sized firm may be measured in terms of tons. Preservation of all the records of all the firms becomes impossible. This problem of what to keep and what to destroy is not easy to answer, and to a large extent must be determined by the type of business. In a manufacturing concern, for example, production records, payrolls, material on the introduction of new machinery,

71

and information on the investment of capital are obviously items of value. In a distributing concern, such as a wholesale grocery, records ought to be kept which would show the assembling and distributing of commodities.

If the professional business historian were consulted, he could offer valuable suggestions to business houses. As a local historian, however, you will generally be faced with the problem of taking what you can find and using it to the best practical advantage for your own purpose. You may learn that too much has already been destroyed. Or you may find yourself embarrassed with a plentitude of records that, in their entirety, are both confusing and difficult to understand. Because of the trees you may lose sight of the woods. If such should be the case it might help you to have some sort of yardstick with which to measure the value of the various records. Such a yardstick was prepared by Ralph M. Hower, editor of the *Bulletin* of the Business Historical Society, and includes the following:[1]

Accounting Records: Nearly all accountancy records are important for they show the pulsations of the business during the year, and reveal the income, outgo, and net profits. These records include daybooks, general and subsidiary journals, ledgers, balance sheets, trial balances, statements of income and expenses, tax schedules, vouchers, payroll statistics, records of the capital invested in the plant—including fixtures, equipment, raw materials and products, budgets, costs of production, auditors' reports, and the methods used by the accounting department. Samples only need be taken of accounting forms, sales slips, invoices, receipts and checks. These samples will show when new methods were introduced and what changes were made.

The Purchasing Department: Enough letters, reports, specifications, memoranda, ledgers and other records should be used from this department to show the methods and policies of making purchases, the items and amounts bought and their sources, the prices paid, and the discounts or other allowances given to the company.

Production Department: It is rather difficult to get records which show the work of a department based on movement. Photographs and working models, either of the plant or of machinery, are a help. If possible, samples should be secured, but these samples will be useless unless they are identified and the date of their production ascertained. Charts of the plant layout, the internal transportation system, plant organization, the passage of materials and work, and any changes in the plant setup should be secured. Any technical reports or descriptions of the methods of production, together with rules of shop discipline, should be saved. Production methods will vary greatly, and enough material should be examined to show what was done and how it was done. Unique documents should

---

[1] *Preservation of Business Records* (Boston, Business Historical Society, Inc., 1940), 20–30.

always be singled out; sampling should be confined only to repetitious material.

Inventory: When a business takes inventory it counts up what it has on hand. The final result is shown in the accounting records. Inventory records, then, are important only to the extent that they show how the inventory was taken and how it was recorded.

Labor and Personnel Records: These can be of great value to the historian. From them he can trace any rise or fall in wages, and see the extent to which seasonal, technological, or cyclical unemployment has affected the workers in the enterprise. These records are apt to be bulky, and summaries, if they exist, may be substituted for examination. Material from these records which show the number of employees; their special skills; the turnover in employment; the rates of pay, including bonuses, overtime, or any other additional payments; stock purchases; working hours; vacations; company benefits, including health and safety services, athletic activities, or any other social, educational, or recreational features; and rules and regulations and anything else relating to working conditions offer a rich field for the researcher.

Sales Department: Many businessmen regard this department as their most important unit. The historian is interested in what was sold, how it was sold, the quantity sold, and where it was sold. The first category of material consists of sales statistics. In addition, material on the number of salesmen, sales districts and methods, dealers and trade channels used, terms of sales, prices, catalogues, contests, and quotas, costs of making sales, and data on goods returned is also valuable. Samples of sales slips, brands, trademarks, packages, and routine correspondence will be helpful. Care must be taken to go through any special reports on sales by executives.

Advertising: The varieties of advertising are almost endless, but one copy of each printed advertisement and each radio script ought to be selected for examination. If possible, information should be secured telling where the advertisement was used and the results. Special features dealing with anniversaries or other notable occasions deserve to be noted. Reports, correspondence, and memoranda dealing with advertising matters are also important.

Statistics: The material of this department consists largely of material furnished by other departments, and need, therefore, only be sampled to show the work of the department.

General and Financial: Material under this heading includes the correspondence of the senior executives and is usually of sufficient importance to be examined thoroughly. Here is where questions of policy are settled, important decisions made, and personalities loom large. All general correspondence should be scanned, important letters noted, and samples taken of the remainder.

Miscellaneous: A number of important records do not come under any

one general heading. They include the charter, franchise, corporate articles, lists of stockholders, partnership agreements, investment records,
mortgages, deeds and leases, code and cipher books, speeches and public
announcements, company publications, and insurance policies. All minutes of meetings of stockholders, directors or other management groups
ought to be examined. Sometimes firms keep a diary; this is valuable and
should be carefully scrutinized. Of even greater value is the annual statement which summarizes the company's history during the year; this
may easily prove to be the most useful single item of business material
to be found.

It may be that you will not need to go directly to business firms for
your data but can find what you want in the libraries. Since the World
War, interest in the preservation of business records has been increasing.
A pioneer in this work, Professor N. S. B. Gras, has gathered at the
Baker Library at Harvard University an enormous collection of business
records. This collection has already furnished material for studies of
Jay Cooke, John Jacob Astor, and the Massachusetts Bank. In the
future, as students delve into this mass of documents, no doubt many
other valuable studies will appear.

Most historical societies have at least incidental material concerning
business history, and a few have taken definite steps towards forming
business history collections. The Minnesota Historical Society has records of fur companies, a number of general store documents, hotel registers, and about a ton of banking records. At first glance it might appear
that hotel registers would contain little information useful to the historian, but an examination of the *Register of the Carimona House* for the
years 1855–1859 reveals much that is of interest. Patrons came to this
Minnesota hotel and tavern from as far away as California, Maine,
Kansas, and Louisiana. Comments in the same or a different hand provide clues to the character or calling of the person listed in the register.
"Drunk as usual" identifies one, and "Turned farmer for life" tells
something of another. Other comments tell of bloody faces at election
time, give the names of candidates for office, and note what their oppo-
nents thought of them.

A number of business history records have been collected at various
depositories in the South. The University of South Carolina has plantation records for the years 1834–1877. These show the cost of raising
cotton and of maintaining slaves, and give the amount of capital invested
in southern plantations. Elsewhere a number of documents have been
gathered dealing with trade in cotton or slaves, but a great deal of further
collecting remains to be done.

Perhaps some examples of the usefulness of business records to the
local historian will be helpful. The first illustrations are of companies
whose files are fairly complete. The records of the Boston Manufacturing
Company and the Lowell Machine Shop consist of ledgers, journals,

time books, shop records, and a few letters. From them we can learn something about the introduction of the power loom into America and the beginnings of the machine age in this country. These materials give the costs and methods used to build machinery in 1816. They also show that early manufacturing in this country was not entirely caused by the profit motive; patriotic citizens, stirred to anger by the War of 1812, wished to make us independent of England and her manufactures, and so they invested capital in factories and machinery. In addition, the papers of the Boston Manufacturing Company are of special interest because this company was probably the first in America to carry through, under one roof, the whole manufacturing process from raw cotton to finished textiles.

Another valuable collection describing early factory conditions is contained in the Slater Papers. These consist of daybooks, ledgers, letter books, production books, payrolls, journals, and various other records, of Samuel Slater, who has been credited with opening the first power cotton mill in America. The records show the slow development in manufacturing skill in this country, furnish wage data, and manufacturing costs, give the movement of labor, and picture the effects of machines on the development of the industry.

Of a different nature are the records of a flour mill of Rochester, New York, dating from the seventies of the last century. The records of this firm, which are complete, have been collected by an expert, Dr. Henrietta M. Larson. The story shows that what kept the firm alive, in spite of heavy competition, was careful management and the manufacture of high quality flour.

An unusual story can also be gleaned from the letters, letter books, and account books of Frederic Tudor, the "Ice King" of early nineteenth century America. In 1806, at the age of twenty-three, Tudor decided that selling ice offered a new field of opportunity for a young man. Before this business could be organized on a commercial basis he had to make a number of experiments to find the best way to build ice houses, to transport ice, and to preserve ice in the home. After these problems were solved he still had to create a want for his product. He developed a market by showing its usefulness in hospitals and for preserving food, by introducing ice cream into new districts, and by teaching people to use cold drinks. As early as 1806 he was shipping ice from Boston to the West Indies, but this foreign trade was badly hit by the Embargo of 1807, the War of 1812, and the panic of 1819–1821. Tudor was not a man to be beaten by adverse conditions; as one market closed, he developed another, and so with the closing of his West Indian market he began to ship ice to southern ports, New Orleans and Mobile among others. After the war and the depression had passed, he returned to his old West Indian markets, kept his new southern outlets, and opened up still others. By 1835 he was shipping ice to India, and at one time Tudor shipped ice to Havana,

Jamaica, New Orleans, Mobile, Charleston, Calcutta, Madras, Singapore, and Bombay.

Account books seem to be the type of business record which most easily survives. Their variety is almost endless, and, when skillfully used, they convey considerable information. The account books of farmers and general stores, taken together, show changing agricultural conditions. From them you can trace the effects of depressions on the farmer's standard of living, shifts in crops, the status of agricultural laborers, agricultural prices, and the effects of new kinds of transportation or of the opening up of new areas. Further, the general store accounts will show its annual turnover, and profits, the difference between urban and rural prices, and the special problems of credit faced by country stores.

The account book of Jacob Adams of Newbury, Massachusetts, during 1673–1693, for example, reveals this farmer-shoemaker as a custom worker in his own home, buying his leather, and selling shoes made on order directly to customers. An interesting feature of this record book is that along towards the end apparently he was no longer selling shoes directly to customers, but was making shoes either for a store or for some middleman. Such an account shows how early the middleman began to intrude between producer and consumer. From account books of the shoe industry in the forties you can trace the volume of business, the costs of production, the number of employees, and the prices of the finished product.

Peddlers have not always enjoyed the highest reputation, and Yankee peddlers, in particular, have often been accused of using shrewd tricks to separate the guileless farmer from his money. Yet the account book of one of these peddlers, for the years 1849–1860, does not show that the total profits were extraordinary. For example, a typical day's sales in 1858 in Rochester, New York, included the following items: a colored picture, a pocket knife, a child's rattle, two song books, a pair of men's rubber suspenders, two baskets, a paper of pins, salve, and some peppermint essence. The total cost to the peddler was 86¢, his retail sales amounting to $1.67, and his profit to 81¢. Usually the peddler's volume of sales was so small that he rarely made over 50¢ a day. The entire earnings of this particular peddler over a period of ten years, not entirely spent on peddling, however, amounted to less than $540.

Advertising is probably as old as business itself. Some types of advertising, such as handbills, tend to disappear quickly and are not easy to find. When found, however, they sometimes contain curious information. One such, appearing in Boston in the middle of the nineteenth century, shows some of the difficulties faced by the early telegraph companies. The handbill offers a $5 reward for information leading to the arrest and conviction of persons breaking wires or glass insulators belonging to the company. A hint as to the source of the breakage is contained in the

76

admonition: "Parents would do well to caution their Boys, in relation to this matter."

Inventories often contain useful information. The first successful iron works in New England was established in 1645 at Lynn, Massachusetts. Fifty-five documents of this concern, covering the period 1650–1685, have survived. An inventory of goods for 1653 lists hammers, anvils, tongs, gudgeons, bellows, and various saws among the assets, and also gives the names of the indentured servants who made up the labor force, together with the cost of their passage over, their food, and their keep.

For those interested in the history of shipping, a number of collections provide voluminous material. Some records contain the cargo lists of colonial ships; others give the story of the East Indiaman and of the clipper ship in great detail. An illuminated logbook from the sixties comes from the hand of a mate who drew pictures of the life and work aboard a ship sailing from Boston for Calcutta and Bombay. The account books of James Emerton of Salem from 1816–1835 show Americans trading with the pirate colony of Madagascar. American merchants sent out hams, fish, textiles, muskets, swords, gunpowder, rum, laces, and looking glasses, and the supercargo bought in return horn, hides, raffia, tortoise shell, ivory, ebony, and gum arabic.

From other shipping records a new picture of the California gold rush emerges. Hitherto it had been known that ships' crews had often joined the rush, and it had been thought that their desertion was caused by the gold fever. The record books and letters of a ship captain sailing to California in the fifties reveal, however, that sometimes crews may have deserted because no funds were available to pay their wages on the return journey. After the discovery of gold, many ships were engaged in taking a wide variety of goods to California. With a whole world competing for the new market, San Francisco became overstocked with goods. For example, in 1850 there was enough chewing tobacco in the city to last the inhabitants for sixty-five years, and there were fifty pairs of boots or shoes for every person. Owing to this glut of goods many articles sold far below cost, and some were dumped on the beach, and some were not even unloaded. As a result a number of ships did not have enough money to pay the wages of the sailors and were forced to tie up in the bay.[2]

Business letters frequently contain much useful information. The letter written by John Perkins Cushing in May, 1837, to the Chinese merchant, Houqua, of Canton, throws light on the panic of 1837–1843. The letter says that in the past two months there had been a complete prostration of confidence and of commercial credit, and that the business world was in complete stagnation. According to the writer, the panic was caused by overtrading in western lands and in railroads, and that speculation in

[2] Much still remains to be written about the history of the shipping industry on the Great Lakes.

77

these had absorbed much of the capital of the country. An additional factor, the letter writer adds, was that British merchants were calling our debt, but that this debt couldn't be paid because of the fall in cotton prices.

The notebook of an inventor may also contain valuable material. A facsimile of a notebook of Thomas A. Edison was found in some records of the United States Court of Appeals. This notebook reveals what was going on in his laboratory during the course of an invention—in this case, the carbon telephone transmitter.

In certain other government records material on business history may be found. Customs records may show the foreign trade of this country. For example, several customs documents for about 1808 reveal that iron was shipped from Russia to Massachusetts and then shipped from there to India. Soap came from Italy and was then carried by Yankee skippers to the island of Mauritius. Tax records are another mine of information. They disclose the ownership and value of real estate, crops, shipping, warehouses, farms, and personal property. They show also how property is divided in the community, the number of rich and poor, the increase or decrease in property holdings, and the effects of periods of depression or prosperity. Estate appraisements reveal the different categories of property owned by an individual and tell something about values. For instance, on one southern estate ten slaves were valued at $2,955 in the early decades of the nineteenth century.

Pamphlets, tracts, and annual reports are sometimes useful. Some pamphlets from the mid-nineteenth century set forth the respective merits of wood and anthracite coal when used in steam locomotives. Tracts frequently disclose the economic thinking of the times. Mathew Carey, early nineteenth century economist, published a tract entitled *A View of the Ruinous Consequences of a Dependence on Foreign Markets for the Sale of the Great Staples of this Nation, Flour, Cotton, and Tobacco.* Written in the depression year of 1820, it was aimed to help in the passage of a protective tariff. Likewise, annual reports may give accounts of controversial matters. The *Fourth Annual Report* of the Delaware, Lackawanna, and Western Railroad Company for 1857 tells of a controversy over methods of finance.

Certain kinds of business historical material are fairly scarce in existing collections. In particular, records of the following kinds of businesses are needed: banks, elevators, mills, printing companies, general stores, mail order houses, department stores, warehouses, credit houses, produce and commodity exchanges, wholesalers, importers, exporters, brokers, selling agents, jobbers, and commission dealers. Information is also needed on service occupations, such as hotels, restaurants, beauty and barber shops, gasoline stations, garages, and saloons. Plantation records[3]

---

[3] A collection of plantation records of the Allston family in South Carolina has been edited by J. H. Easterby and will be published by the Beveridge Memorial Fund of the American Historical Association.

and farm diaries and account books are not well represented in present collections, but sufficient material on all of these can probably be found by the earnest seeker. Mine records need to be observed. Transportation material, such as the records of bus, taxicab and trucking companies, is scarce and offers a field scarcely touched by investigators. Railroads and canals have been better chronicled. The list of possibilities is far from exhausted; many opportunities await the local historian of business.

CHAPTER VI

CHURCH RECORDS AND CEMETERY INSCRIPTIONS

THE local historian ought also to keep in mind the importance of well kept church records as a source of data. Often the minister or circuit rider arrived with the earliest settlers. Perhaps even before the village became incorporated a strong denominational organization existed. Long before the newspaper began to relate the affairs of the community, the church records had been mirroring its religious, social, moral, economic, and educational life.

One example will serve as an illustration. Settlement at Parkville, Missouri, began in 1837; the town was laid out in 1844; the population had reached 300 by 1850; the first newspaper started publication in 1853; the town minutes commenced in 1855. Note, however, the first historical sketch of Parkville as it appears in the Presbyterian Church Records. Page one begins:

Until the year 1837 this country was trodden by the careless step of the Redman. As soon as it was ceded to the United States a vast tide of population flowed in to possess the land. Many who came were those who had escaped from the restraints of Society to these ends of the earth.

But God who often scatters his people to assist in laying the foundations of Society sent some religious men also. There were some Methodists and Presbyterians located in this vicinity and many of the 'Hard Predestinarian Baptists.' These last, however, have no intercourse with any other denomination and are violently opposed to every Benevolent enterprize of the day.

It is not known by whom the first sermon was preached here.

At an early day there was occasionally Campbelite preaching.

During 1839 & 40 Our Methodist Brother Barker visited us from time to time.

The first Presbyterian sermon was delivered by Rev. Edmund Wright of Weston in November 1842. . . .

His visits were very acceptable. There had been previously some attempt to sustain a Sabbath School and Bro. Wright greatly promoted the cause by aiding them in procuring a library a part of which came as a donation.

The following winter a Sabbath School and Bible Class were sustained.

As it was not thought expedient to organize a church, a temporary union was had with the Methodists, with whom we always had the most fraternal intercourse.

In June 1843 this place was favored with the labors of Rev. Charles Lord a Missionary of the American Home Missionary Society. Mr. Lord remained but a short time when he returned to Mass. for his family. In the fall he came again, but in a short time left for Independence. . . . Mr. Lord preached one half of the time with us for some months subsequent.

Observe that all the foregoing occurred before the town had been laid out—a whole decade before the newspaper began to chronicle its weekly happenings. The record continues:

In the year 1844 a town was laid out here by Geo. S. Park Esq. the proprietor which received the name of Parkville.

This year Mr. Wright visited us several times and the Sabbath School was continued as before.

In April, 1845, the 27th day, Rev. Messrs Wright and Lord met here by previous appointment for the purpose of organizing a Presbyterian Church.

For many months in this year there was no preaching in town of any kind. It was exceedingly sickly here and throughout all the West. Great numbers died. There was neither health or strength to attend to the Institutions of the Gospel.

The record continues until March, 1849, when the Rev. George S. Woodward of Pennsylvania arrived. He found only three members of the Presbyterian Church, but he was so energetic that a parsonage was soon erected and a movement launched for a place of worship. The subscription list started out with this heading:

Every prosperous and thriving village has its houses of religious worship. A neat edifice is not only an ornament to a town, but speaks well for its morals, good taste & public spirit. And no town which looks to a healthy growth and wishes to hold out inducements for good & intelligent citizens to settle among them will be long deprived of one.

The sound of the church going bell is fraught with too many pleasing associations, not to desire to hear its tones from Sabbath to Sabbath.

This activity stirred the Methodists to build a church and the Baptists to organize themselves into a congregation. The year 1851 saw two denominations in Parkville, each without a building. The year 1852 saw three, two with new church structures. All this, be it noted, occurred before the newspaper began publication or the town was organized as a governmental unit. It will be seen, therefore, that if the proper church records can be found, they, rather than the town minutes or the first newspaper, may provide the first written account of your community life.

"If the proper church records can be found"—ah, there's the rub! The early religious documents of any community are almost always hard to find. Everyone you inquire of remembers having seen them or heard of them, but nobody seems to know where they are. Their rightful place is in the hands of the minister or the clerk, but sometimes these individuals have moved away and taken the records with them, intentionally or unwittingly. The clerkship in many churches changes fast, and the ministers seem to change even faster. Houses and churches burn, and the records are lost by fire, by flood, or in other ways. Sometimes the papers of a church temporarily inactive have been placed in the keeping of one nearby and somehow have never been returned to their rightful owners.

At other times a clerk, appreciating their historical value, has placed the records in a safe place for preservation, but unless there is some definite records at the church, no one knows where they are.[1]

There is, however, a brighter side to the picture. Often you can locate materials which even church members in your community have believed lost or destroyed. If you think that some former pastor may have the records, you may trace his whereabouts by asking the present incumbent where the former pastor is now living. Usually each denomination publishes a yearbook which contains information about all churches and the location of all ministers. If the records you are seeking are those of a strongly centralized group, such as the Roman Catholic, the Episcopal, or the Methodist, it is possible that they have been sent to the immediate headquarters of the particular church. A number of church organizations maintain archives either in their national or state headquarters where they deposit old records of active and abandoned churches. Historical societies and state libraries sometimes make specialties of such records. A notable collection is the Samuel Colgate Baptist Historical Collection at Colgate University, Hamilton, New York.[2] The larger sects have their church historical society libraries and these, together with their theological seminaries, often become depositories of official records.[3]

While the Historical Records Survey was active they attempted the listing of approximately 64,000 church units, or about one-fourth of the total number in this country. They published volumes for the Catholic Church of New Hampshire, the Moravian Church of Wisconsin, the various Baptist bodies of New Jersey, as well as inventories of other denominational groups. These church archives inventories give a brief historical sketch of each unit and indicate the dates and number of volumes for each set of church records.[4]

You will find a great difference among the various denominations regarding their earlier records. Of the main Protestant groups, probably the most careful were the Presbyterians, Congregationalists, and Episcopalians. The Catholic clergy also kept good records. One of your difficulties may be in reading the records of a group which started out using

---

[1] A good many of the records of the several Presbyterian churches in Columbus, Ohio, have been deposited in the Department of Documents at the Ohio State Archaeological and Historical Society Library, which also has a number of papers of the Methodist Conferences for Ohio.

[2] Doane, *Searching for Your Ancestors*, 135–136.

[3] The Department of History of the Presbyterian Church, 520 Witherspoon Bldg., Philadelphia, Pa., has a large collection. The Presbyterian Synod of New York, through its Committee on Archives and Historical Materials, has been collecting and depositing information about its churches in the Auburn Theological Seminary, Auburn, N. Y. Drew Theological Seminary, Madison, N. J., has a large collection of Methodist historical material. The minister of each local church can give you the addresses of the church historical society or the theological seminaries. Letters can be sent to these asking if the missing early records are to be found there.

[4] Evans, *Preservation of the Nation's Records*, 2–9.

a foreign language. If the language is German, Dutch, Swedish, Norwegian, Polish, or some other rather common one, you will probably find some members of the local church who will translate the old records while you write down the pertinent facts. Often the minister can use the language or suggest the name of someone who can.

The genealogist, Stiles, suggests:

In the good old days, when a minister held his charge over a congregation for forty or fifty years, or, as sometimes happened, during his whole active life, the pastor generally kept a private memoranda of births, baptisms, marriages and deaths, as well as of many other domestic and social events occurring among his flock, or even in the community at large in which he lived. This record was (according to the character of the man himself) apt to be interspersed with comments and references which rendered it most interesting and valuable to the historical and genealogical student. . . . The discovery, in some old garret or in the possession of his descendants, of such notes, or diary, is a veritable 'bonanza,' and in the older settled communities its *possible* existence should always be borne in mind, and ascertained, if possible, by diligent search.[5]

You may think that church registers record only such data as baptisms, births, marriages, deaths, and burials. Actually, however, they often include much more information of value. In such records there might be a list of all previous clergymen with the dates of their service. Occasionally, an early minister made use of the registers to enter curious happenings, such as accounts of accidents, storms, frosts, fires, and and floods. One custom, not entirely obsolete even today, was for certain denominations to hold trials for breaches of church discipline and of the moral code. In some of these trials the accused was a member of the clergy but just as often a lay member of the church was brought to trial for what might today seem to be a trivial offense. In Parkville, Missouri, during the fifties, for example, a Mrs. Alvirah Bates was brought before the Presbyterian Church session for "having attended a 'ball,' engaged in dancing and long neglected the Ordinances of God's house," and several years later the same church tried a John McWilliams and his wife for playing cards.[6]

Among other things, such minutes show that the early residents were real flesh and blood men and women, subject, just as we are, to fits of temper, moral lapses of one degree or another, perhaps guilty of profanity of bearing false witness, of playing cards or dancing, or of breaking the fourth or the seventh commandment.

Naturally, one has to be cautious in dealing with church trials. Mem-

---

[5] Stiles, *Handbook of Practical Suggestions*, 26–27. While such a diary could hardly be called a church register, to all intents and purposes it might very well be classed as such.

[6] The two cases appear in the *Minutes of the Session, Parkville Presbyterian Church* Parkville, Missouri. Similarly interesting church trials may be found in the reports of the Methodist Episcopal Church among the papers in the Samuel Williams Collection at the Department of Documents, Ohio State Archaeological and Historical Society Library, Columbus.

bers of other denominations may have been equally guilty of objection-
able conduct, and it is hardly fair to quote from, say, the Presbyterian
records just because these happen to be extant while the others may have
been destroyed or discretely kept from your eye. In all matters of this sort
you will do well to talk over questionable items with the denominational
pastor. If he will not permit you to quote *verbatim et literatim* some of the
more entertaining instances of church discipline, perhaps he can be in-
induced to let you do so by substituting A, B, and C for the leading
participants. Failing to secure his consent even to that, he might allow
you to use the information on condition that you cloak the identities
both of the participants and of the church involved. The exact recording
of a church trial is not essential to your history. It is highly entertaining
at times, but much can be done, and in a tactful way, to set forth almost
the same thought without giving offense to anyone. It is well to consider
in advance the predicament in which you may place the clergyman who
will later be approached by an irate parishioner with the threatening
question, "Did you let the writer of that new history of our town have
access to the church records of the trial of my grandfather in 1875?"

In addition to registers of baptisms, births, marriages, and deaths,
there should be other record books and minutes in the keeping of the
minister or the clerk. These may list all members who have ever belonged
to the church, together with the dates of admission, dismissal, or death.
Such entries often prove valuable, for they state from what church each
member has come or "brought his letter," or to which church he has
been dismissed or "taken his letter." The board of elders and the board
of trustees, by whatever names these boards are variously known, are
in the habit of keeping a record of their meetings. These minutes are informative and helpful. If the elders' records are complete, you should
be able to compile a list of past clergymen together with their years of
service, their salaries, and perhaps the general esteem in which they were
held. If the minutes of the trustees are complete, you should be able to
find when the original church building was erected, who subscribed toward it, what it cost, what fixtures it had, and what repairs and altera-
tions it received and when. You will find that in many communities, in
spite of the ofttimes bitter denominational rivalry of the period, non-
members and members of other faiths joined with the regular members in
giving toward the erection of each new church.

In addition to these records, the clergyman or church officers may
have a collection of reports, anniversary programs, commemorative sermons, and miscellaneous papers which may add to your store of knowledge. You may even find that the church celebrated a fiftieth or a hundredth anniversary not so many years ago, and that on that occasion
someone published a small history of the church, or an anniversary address in which a good deal of local history is interwoven. Such a discovery
may save you time and effort, but you should not be content until you

have secured permission to glance through and take notes from the actual church records.

You will probably not have any difficulty to get access to the records of your own denomination. If so, start there, and then go on to the next most approachable clergyman. If the community is large, you may have difficulty in being kindly received by all the ministers of the various churches. Some may, and perhaps with reason, be suspicious of your good intentions. Some may be very busy, unwilling to give the time which your searching of the church records may require. Ministerial associations are often found in towns and small cities and perhaps a letter of introduction from your pastor to the other ministers of the town may give you the entry you desire. The Englishman, Humphreys, gives some solid, if somewhat entertaining, advice on the proper approach to some less approachable clergymen who, in this country, happily, are few. With the British clerics in mind, he advises that you go around to the church building and

take notes of all you see. Gather sympathy and do not alienate anyone. It is important also to make friends with the parson at an early stage of your pursuit, and if by luck he appears on the scene and no service is about to take place, speak to him and ask if he has a few moments to spare to tell you anything he knows. Be modest and presume that he knows a great deal more than you do. Perhaps he will walk round with you and point out . . . pieces of carved stone from some much earlier building. Listen to and take in all he has to say. Tell him you are making notes upon the history of the church and parish, and that you hope you may count upon his help. Diplomacy is essential with the parson, especially on a first visit. Do not forget that he has the custody of the valuable parish registers and other parish books necessary to your purpose . . . if you make out a good case he will probably allow you eventually to sit in the vestry or even in his own house to make extracts. The parish chest nearly always contains many other books and papers besides the actual registers. . . . Before you say goodbye to the parson on this first visit, propitiate him in every way you can, and when you tell him you intend to come often . . . look him straight in the eye and see if he appears as though he could bear it. Ask if there is any special day or hour when he is more free than another to give you a few minutes. Do not try to bounce him into doing anything. Find out from him on this first visit if there is anyone known to him in the village, or out of it, who is specially interested in the history of the place, and to whom you could go for further assistance. Also if he knows of any printed or manuscript accounts of the place. Do not take up too much of his time at first, but when you have parted with him, and used your best smile in so doing, walk around the churchyard alone and look at some of the names of families on the stones.[7]

It is advisable to show to the pastor what you have written. He is a well educated man and is certainly better acquainted with his own church than you are likely to become through your own reading about it in the registers. You may have more data about its past, but he may be able

---

[7] Humphreys, *How to Write a Village History*, 10–11.

to interpret the data more correctly. He is familiar with the shades of difference between his own and other churches, and he will be able to correct unintended errors and omissions. The various sects differ so much in their forms of government, in the titles of their officers, and in certain of their religious beliefs and practices that you will do well to consult the local clergyman in order to be sure to use the correct terminology. Remember, however, that it is your history and not his, and draw your lines accordingly and in proportion to the prominence of the church in the history of the town or community.

In your chapters regarding religion you will, of course, not want to offend the feelings of any group. There is a technique in writing which clearly sets forth the special beliefs to which a sect may subscribe, but does not hold them up to ridicule. If you are unable to write that tactfully, it is best to remain silent on the subject.

You may find that the strongest church or churches of the early days are now defunct through some strange turn of the wheel of fortune. You will probably run across one or more defunct churches and may not be able to locate their records, try as you may. Inquire among old residents whether they know of any children or grandchildren of former prominent members of this nonexistent church. Look up these individuals and learn all about their forebears' church and the possible whereabouts of the records. It may be that they are reposing in some local attic or in the archives of a church historical society or at the church's headquarters.

Again, you may run across references to these defunct churches, as well as others which are still flourishing, in one of the regional or state histories which have occasionally been published for one or another of the sects. The two following excerpts, found in such a volume, helped to complete a picture of the early days in the Parkville Presbyterian Church. The Minister, who served from 1845 to 1848, wrote:

There are but few Presbyterians here, and no preaching at all. Mr. Park, the proprietor, is from New England and is very anxious to have a minister permanently located. He and his brother-in-law, Mr. Parsons, will supply all my immediate wants of board, horse, etc. I find this place where I am to board to be one of the pleasantest places in all the Platte. Yes, will you believe it, it is in a corner of the State of Maine! Mr. Parsons is from Maine. Mrs. Parsons is the very life of the church.

Another minister left an interesting glimpse of the simplicity of Parkville church life about 1850 when he wrote: "Our good elder came to the service, clad in his red blanket overcoat with black fringe, a bottle of wine in one pocket and two blue tumblers in the other, with the bread wrapped in a paper." (These preparations were, of course, for the communion service.) These two passages were from letters written by Parkville pastors to ministerial friends elsewhere. Naturally, one could not find such letters in the local community, but they somehow drifted into the possession of the writer of a presbyterial history.

Be on the watch also for autobiographies or biographies of prominent clergymen. Preachers of the frontier days in the Central West were in the habit of writing their memoirs in their first years of retirement from active service. The more a minister had traveled about and the more experiences he had, the more likely he was to write an autobiography. Peter Cartwright's life is a good example.[8] One such autobiographer, who had served the Parkville Presbyterian Church immediately after the Civil War, said that as the men at church sat down after singing a hymn, the thud of revolvers in hip pockets drowned out the closing of the hymn books—quite a commentary on postbellum pioneer conditions.

CEMETERY INSCRIPTIONS

Cemetery inscriptions can provide historical data; sometimes they are the only source for certain years when the birth and death records were kept by neither the town nor the churches. When a new country was first settled, the dead were buried on the individual farms and in some places family burying grounds are still continued. Certain parts of the country have numerous private cemeteries of this sort. Usually, however, the village or town soon set aside a plot of ground to be used for this purpose, often placing restrictions on its use, such as requiring residence in the town before an individual could be buried there. These restrictions were always hard to enforce, however, because of complex relationships, varying residences and occupations. Gradually the private, family cemeteries gave way to the common cemeteries. Often the very existence of these early graveyards has been forgotten. Not two miles from where the writer once lived is an abandoned cemetery wherein from thirty to fifty bodies were placed between 1837 and 1857, yet only a few people in the region today know of this old graveyard or anything about the people buried there. Such cases may appear in your community and are often to be discovered by asking old residents.[9]

For the sake of preserving for the future the fading inscriptions on old stones, and for what immediate use you yourself can make of them, it is advisable to have the old stones recording deaths before, say, 1875 copied, including such matter as Scriptural passages, bits of poetry, etc. If this may seem to be too big an individual task, it might be arranged for a troop of Boy or Girl Scouts to do it. In one town of 650 population, all stones from 1837, when the community began, to 1875, were copied off in less than four hours by one student. These inscriptions, being readily accessible when copied, were frequently referred to in the course of

---

[8] The manuscript of his autobiography has recently come into the possession of the Ohio State Archaeological and Historical Library at Columbus.

[9] There is still some controversy about the exact burial place of Johnny Appleseed (John Chapman), though a recent report of a commission appointed by the American Pomological Association seems to have authoritatively settled the question. See *Ohio Archaeological and Historical Quarterly* (Columbus), LII, 181–187 and 276–284.

writing the town's history. It is advisable to make a rough plan or map of the cemetery, noting conspicuous trees, entrances, monuments, etc., and as the copying of inscriptions proceeds, indicating on the map the location of the stones. The inscriptions can be written in a small notebook and each one numbered, an identical number being placed on the appropriate cemetery map. This will allow you to return at once to the stone if, for any reason, you want to verify names, dates, lettering, etc., as may sometimes be necessary on barely legible stones.

After you have become thoroughly familiar with the cemetery, induce one or more old residents to go there with you. They can point out the relationships which existed between various families. The very sight of old stones marking the resting place of old inhabitants will loosen a flood of recollections that may be of considerable historical value.

Inscriptions in stone sometimes weather so quickly as to be difficult to read. Familiarity with local surnames will make it easier to decipher names. Your greatest difficulty will be with figures, for every digit from 0 to 9 has at some time been mistaken for one or more other digits. The figures 3, 5, and 8 are often confused; so also are 4 and 1, 4 and 7, 5 and 6, 7 and 2, and 6, 9, and 0. Spring and autumn are the best times to copy inscriptions and the best hours of the day are those when the face of the stone is a little in the shade. Rubbings can sometimes be made of difficult stones. This is done by laying a large piece of thick paper flat against the surface to be copied. Then use the flat side of a large colored crayon to rub over the lettering. If you desire to photograph a monument for inclusion in your book, it is advisable to go over the letters with chalk to make them more readable.

If your community is less than a century old, you may be surprised that you cannot find the names and stones of persons you know to have been the pioneers. This is not hard to explain. One of several things happened. They may have died before stonecutters migrated to the community, so no stone was ever erected. A wooden marker may have been used and never replaced when it rotted away. An unsuitable, badly inscribed native rock may have been used and later removed. The pioneers may be buried in some forgotten private cemetery. Again, they may have been interred in a burial ground in an older village or town nearby.

It is possible that the inscriptions in your cemetery may already have been printed in a book or magazine article. This has often happened in cases where the graveyards are historic or contain prominent national figures. A central western county collected and mimeographed all the inscriptions in the public and private graveyards within its bounds. Printed records of inscriptions, if they exist, will probably be found in the local and state historical society libraries.

Mention has been made earlier of the fact that some states require that cemetery inscriptions be copied and sent to the proper office along with other vital statistics of the community. In North Carolina, workers of the Historical Records Survey have abstracted and placed in the search room of the State Historical Commission, in Raleigh, vital statistics from more than 225,000 tombstones in every part of the state.

The historical data to be found on burial stones are of several kinds. Naturally, they give the name and birth and death date of the individual. They often give the wife's and children's names, and sometimes even the marriage date. Not infrequently they include the place of birth of the individual and this may be your only clue to the early home of some prominent settler. Very often they tell in what manner death came, naming perhaps cholera, a battle, the falling of a tree, a drowning, or some other accident. Occasionally a brief biographical sketch is given.

Often odd and amusing thoughts and sentiments, and even irreverent jingles, may be found inscribed. These if introduced into the history may add flavor and humor to your narrative. Jacobus, the genealogist, states that the following epitaph of Dr. Isaac Bartholomew, who died in 1750, is traditionally ascribed to his widow:

> He that was sweet to mi repose
> Hath now become a stink unto mi nose.
> This is said of me:
> So it shall be said of thee.

Jacobus also records the following:

> Here lies the Mother of eight:
> She might have had more, but now it's too late.[10]

Another genealogist records two epitaphs, one written by a man who believed in placing his advertisements where people were most likely to see them:

> Here lies Jane Smith, wife of Thomas Smith,
>   Marble Cutter.
> This monument was erected by her husband as a
>   tribute to her memory and a specimen of
>   his handiwork.
> Monuments of this style are two hundred and
>   fifty dollars.

> Underneath this pile of stones
> Lies all that's left of Sally Jones.
> Her name was Lord, it was not Jones,
> But Jones was used to rhyme with stones.[11]

---

[10] Jacobus, *Genealogy as Pastime and Profession*, 5, 13.

[11] Stetson, *Art of Ancestor Hunting*, 55, 56. He also includes the brief inscription: "I was somebody, who, is no business of yours." *Ibid.*, 55.

PART II

WRITING LOCAL HISTORY

Chapter VII

THE TECHNIQUE OF GATHERING AND ORGANIZING LOCAL HISTORICAL MATERIAL

Now that you have become familiar with the various sources of information and know where to find them and have selected which ones will be most helpful for your particular subject, the next step is to take notes in as concise yet adequate a form as will later enable you to have sufficient data for the writing of your history.

What follows is the result of the historian's long struggle with method. It is quite frankly a counsel of perfection. Much of it is obvious. Much of it you already know. A great deal of it may have no interest to you. But you may well wish to delve into the intricacies of perfect method so we have provided you with the latest and best tools of the profession

BIBLIOGRAPHY SLIPS OR CARDS

First of all, when you make your rounds at the various libraries, you will find small call-slips provided on which to write the author and title of the book and the call number as indicated in the catalogue. These slips are handed to the library attendant who uses them to find your books for you. In order to save yourself time and labor, it is helpful to carry with you a scratch pad of 3″×5″ size blank slips and a piece of carbon paper similar in size. You can thus be making a duplicate of each call slip for your own use at the same time that you are filling out the original slip for the librarian. By marking in the upper right hand corner a symbol for each library you visit (for example, LC for Library of Congress; MH for Minnesota Historical Society; or OAH for Ohio State Archaeological and Historical Society) you will later be able to have a record of each volume you use and will have no difficulty in retracing your steps should you find it necessary to consult the same book twice. You should also use similar slips for each map, manuscript, newspaper, periodical, public, business, or church record, microfilm roll, or photostat you examine, and even for each interview you attend. These slips will be your own card catalogue to your personal library of notes and later will form the basis for your bibliography.

While you are examining the various materials you will want to make additional notations on your bibliography slips. First of all, you will want to note the full title of each book or magazine (the call slip may have had only an abbreviated title), then you will want to indicate the place and date of publication, the edition, and the publisher; if it is part of a series you should note the series, volume, or part number; if a map you will want to indicate its size, color scheme, and scale, as well as its subject and date; if a newspaper, you will want to mark down the city (if this is not part of the title), the month, day, and year, and the name of the editor (if you can ascertain this). On the reverse side of your slip you may want to make special notations, such as which chapters or pages are particularly helpful for your subject, whether you think the statements are reliable or ought to be checked against another authority, etc. Make all these notations at the time you are examining the book, paper, or other type of material; do not wait until your impressions get cold.

NOTE-SLIPS OR CARDS

Now you are ready to take notes. Writers have discovered that slips or cards of either $4'' \times 6''$ or $5'' \times 8''$ are the most convenient size for note-taking. The former size is perhaps even better than the latter, for it is large enough to allow for ample quotation of paraphrasing, yet small enough to file in an empty shoe-box, and empty shoe-boxes make excellent and inexpensive filing equipment for the local historian.

Whether you type your notes, use a pen, or a pencil, will depend upon the library in which you do your work. Most libraries will not allow ink to be used, especially if you are taking notes on valuable manuscript material or rare books. An indelible pencil or a medium soft lead pencil is your only recourse for note-taking at such places. At a few libraries you may be permitted to bring a portable typewriter or to use a typewriter provided for patrons. Generally, however, a stock of well-sharpened pencils and sufficient slips or cards for the day's stint are your best tools for note-taking.

When writing your notes, try to confine each slip to a single idea or topic. Combining several topics on one slip, just because these happen to come from one book or are on the same page, is poor economy and will lead to confusion when you begin to organize your material. Your notes are like the pieces of a jigsaw puzzle and if you will fasten together unrelated topics or pieces it will make it more difficult for you when you try to fit in all the related parts.

Leave a wide margin at the left side of your note-card—wide enough to indicate in brief form the author and title of the book (if a magazine, the title of the article, as well as the name of the magazine), the volume number or other division (if any), and the page or pages from which your note is taken. Do not neglect doing this on every card—otherwise your note-taking is blind effort without benefit of authority to support it. Leave also a wide margin at the top of your card. In the upper right hand corner, try to put (as accurately as possible) the place and date for each note you take, that is, the place and date of the material you are noting, not of the time you are recording it or even of the time it was recorded by the author. For example, you may be noting an item on the settlement of the town of Chillicothe, Ohio, in 1803; you find the item in a history volume written in 1848 in Marietta, Ohio, and you are now noting it at Columbus, Ohio, in 1943, but, obviously, the items for place and date which you want to indicate at the right hand upper corner of your card are "Chillicothe, 1803." If you are not sure of the time or place where the action occurred but are guessing, indicate your guess with a question mark, thus:

Chillicothe [?]

March, 1803 [?]

When you begin to arrange your material for writing your history you will find it an invaluable help to have the approximate time and place for each bit of information.

Do not try at this stage, to give headings or subheadings to your notes. Leave that for later, after you have studied the succeeding chapter with its model outline and have determined what the main topics and subtopics of your own outline should be.

NOTES ON PRINTED WORKS

There are several ways of taking notes. One is to copy the exact words of the author. This is the lazy man's way of historical writing, unless you are planning to edit selected documents or excerpts from the materials you use and do not intend to do any interpretative writing of your own at all. Another and better way is to read the paragraph or page at least twice (once for general sense and a second time for detailed analysis), and then to try to put the idea expressed by the author into your own words, copying verbatim only such words, phrases, or sentences as are so expressive or colorful that you want them exactly as the author said them. This second method will insure your understanding what the author is trying to say, for unless you understand his statement you will not be able to paraphrase it in your own words.

A third way is to "boil down" the author's statement to as brief a form as possible, that is, giving a summary. In taking notes it is not advisable to do much summarizing, unless you are certain that the subject summarized is one which you will not need to discuss in great detail later on. It is better to paraphrase at the note-taking stage and then to summarize when you begin to write. Rather have too much than too little when taking notes.

When copying the author's words be careful to copy exactly; notice which words are capitalized and which ones are italicized (underline italicized words when writing or typing); include all punctuation marks; be careful of paragraph indentions, and above all be sure to enclose the quoted part in quotation marks. If you find a quotation in the part you are copying, be careful to use single quote marks both at the beginning and end of this quotation within a quotation.

"John Henry caustically rebuked his political opponent by telling him: 'That was a stupid way to steal my thunder.' "

95

If the material you quote or paraphrase begins on one page and continues over on the next, a simple way to indicate the stopping place on your note is by making a slanting line at the place where the page ends. For example:

"Long ago it was considered fashionable for the ladies to wear/bustles on the skirts and puffs at the sleeves."

Some writers even write the page numbers thus:

"ladies to wear [56/57] bustles."

Oftentimes you will want to omit parts of a quotation and include only the most pertinent words or phrases. Be careful to indicate on your note-card that you are making such omissions. If the omission is at the beginning of a sentence use three periods (the technical name is "ellipses") after your opening quotation marks and do not begin the first word with a capital letter (unless, of course, that word already has a capital letter). For example:

". . . thus the city fathers met in secret conclave to discuss ways and means."
". . . Roberts spoke sharply to the assembly."

If you omit material in the middle of a sentence, indicate this also by inserting three periods for the omitted part. For example:

"Once in a while . . . strangers rose to eminence . . . after a brief period of residence."

Be careful, however, not to omit such parts of a sentence as will change the meaning. For example, the original sentence may read: "Every written record that can be found indicates that John Doe was a thrifty, hardworking, honest, upright, albeit, a somewhat eccentric individual." If you should take from this only the following part: "Every written record . . . indicates that John Doe was . . . a . . . eccentric individual," you are guilty of giving the wrong emphasis to the meaning of the original sentence. Even worse is a twisting of meaning such as taking the sentence, "Above all, the border county delegates to the convention were very much against violent abolitionism and shied away from all discussion of either pro- or anti-slavery topics, though they did include a mild plank favoring abolition as a concession to the opposing faction from the northern counties," if you quote from it only the following, "The border county delegates to the convention . . . include[d] a . . . plank favoring abolition . . . ."

If the omission occurs at the conclusion of a sentence, use four periods to show that the sentence ended at that point. For example:

"John Jones made a fortune and then retired to live comfortably on his income . . . ."

If you are quoting the last part of one sentence and omitting the first art of another, indicate it thus:

"John Jones made a fortune and then retired to live comfortably on his income. . . . his grandchildren found themselves penniless in the early thirties and the tradition of shirt-sleeves to shirt-sleeves was thus again demonstrated in the Jones family."

If, however, the omission includes the last part of one sentence as well as the first part of the next, use four periods to show that a conclusion of a sentence occurred at some point in the omitted part:

"When the immigrants began to enter . . . . a new industrial prosperity developed in the region."

If you are quoting something with a part omitted from the end of one paragraph, but complete from the beginning of the next, do it thus:

"That way the citizens felt that they were actively participating in their town government . . . .
"Nevertheless, a few grumblers existed to disturb the equanimity."

If there are omissions at the end of one paragraph as well as the beginning of the next, both should be indicated like this:

"Often the circuit preacher would stop at Centerville on his regular rounds . . . .
". . . The schoolmaster, too, was an important figure in the community."

If you skip an entire paragraph, run a line of periods across your card, like this:

"Frequently, the men-folks returned from hunting and found their wives enjoying a quilting-bee."

. . . .

"The advent of the railroad and the introduction of the telegraph and telephone changed the lives of this community quite drastically."

Sometimes, your quoted portion needs amplification, a name inserted, a date added, a verb supplied, to make the material quoted more intelligible. Such additions are called interpolations and are permissible as long as you are careful to enclose the interpolated part in square brackets—parentheses are not the proper form of punctuation to use, for your author may have used these himself and later you will find yourself doubting whether the insertion was his or yours. Example:

"Ten years earlier [1820?], the village was only a spot on the state map. Today it is considered an important metropolis and center of industry. An early chronicler [Thomas Green] informs us . . ."

Be very careful to copy your quotation exactly as it is, even if there are misspellings, questionable dates, or ungrammatical phrases. To protect yourself insert *sic* in square brackets after every such deviation which you know to be incorrect, or put the correct form in square brackets following the author's error: Example:

"Then suddenly Laurence Thomas [Thompson?] rose to his feet and proclaimed the sentiment of everyone in the room when he declared that not only freedom of the slaves but the solidarity of the Union was at state [*sic*]."

97

Do not work at top speed until the closing bell drives you from your materials. Try to reserve a half hour or more before laying aside your notes in order to check for errors. This may seem a bore and a waste of time, but it will save you many a second trip to the library, and if you are doing your research in another city, such a check is doubly important. While checking, make sure that you have copied dates correctly, spelled names accurately, and that your notes are plainly written. The digits 3, 5, and 8, for example, are often confused; 4 and 1, 4 and 7, 5 and 6, 7 and 2, and 6, 9, and 0 are also often mistaken for each other. Be sure your vowels are plainly written as well as the letters n, m, w, T, F, L, and S. One can never be too careful in avoiding errors when taking notes and only by a meticulous checking will you be able to find these errors before it is too late.

NOTES ON MANUSCRIPTS AND SPECIAL MATERIALS

When taking notes on manuscript materials such as deeds, wills, diaries, and letters you must be on guard for a few other hazards. First of all, you must remember the change in the calendar after 1752 and the consequent possible confusion in dates around this period. There are eleven days difference between the Julian (Old Style) and the Gregorian (New Style) calendars. That is why George Washington's birthday was on February 11, Old Style, but on February 22, New Style. Then, too, it is always best to be cautious about letters written during the first few days of the month of January. Quite often the writer will forget and keep writing 1832 when it is 1833 that he meant to record.

Spelling of names of persons and places may also cause you considerable trouble. The people of several generations ago were none too well schooled and spelling was not as rigid as today. Sometimes they wrote even their own names in two or three different ways. Thus Backhouse may appear as Backhus, Backas, Bachus, Baccas, and Bacchus. The town of Sandusky, Ohio, for example, had the following variations: Ostandousket, Sandosque, Sandusket, Sandoski, Sandouski, St. d'Osquet, St. Douskie, and Sandusky.

Just as you may be careless in writing dates or may write a hand difficult to decipher, even more careless were your forefathers, and when examining their letters, diaries, account books, etc., you must be on the alert for errors or confusions. The letters "u" and "n" look very much alike and certain capital letters may be difficult to decipher in long hand script. Signatures are even more difficult, for these are notoriously illegible. You must remember that the long "s" ∫ was in use throughout the early period of American settlement, especially when with another "s" in words such as "masses," "classes," etc. This long "s" is especially confusing when trying to decipher a signature.

You must also guard against too rigid an interpretation of terms of family relationship. In olden days the term "cousin" was often applied to almost any relative and "brother" or "sister" might be a true brother or sister or a brother-in-law or sister-in-law, a step-brother or sister, or even a member of the same church. The terms "uncle" and "aunt" were also loosely used. All these possibilities for error and confusion must be watched and guarded against constantly.

Finally, when using unpublished material, remember not only to indicate the name of the collection, the names and places, and dates, but also the library where this collection was found. Since there are not likely to be duplicates of unpublished material this last bit of information is of great importance to anyone else who may want to use the same material. When making note of a letter include, for example:

John Jones to Henry Smith, Jackson, Michigan, January 14, 1837, Henry Smith Papers, William L. Clements Library, Ann Arbor, Michigan.

It may be that some of your notes will have to be based on photostatic or even on microfilm copies of materials located in distant libraries. Methods and cost of securing such materials have already been discussed in an earlier chapter. Your problem now is to reduce these physically peculiar types of research materials to the common denominator of the note-card. Your photostat will present little difficulty, for it is easily read with the naked eye, and you can treat it just as you do a printed or manuscript source on ordinary paper. Remember, however, to indicate on your note-card that what you have used is a photostat of the original. In order to read microfilm copy it is necessary to have some sort of a reading machine and you will be obliged to make your notes while watching the film in the machine. This may be a bit tedious and hard on the eyes; do not plan, therefore, to do much microfilm reading at one continuous stretch.

Do not forget to make note-cards for your personal interviews. In order to fit into your plan for your local history these will have to be summaries or condensations of the fuller notes of your interview with enough direct quotation for emphasis and flavor. If you have done a good job of note-taking promptly after each interview you will not find it too difficult to rework the information into briefer note form and to break it down into single units.

NOTES ON MAPS AND ILLUSTRATIONS

When recording the maps which are useful to your history you may want to make tracings of some portion or even of an entire map. If the librarian allows you such reproduction you may trace lightly with a soft pencil on a sheet of onion skin, tissue paper, or standard tracing paper. Be careful not to press too hard so that you will not deface the original map. Once your outlines are traced, remove the original map and copy the indications such as rivers, towns, etc., or the shadings and other markings that make your map distinctive. This is your initial step in map-making. If you wish to use this map in your book it will be necessary either for you to draw it in india ink or to have someone else make the drawing. Such ink is easily photographed for publication and even if your volume is not published it still insures the safeguard of having a map which will not fade. Charts and graphs may also be traced and then redrawn with india ink.

Your bibliography card will, of course, indicate as much data as possible about the map, what it illustrates, its date, its scale, its size, when it was found, who drew the original, etc. Your note-card, however, need only say that on a certain subject you have this particular map to include. Some writers attach the transparent tracing to a note-card, fold it to the size of the card, and give it a subject heading. This is advisable, however, only if your map is a temporary one. Do not fold your good, india ink map, or a photograph of a map, for the folds may show when reproduced for publication.

The pictures you want can, of course, be reproduced only by some photographic method. As you come across photographs of interest to your history you may want to make note of these, giving a brief description, perhaps copying the legend and indicating the size. Be sure to indicate on your bibliography card where you saw the picture, for pictures, maps, and other illustrative materials are not always easy to find a second time should you fail to locate their exact position when you first see them. In addition to any pictures you reproduce, you will, perhaps, also have some of old buildings or other still-existing landmarks, taken either by yourself or someone else, and these you will also want to add to the collection.

It is best to group all your illustrative material together for the present, that is, keeping all your pictures and information on them in one group, your maps in a second, and your charts and graphs in a third. Later, when you begin to organize your notes you will be able to separate these groups and fit them into the proper places in your history.

Assuming that you have followed faithfully all the possible avenues leading to material about your history and have taken careful bibliographical and card-notes on all these available historical materials, you should now have a great number of cards or slips, enough to fill at least several of your handy shoeboxes. These notes, then, are the mortar from which you will fashion the bricks for the erection of your historical edifice. Before you can begin to build, however, you must have an architect's plan for the shape, size, and design of your structure. Such a plan is what your outline will be.

Your outline will not be an exact duplicate, even in part, of the model outline presented in the next chapter. You do not want it to be. Yours will be an original piece of work and while you may, with profit, pattern your outline after the model one, it should be your very own in design and intricacy; even the finer touches should be yours though the bold pattern or outline may follow the guiding model of the succeeding chapter.

Before making your outline, study your notes; read and reread them; group together those that belong together. Decide whether you want to put all items that happened at a certain time in one group (that is called the chronological arrangement) or those that are similar in subject matter (a topical arrangement). Within either arrangement, you will find it necessary to group by date or by topic.

Next, insert guide cards and decide on your main topics. If you choose the topical arrangement (and this most writers do),[1] your guide cards will bear the labels of your main topics. Under each main topic, you will, of course, have as many subtopics as necessary. These subtopics (or subject headings) may be written in at the top of each note-card. You may also indicate the main topics on your note-cards or you may let your guide cards suffice for these.[2]

As you analyze your material you may find that some of it could fit into more than one topic. In one place you will want to deal with it in detail and in another just refer casually or in summary. Leave your note-card at the spot where you want to use it in detail but make a cross reference card at the other place, to remind you that you have such material available.

After reading carefully and referring frequently to your model outline to make sure that your general pattern is correct, you may find gaps in your research and have to fill these in by further searching and note-taking. It may be, however, that it is impossible to do a complete job and in such a case you will be forced to circumscribe the scope of your local history and write only on as much as you can adequately unearth in your search for information.

Now that you have all your cards grouped in the proper main topics and subtopics, you are ready to proceed with your architectural blueprint, that is, your outline. Once you have that down on paper, you will, perhaps, begin to see certain flaws in order of sequence and you may wish to regroup according to what seems to be a more logical arrangement. This will mean shifting of note-cards as well as guide cards.

Finally, you will reach what seems to be the best possible arrangement for your material. Your next step is to begin the actual writing. For suggestions and hints on how to transform the bricks of research into an artistic, logical architectural pattern of local history, according to the blueprint of your outline, turn to Chapter IX.

---

[1] An example of the chronological arrangement of writing is Paul M. Angle's *Lincoln, 1854–1861; Being the Day-by-Day Activities of Abraham Lincoln from Jan. 1, 1854, to March 4, 1861* (Springfield, 1933).

[2] You can make your own guide card by pasting a strip $\frac{1}{4}''$ to $\frac{1}{2}''$ wide part way across the top of a blank note-card.

CHAPTER VIII

A MODEL OUTLINE FOR A LOCAL HISTORY

IT is hoped that the model outline presented in this chapter will be found suitable, with adaptations, to all local areas in the United States, be they villages, towns, cities, counties, or even larger geographical regions. This outline is not meant to be taken as a whole, and to follow it in every detail would perhaps require more time and effort than any one writer of local history can afford. It may be desirable for you to limit consideration to the political, the social, the economic, or some other phase of the subject, or it may be best to try to cover only a certain period. In such a case, parts of the outline will not be needed. While you will almost certainly need to modify the outline in some ways it is hoped, however, that the suggested treatment will prove useful both in preparing your outline and in determining what historical information you should seek in order to cover the field properly. After some of the main divisions of the outline, comments and suggestive questions are included, to explain it and to suggest fruitful avenues of research.

The first three topics can be used for almost any community, and should be discussed only once—at the beginning of the narrative. Topic number four, and those following, may be used for any chronological period; and then repeated for later periods. If the history is to be broken into three chronological periods; e.g., the topics could be used as follows:

A. *The Early Period* (1750–1800); *Topics,* I, II, III, IV, V, etc.
B. *The Middle Period* (or "From the Revolution to the Civil War," etc.)
C. *The Later Period* (1865–   ) *Topics,* III, IV, V, etc.

The author will have to decide into how many chronological periods he wishes to divide his narrative. Frequently the major wars will serve as good divisions; e.g., the Revolution, the Civil War, the First World War. If the community is relatively new, the topics might all be discussed just once for the whole story; but usually two or three major periods will have to be considered for all the topics the author desires to include. Special chapters can be inserted within the outline of topics which follows—although they are not listed therein—on special upheavals or crises in local history (e.g., "the community and the Civil War"; "the great fire of 1904," etc.). It will not usually be desirable to repeat many of these topics for more than two or three chronological periods; since the story might then become too long or too complicated.

A skeleton outline of all major topics is listed below, so that their scope and sequence can be seen as a whole. After this, each topic will be listed with subheadings and with some comments thereon. The sequence here given does not necessarily have to be followed exactly—e.g., topic VII

102

("Population") might well be inserted above as number V, after IV ("Economic Developments"). But in most cases the topics as listed fit into one another in a fairly logical order.

SKELETON OUTLINE

I. Geography—Topography
II. Antiquities—Indians
III. Pioneer Settlement
IV. Economic Developments
V. Political Developments
VI. Religious Development
VII. Population History
VIII. The Family
IX. Education
X. Newspapers, Publications, and Libraries
XI. Social and Fraternal Organizations
XII. Other Cultural Activities—the Arts
XIII. Science and Technology
XIV. Law
XV. Social Problems and Reform
XVI. Recreation
XVII. Folk Lore
XVIII. Technical Format

I. *Geography and Topography*

1. Situation, size, physical characteristics of the area
2. Natural resources—mines, forests, fisheries, etc.
3. How these influenced settlement, and determined its present economic and social conditions
4. Soil—its kind and quality and the effect of the soil on the type of agriculture
5. Climate

The population makeup of a geographic region often depends upon the kind of soil, the natural resources, the physical environment, etc. Thus Swedes, French Canadians, and a sprinkling of Irish, Scots, and Poles are attracted to the logging regions of the Pacific states, while a mining area attracts another immigrant element. The appearance and social conditions of a logging camp, a mining town, or a farming community are largely a result of the technological processes involved and these all have their roots in the geography of the region.

Two geographers, C. Langdon White and George T. Renner, have emphasized the importance of these elements in the history of communities:

Although human communities occur from the Equator almost to the earth's poles, their distribution is far from uniform. Contrary to general belief, the distribution of mankind over the earth's surface is not due to mere chance, nor to human desire. Human communities are tied by ecological relations to the earth which gives them sustenance. The earth varies locally in the amount of protection which it lends, the opportunity for migration which it presents and the natural resources which it affords. Consequently, the amount of population which it will support varies greatly from place to place. Thus the distribution of society is purely an ecological matter. Human communities are localized, concentrated, or disseminated because they are adjusted to the physical characteristics of the earth on which they exist.

Communities are also differentiated one from another, and given specific characteristics for the same reason. . . .

. . . Therefore, what peoples will inhabit a given area, what use they will make of the resources of that area, how large their communities will be, how those communities will be organized and what standard of living they will possess are largely a matter of ecology.[1]

Another writer on the same subject points out that "a description of the nature of the soil and of the natural features . . . hills, rivers, streams and so on—is fundamental to our purpose, for on these do the site of the village and the activities of the inhabitants depend. It is hardly an exaggeration to say that geography is the basis of history."[2]

II. *Antiquities—Indians*

1. Indian mounds, rock-carvings, copper and stone implements
2. Indian life and civilization
3. Indian-white relationships during the early years
4. Indian treaties and removal of Indians from the area

If Indian relics, mounds, and evidences of earlier civilizations are to be found, these should be described according to the degree of their importance. Notable collections of Indian relics gathered from the neighborhood, either in private hands or in museums, should be mentioned and described. We can understand and appreciate our own civilization better if we are informed of the earlier civilization that once existed on the very hills, beside the same waters, and in the same valleys that we now inhabit.

III. *Pioneer Settlement*

1. Conditions which made the area desirable as a home
   Indians—absent or still present when settlement began
   Land—wooded or prairie
   Transportation—difficult or relatively easy
   Sources of income—immediate or to be developed
   Markets—nearby or far away

---

[1] White and Renner, *Geography: An Introduction to Human Ecology* (New York, 1936), 11–12.
[2] Wake, *How to Compile a History*, 29.

2. Character and composition of the early settlers
   Nationality by birth and parentage—native American or immigrants
   Home of settlers immediately preceding their coming
   1) Route followed from the old to the new home
   Motives which led to their coming
   Old-home occupations of settlers compared with the new-home activities
   Special characteristics of the early settlers
   Relations between different racial or national groups; *e.g.*, whites and Negroes; French, Germans, and British, etc.
3. Biographical sketches of outstanding pioneers
   The "founders"
   Their chief supporters and advisers
4. Map of the area shortly after settlement
   Explanation of details and matters not readily apparent

In some regions French, Spaniards, or Germans predominated before the English-speaking Americans moved in. When writing about such localities one should treat of these non-British groups. The French were especially active in the upper Great Lakes region and in the Mississippi Valley and its tributaries. The Spaniards were aggressive in the Southeast and the Southwest. In a few regions there was considerable overlapping of activity by the French and Spaniards, and in such areas both should be accounted for. In parts of Pennsylvania and the up-country of the southern seaboard, a pioneer German element was predominant.

It is well known that certain regions were only slowly opened to white settlement because of the difficulty of reaching them, or because of fear of the Indians, or because they were wooded instead of prairie land. Prairie lands were readily changed into farming areas, but timbered land of the stubborn sort grudgingly yielded perhaps five acres per year to the plow.

Often a new settlement experienced a mushroom growth, only to dwindle away almost to the point of extinction when the early sources of wealth were exhausted. Other new settlements had all the natural resources needed for a flourishing community, but lacked good transportation or nearby markets.

It is important to note whether or not the early settlers were homogeneous, whether they were native Americans or immigrants from abroad. The original home of the early settlers is important, for these pioneers tended to set the social "pattern" and make it Yankee, Southern, European, or something else. Were the settlers able to follow in their new home the occupations to which they had been accustomed? Whether they did or not may account for the degree of success they experienced. European immigrants in many cases have been unable to continue the occupations they were acquainted with in the Old World.

Be careful not to eulogize the pioneers uncritically. They did not all possess outstanding characteristics. Some were the scum of the earth, fugitives from justice, ne'er-do-wells at home, misfits, "as great a lot of ruffians as ever escaped the gallows." In the main, however, the early settlers were neither good nor bad, but were mere ordinary men, women, and children, just as we are today.

Care should be taken to distinguish real settlers from speculators whose influence in the early social, religious, and economic life was nil, or almost so. Because the early names entered for land purchase were American does not mean that American ideas, customs, and practices prevailed from that time onward, for "some of these were speculators taking up numerous tracts for resale to settlers."[3]

An excellent book to refer to when writing this particular chapter is *An Introduction to the Study of Society*, by Albion W. Small and George E. Vincent.[4] One section of the book is devoted to an anonymous community (really Topeka, Kansas), and describes how the arrival of the first "prairie schooner" started the evolution of the settlement into a flourishing city.

A map, by all means, should be included in this chapter. It should show, so far as ascertainable, the original Indian trails, the early highways, the first settlements, and homestead sites. If it is on a scale of sufficient size it can show the natural physical features, the names of each settler on his tract, and other information important for the period.

IV. *Economic Developments*

    1. Transportation, trade, and communications:
        General relations to other communities, sections, countries
        General nature of trade, in relation to agriculture, manufacturing, etc.
        Frontier trade—furs, etc.
        Roads, rivers, and canals
        Maritime trade
        Railroads
        Telegraph and telephone
        The automobile
        Air routes
        Mail services

    2. Agriculture:
        General ideals and methods
        Subsistence farming
        Lumbering and forestry
        Money crops—their relation to trade
        Machinery and implements
        Rotation and fertilization
        Animal husbandry
        Capital—owning, mortgages, renting, share-cropping, etc.

---

[3] Schafer, "Documenting Local History," 10–11.
[4] New York, 1894. This book is mentioned because it will probably be found in many public and school libraries. It contains several maps showing how Topeka grew.

3. Manufacturing:
    Early handicrafts
    Inventions and machinery
    The factory system
    Private business and corporations
    Banking and finance
    Labor and the unions
    General business relations
4. Maritime activities:
    Fisheries
    Shipbuilding
5. Extractive industries:
    Mining, oil, etc. (Lumbering might also be considered under this heading, if the forests were simply cut down without any reforesting)

In dealing with economic developments as with all others, note what skills, habits, or attitudes the settlers brought with them into the new community. Were they, for example, good farmers at the start? Certain groups, like the "Pennsylvania Dutch," had inherited a superior tradition in farming, and this exerted a real influence on their agriculture.

Perhaps in dealing with agricultural development certain definite periods can be indicated. Some regions have had decided turning-points, due to a change in the crop or in the use to which land was put. In the South, the Civil War, with the abolition of slavery, brought radical changes in farming methods. In the immediate vicinity of large cities in the Central West the land was cleared ready for agricultural purposes; wheat farming was carried on extensively; in time this gave way to dairying, often by the cooperative method or by the sale of milk to the cities; finally, as in all communities, modern methods of farming caused other changes in the mode of life of farm families. Certain regions today raise crops wholly unknown a generation ago. General farming may have given way to specialized farming, but in time the general farming may have been resumed. Schafer points out that

from the census of agriculture one can describe the kind of farming carried on in any given township, and tell whether wheat growing, stock raising, dairying, or specialized crops were emphasized. Since the census also tells us who are the cultivators, a correlation between cultivators and products can be made which shows what type of people are growing wheat, what type dairying; who are the onion kings, or the sugar-beet growers, and what family or hired labor supply the general group employ.[5]

While all industries should be treated, stress would be laid upon those which are predominant or were so at one time. Were there old-fashioned peddlers, gipsies, traveling knife-grinders and chair-menders in the early years? If so, how long has it been since they stopped coming? A study of early business methods and ethics would be revealing. The "service"

[5] Schafer, *Trans-Mississippi West*, 305.

idea, stressed so much today, was unknown a generation ago. Competition was keen between rival dealers, and often unscrupulous.

Maps may be utilized to show the early routes of transportation. If the dates can be determined for the beginning of each new route or method of transportation and communication, these should by all means be included. A good deal of romance is interwoven with the early methods of travel and this should be mentioned. Stage-coaching days, steamboating days, sleighing days, covered-bridge days and covered-wagon days— the mere mention of these brings up memories of the past.

If your community is on the route of an old national road, it may have witnessed stirring scenes. Statistics of the number of wagons passing certain towns in a single day have occasionally been preserved. The great dispersion of population took place in the decades which followed the Revolutionary War. Families moved from one pioneer settlement to another until they finally scattered throughout the entire country. Where there were canals and bridges, toll rates and records may still be found in various depositories. It is important to chronicle the coming of the railroad to your town or community and to show the results. Your town may have been one which protested against this development. Or your community may have opposed the coming of the automobile. In 1905 the call for a mass meeting in Mexico, Missouri, read:

> We the undersigned citizens, deeming it necessary for the safety of our families and believing that the automobile is a menace to the lives of our people and of the prosecuting of our callings, do hereby give public notice that there will be a mass meeting held in Mexico (the county seat) at the court house on Saturday, September 23, at 2 o'clock p.m. to consult as to the best means of controlling this evil.[6]

While such reactions to new means of travel are interesting and may have had some justification, the important thing is the change in community life which they produced.

This chapter should also include a list of the early trades and the manner of conducting them—shoemaking, stone quarrying, harness making, blacksmithing, carpentering, wheelwrighting, dressmaking, tailoring, barbering, stone constructing, weaving, brick making, butchering, etc. The apprentice system should be discussed and its extent estimated. Wages should be given for unskilled labor. Hired laborers on farms and elsewhere might be investigated. Did the community have an influx of seasonal labor at harvesting time? Where did it come from? How many remained to become residents? What was the effect on the community of the seasonal labor? These and many other questions shed light on the social conditions of the community.

---

[6] *Ibid.*, 170. One suggestion was that "those who were determined to operate the nuisances build themselves private roads and stay on them."

V. *Political Activities*

1. Original form of local government
2. Changes in charters, boundaries, status, etc.
3. Prominent officials
4. Rise and progress of political parties, their local programs, elections, etc.
5. Degree of efficiency and honesty in local government, financial policies, etc.
6. Relation of government to other institutions (churches, schools, social problems, etc.)
7. Civic services:
    Water
    Sewerage
    Gas and electricity
    Fire and police protection
    Public recreation facilities
    "City planning"
8. Civic reform movements

The story of local government is the most obvious and perhaps the most important aspect of community organization. Most settlers were familiar with either town or county administrations, and were anxious to reestablish these in the new communities as soon as possible in order to maintain law and order, and provide schools and public services. Observe how they went about reestablishing the governmental forms to which they had been accustomed; and to what extent, if any, new conditions led to modifications of the same. Soon the community was interested in its relation to the state and nation, as well as in its own immediate affairs. This brings in the story of political parties and elections. Distinguish between the theory of how institutions like the town meeting or the county commissioners were supposed to work, and how they actually operated. The development of local services, like police, fire, and public health protection, was often picturesque as well as important. Keep in mind the relation of government to the community as a whole: *i.e.*, to religious feeling, public opinion, and to other aspects of community life.

VI. *Religious Developments*

1. Early religious life
2. Development of the major denominations (doctrines, government, ritual, morals)
3. Minor groups
4. Interdenominational relations
5. Moral attitudes in churches, and their relation to social problems, law and order, civic reform, etc.

Although large numbers of people in the early colonies were not church members, the religious life was usually a significant part of community activities. Most of the colonies had established churches which, especially in New England, exercised great influence in governments, schools, and other phases of community life; but during and after the Revolution, intolerance broke down because of the diversity of denominations and the force of Revolutionary liberalism. The prevailing characteristics of American religion by about 1800 were the diversity of denominations, the ferment of religious revivals, reviving orthodoxy, appearance of new sects, and puritanism in morals. This was usually the "atmosphere" in which local communities developed after that date. Note how it affected any given local area; and to what extent, if any, this community was exceptional in these matters.

After general religious conditions have been discussed, something may be said about the development of particular denominations or individual churches (parishes). Keep in mind, in considering a particular denomination, such essential matters as its general theology or doctrines, forms of church government, ritual and ceremonies, character and activities of the clergy, attitudes towards morals and such institutions as the schools. Recall that some institutions, not strictly denominations, had a more or less religious character; e.g., the Masonic and other fraternal orders, the Salvation Army, the YMCA, the YWCA, and the Knights of Columbus.

These matters should not be gone into in great detail, for general trends affecting all sects are of greater significance—the revivals, the attitude of churches toward such social problems as temperance and slavery, and interdenominational relations (e.g., Catholics and Protestants). In particular cases, however, the development of individual groups (e.g., Catholics, Quakers, German churches, Slavic churches, etc.) may be especially important.

Care should be taken to give each church its due, and yet not to fill the text with unnecessary details or fulsome praise. The part religion played in the community at various epochs should be clearly indicated. Finally, the losses or failures of the churches, as well as their achievements, should be frankly considered. Religious scepticism and indifference, as well as belief, may deserve a place in your story.

VII. *Population History*
　　1. Birth and death rates
　　2. Growth or decline of total population
　　3. Migrations:
　　　Immigration
　　　　Statistics
　　　　Racial or national groups
　　　　Treatment of immigrants
　　　　"Americanization"
　　　　Influence of immigrants
　　　Emigration
　　　　Causes and destinations
　　　　Selective influences?
　　　　Results

The chief phases of population history to be considered are the natural increase or decrease (birth and death rates) and migrations. A brief discussion will usually suffice for the first. A high birth rate was usual until after about 1860, with large families. This resulted from both economic need and prevailing religious attitudes. After about 1800, and especially between 1840 and 1850, and again after 1900, the birth rate declined. Death rates were also high until nearly the last date. Federal or state census figures will show how far a given community reflected these trends.

Not all communities have been subject to major migration movements, but some have gone through several. The census reports reveal their extent. In industrial areas Italians, Greeks, Poles, Jugo-Slavs, Bulgarians, and others have made up a large part of the labor supply. In agricultural areas the rural population still consists largely of the descendants of the New Englanders, the Irish, the English, the Welsh, the Scots, and the Germans. A writer on Connecticut gives us a picture of the importance of immigration into that state which, in spite of its long colonial history, now has a population almost two-thirds of which is either foreign-born or of foreign-born parentage.

The casual traveler through the Connecticut countryside will hardly note that instead of Yankee farmers it is mostly former inhabitants of Russia, Poland, Italy, and their children who are tilling the fertile soil in the valleys and the less fertile land of the hills . . . .

He goes on to say that not only the farming but also the manufacturing, the finance, the political life and the religious spirit are all being gradually permeated with individuals of foreign extraction. He concludes, however,

Yet, over and above all these diversities a remarkable unifying force is discernible, a force that seems to be constantly working towards an elimination of distinguishing peculiarities and which, under favorable conditions, may eventually lead to a certain degree of cultural homogeneity.[7]

What is true of Connecticut is true of most other New England states, and to a lesser degree of some of the other states in the Union. Each immigrant group has contributed something of value to the community.. It may be labor, an appreciation of one of the fine arts, a tempting dish, a type of architecture, worthwhile customs, new crops, a new religious emphasis, or new trades and occupations. Wisconsin published a special

---

[7] Samuel Koenig, *Immigrant Settlements in Connecticut: Their Growth and Characteristics* (Hartford: Connecticut State Department of Education, 1938), 9–10. This is a 68-page publication of the WPA, through the agency of the Federal Writers' Project for the State of Connecticut. Pages 24–58 are devoted to the characteristic features of the various immigrant groups. Pages 59–68 contain a valuable bibliography of each immigrant group and of immigration in general. The book should be valuable in any state if only for the bibliography.

bulletin on its foreign groups, and no doubt information on this subject may be found in a number of other state historical societies.[8]

In this connection it is well to look at the attitudes of those who have lived long in a community towards those newly arrived. The role of social isolation, as in the case of strangers, such as Negroes, Jews, or the foreign born, tend to isolate these groups into one section of the community. What role do the attitudes of the natives play in isolating these groups both geographically and socially? What was the reaction to the foreign club, church, or old world festival? Strange words may appear in the records of your community. For example "Stirabout" (oatmeal and milk) indicates that Irish immigrants were among the early settlers.

In many small communities names were changed for various reasons. Hostility toward foreign groups practically forced them to hide their identity. How many of the early fathers of your town became good Americans merely by changing from Klein to Little or Small? How many Schwartzes became Black or Solomons became Sullivan? The hearings before the Senate Committee on Immigration formulating our present immigration law explain much of the history of name changing. The changing of names suggests hostility to persons who could be identified as foreigners or strangers in the early history of American towns.

By what social process was unity of action achieved? Did the colored Civil War soldier symbolize the essential common purpose when he visited the schools on Memorial Day? In terms of town pride what ceremonials or rituals or days of celebration permitted harmony even for just one day? What effect did this union of effort for the promotion of civic achievement have on later relations between and among groups which previously were divided by ancestry, traditions, symbols, prestige, and status? For example, the annual Cattle Show is a completely competitive affair. Jellies, vegetables, horses, cattle, plowing matches, "five dollars for every minute," anyone could resist the itinerant wrestler, and so on, frequently reversed the traditionally held attitudes of efficiency and industry. Did such results play a part in admitting previously socially isolated groups into organizations composed exclusively of a selectively determined membership?

Not only has there been migration into the community, but many communities have also experienced an emigration. The reasons for this exodus have often been as varied as those which caused the immigration. There has always been a period of agitation and moving about following a war or a grave financial panic. Samuel Koenig, in discussing such movements, says:

Toward the end of the eighteenth century, the steady increase in population was counterbalanced by the first wave of westward migration from Connecticut. At first, the colonists had been satisfied to cultivate the relatively poor land which

---

[8] *A Study of the Foreign Groups in Wisconsin, Bulletin of Information* No. 3, December 1897. The bulletin contains 22 pages.

makes the State unadaptable for extensive agriculture, but when a trail to the west was blazed, the exodus began. Connecticut Yankees settled in most of the states between the Atlantic and the Pacific. Many towns in Ohio, Missouri, and other midwest states owe their origin to natives of Connecticut. More descendants of early Connecticut settlers live in several western states than in Connecticut itself.

The natives of Connecticut did not by any means confine their migrations to the middle west or far west; the stream flowed in practically all directions. First, there were the more fertile lands in New England. Many Connecticut emigrants found their way to Massachusetts, Maine, New Hampshire, and Vermont. New York, New Jersey, and Pennsylvania were among other eastern states that received considerable numbers of former Connecticut inhabitants. Others could not resist the mild climate, the fertile soil, and the abundance of slave labor in the South, and settled in Dixie Land.[9]

What is here said of Connecticut could be said of many other eastern states.

One of the more important aspects of population movement to look for is why certain types of personalities migrated from their original habitat and settled, let us say, in your community. Is there a selective factor that leads a person to leave one place and settle in another, aside from the obvious fact that employment is more likely in the new community or that he has been involved in some sort of disturbing activity in his home town. How did his fellow townsmen feel when he left? Were they relieved or was he the instrument through which the changing attitudes redefined the issue or problem involved? For example, a Baptist minister accepts a call to your town because the more conservative elements in his previous church objected to his daughter dancing or serving tea.

A glimpse of the restlessness which pervaded many regions throughout the country is afforded by the example of Platte County, Missouri. This and the other counties to the north, called the Platte Purchase, were thrown open to settlement in 1837. Immediately a flood of settlers flowed in from other Missouri counties and from Tennessee, Kentucky, and Virginia. Before a year had passed Platte County had a density of twenty to the square mile, whereas Missouri as a whole, which lay to the east, had a density of about four and a half. The influx continued for several years. Just as suddenly, an outward movement began. Paxton, the annalist of Platte County and himself a witness to the movements, gave a year-by-year account of the departures for the next twenty-five years [10]

The migration phase of American history, one of the most romantic of all, should be given as it affected your community. This chapter should have a statistical table showing the total population at each decade, as well as the totals for the various immigrant groups if they can be determined.

---

[9] Koenig, *Immigrant Settlements in Connecticut*, 14.

[10] W. M. Paxton, *Annals of Platte County, Missouri* (Kansas City, Mo., 1897), 52, 54, 68, 69, 71, 110, 120, 152, 188, 399, 400.

VIII. *The Family*
    1. Courtship, marriage, remarriage, and divorce
    2. Moral standards
    3. Personal and property rights of husbands, wives, and children
    4. Birth rates, and status of children
    5. Special phases of family life—religious, educational, recreational, economic, etc.

The importance of family life in the community is obvious, and facts about it are often scattered through local histories in relation to manners and customs, or in terms of particular families. Domestic relationships, however, have a history in themselves, which may well be brought together at one place in your narrative. The family changes, just as do governments or churches. The average family of 1800, for example, with many children and strong parental authority, was quite different from that of 1940, with few youngsters and lessened discipline. The children in the earlier family found most of their life centered in it, from their daily chores to their recreation; whereas in recent times much of their interests focus outside, in the schools, scout-troops, movies, etc. The transition, which is partly due to the change from rural to urban living, is less marked today in farming areas.

The status of women in the family has also changed greatly. Customs of courtship have been modified; a wife's control over her person, property, and children has increased; divorce has become more common. The connections between relatives and the sense of family interdependence seem to be less marked. Such trends have led some observers to speak of the "disintegration" of the family, though this may be an exaggerated view. In any case, many persons still feel that home ties are the strongest; and the whole story of trends in family life is therefore one of the most essential in the history of any community.

What role did parents and older persons play in the selection of marriage partners? What was the position of children in the family? Was the family name of positive prestige value, or did personal achievement and status confer recognition upon the family name. How did the residents of your community react to women smoking, using cosmetics, wearing short skirts, getting bobbed hair cuts, having children out of wedlock? Were "state" children regarded as "love," or illegitimate children. For example, in one small town the children of the village were forbidden to play with children placed out by the State because the parents believed that all "state kids" were illegitimate and so contaminated. What role did adopted or foster children play in your town? Did they become delinquents or leaders? Whom did they marry in terms of status and class standing? What was the local reaction to their success or failure?

The story of the family is one that has been largely overlooked by general historians. Arthur W. Calhoun's *Social History of the American Family* is the only work which attempts to cover it comprehensively, and this is often based on fragmentary information. Local histories which contribute real information about family life will therefore add greatly to our knowledge of this topic for the country as a whole.

IX. *Education*
    1. The first schools
    2. Church and other private schools
    3. Public schools:
        Elementary and secondary
        Curriculum; and extracurricular activities
        Teachers and teacher training
        Methods of teaching
        School administration
        School financing
        School building and facilities
        Special schools
    4. Higher education
        Church colleges
        City or state universities
    5. Adult education
    6. General influence of schools on the community, and vice versa

All of us know that the schools of today are very different from what they were fifty, seventy-five, or a hundred years ago. The main differences should be noted. Teachers used to be "hired" more for their ability to wield the rod than for their educational attainments. In some places they had to adhere to the "flat earth" theory (not to mention the anti-evolutionary emphasis of some states today). Did boys and girls attend the same school? How was the teacher paid? When did a student usually stop his education? Were the early teachers schoolmasters or schoolma'ams? Were the early schools connected with the churches in any way? What subjects were taught? When was the high school added? When were the schools consolidated and what effect did this have? How have state laws affected the local schools? Were McGuffey readers used? Was religion taught? When did sports and athletics first come into the program? To what extent did the early school of your locality compare with the following description:

An enterprising young man, claiming to be a teacher, would walk into a community unannounced, and make the rounds with a written contract, binding each subscriber to pay to the said teacher a stipulated sum per pupil, for a school term of usually three months.—There was no such thing as a building fund; every able-bodied man in the neighborhood was expected to lend a hand in cutting and hewing the logs and to be at the 'house raising.' All were there and log upon log, lengthwise at the four sides, crossed at the corners of the house, and notched down, was placed in succession one upon another until a fairly rectangular parallelogram was carried to the proper height of one story; then logs were drawn inward at the sides for the support of the roof and continued upwards at the ends for gables, until the apex of the roof structure was reached, and the whole was covered with clapboards, from three to four feet long, which were weighted at intervals by poles running lengthwise of the building and across the boards, no nails or other iron material being used. The house was then chinked and daubed, after places had been cut out of the walls for one door, one or two small windows and a large fire-place. The door was made of common up-right boards hung on wooden hinges and fastened with the traditional latch-string lock. The floor was made of puncheons laid on logs for joists. The chimney was on the outside and at the gable end of the house, opposite the door. The heating was from the fire-place and ventilation through the stick and clay chimney; the intake of fresh air was 'where it listeth.' The plumbing was a neighboring spring, a wooden pail and a drinking gourd.

The furniture consists of a writing desk, made of a board, horizontal in its length, and inclined upward in its width, with the upward edge against the side of the house and fastened. For the children, the seats were puncheons, having near each end, on the under side, two auger holes, in which legs were inserted. For the teacher, a small table and an old-fashioned round-legged chair, seated with split bark of the hickory.[11]

Not every community is blessed with an institution of higher learning. Communities which possess them have a finer cultural life than others unless other factors enter into the picture. Higher institutions attract cultured people who desire to live in the atmosphere of a college town or who wish to send their children to college. Your chapter can be expected to supply only a brief history of the educational institution in your community, for to treat this subject adequately a whole volume might be devoted to that subject alone.

X. *The Newspapers, Periodicals, and Libraries*
   1. The early newspapers, their origin, growth, and influence
       Political affiliations and part played in local politics
   2. Discontinued newspapers, origin, growth, and influence
       Political affiliations
       Reasons for discontinuance, merging, etc.
   3. The present newspaper, origin, growth, and influence
       Political affiliations
       Its policies for the local community
   4. Periodicals, magazines, and journals
       Origin, growth, influence
   5. Location of the files of present and defunct publications
   6. Libraries—private and public

Nearly every newspaper has been connected with one or another of the political parties. Often a paper was established to champion the political views of a party, or to promote certain ideas. There are probably more defunct newspapers than existing ones. Each played a part during its lifetime. To evaluate the importance and influence of each may not be easy, but it is worth attempting.

---

[11] Quoted by Ellis, *Civic History of Kansas City*, 188, from an address by Joseph L. Norman at the laying of the corner stone of Thacher School, May 23, 1900, and published in the *Report of Public Schools of Kansas City* (1900), 123–124.

Newspapers often played a major role in influencing public opinion on other matters besides politics. This might be a good point at which to compare this influence with that of other factors—*e.g.*, the pulpit; and, later, that of the movies or the radio. In other words, one might comment here on the way in which public opinion was formed in general.

The type of periodical usually called a magazine was often devoted to a particular interest. Thus there were agricultural journals, church and family magazines, and temperance periodicals. These might be more appropriately described under such other main headings as, respectively, Agriculture, Religion, and Social Reform. General literary magazines, or "journals of opinion," usually appeared only in the larger cities; but where they existed, they deserve consideration.

The history of your public library, your local historical society, or your community's private library may be a story worth recording. The date when a community first reached that stage in its cultural life that it felt the need for books might prove of interest in your research. The incidents that led to the organizing of a group to support such a literary venture, the early struggles, the growth of the institution, the present status, all are facts worth chronicling.

XI. *Social and Fraternal Organizations*
    1. Origin and growth of each
    2. Purpose and special field of activity
    3. Relation to whole community

This chapter should take up briefly the history of such organizations as the Masons, Knights of Columbus, Knights of Pythias, Odd Fellows, Grange, Daughters of the American Revolution, American Legion, Parent-Teachers Association, Women's Clubs, Chamber of Commerce, Rotary Club, and others. In communities of several thousand population, the number of such organizations is likely to be a score or more. It may be necessary to choose the more important in each category and give merely a brief history of each, but every organization, past and present, should be listed in some manner, giving the facts as to its origin, date, importance, and statistics. When possible, note also its general place and influence in the community.

You will have to use your own judgment as to whether, in certain cases, these organizations should also be noted in connection with other topics. Thus the Masons might be discussed in connection with the story of the Protestant churches; or the Knights of Columbus in association with Catholicism.

XII. *Other Cultural Activities:* The Arts
    1. Household arts—cookery, wines, textiles, etc.
    2. Minor arts—costumes, furniture, silver, glass, pottery, embroidery
    3. Fine arts
        Music—folk songs, singing societies, orchestras, etc.

Dancing
Painting and sculpture
Architecture—old houses, construction, architectural styles, etc.
4. Literature
Taste in reading—relation to libraries, periodicals, etc.
Literary societies
Original work
5. Professional groups and schools (musicians, architects, etc.)
6. The stage
Amateur theatricals
Pageants
Theaters; vaudeville
Minstrel shows
"Movies"
Opera

The story of minor and household arts is closely associated with family life, and might be discussed in that connection, if the author prefers. Tastes in food, furniture, textiles, etc., were determined in families, but they also were characteristic of communities as a whole. Materials and styles in clothing, household utensils, and furniture were not only essential matters in daily living, but also provide the "atmosphere" for certain periods. Nearly everyone, for example, is interested in the quaint costumes, the linsey-woolsey coverlets, and the trundle-beds of the Puritans.

Taste in such matters also had sometimes a more serious significance. Thus bad habits in eating—the "grease and grits" diet in the South—had an unfortunate effect on the public health of some regions. Most early Americans probably ate too heavy and starchy foods, partly because it was impossible in winter to secure a more varied diet. Their drinking habits were also frequently bad. Such matters could be discussed at this point; or later, in connection with health or with social reform in the community.

The fine arts may be treated under two subheadings, relating respectively to the popular and the sophisticated forms. Thus popular music and dancing—jigs, folk dancing, ballads, square-dancing, the waltz, modern syncopation—are one story; orchestras, choral societies, and the opera constitute another. Folk paintings, or "primitives," are a different theme from the work of professional artists. Similarly, the taste and construction of houses built by farmers or local carpenters can be distinguished from the work of professional architects. The same distinction can even be made in literature and the stage, that is, between the writings published by local amateurs in the newspapers and those by recognized writers; or between amateur theatricals or pageants and those put on by professionals. In large towns, considerable attention should be given to the sophisticated forms.

XIII. *Science and Technology*
1. Local inventors
2. Technological developments in factories, transportation, agriculture, etc.
3. Original work in "pure science"
4. Scientific institutions and professional groups (engineers, chemists, etc.)

On the whole, science has had a greater hand in remaking the modern world than has any other factor. It is therefore important to note (1) whether any original scientists or inventors worked in a given place; and (2) how new scientific devices or inventions were introduced, and how they affected the community. In large towns the founding of schools or museums and the activities of scientific societies were often of great significance.

XIV. *Law*
1. Civil law
    Common law—civil
    Statute law (local, state, and federal)
2. Criminal law (see above)
3. Court organization and procedures
4. The legal profession—training, place in community, in politics

The history of law is another vital subject which has been largely neglected in most histories, probably because it is so technical. Any information you can secure for local areas will eventually add to our knowledge of the whole subject. You may get valuable advice from old lawyers on this theme.

Among the variety of sources which indicate the attitudes which underlie actions is the content of the criminal law. What offenses were regarded as important? Sabbath breaking, gambling, blasphemy, idleness and so on have been punished in many communities. What brought about a change in attitudes toward these forms of conduct? Sabbath breaking, a purely religious affair, becomes a crime. If your community depends upon fruit growing and essential labor must be done on the Sabbath, how did the preacher meet this problem? If your community depends upon wheat growing how did the preacher justify the prohibition of labor.

More frequently than otherwise the influence of formal statute law upon the conduct of persons in small communities is practically nonexistent. Conformity to the rules and regulations of town life is secured through gossip, ridicule, tradition, custom, family status, rumor, or social isolation or alienation. "What will the neighbors say?" is a more certain and powerful social control than the threat of "the law." Such close face-to-face relationships are projected into village and town life or even city neighborhood life and are themselves a means of regulating conduct. Phrases such as "nice girls do not do those things" or "Did you hear about the Johnson boy?" tend to develop a unity of opposition toward the different or nonconforming type of conduct.

119

In the study of crime and delinquency in your town you should try to learn whether the offenders were native- or foreign-born, and if the latter what country they came from. What methods were used? What crimes were commonly committed? What attitudes were held toward offenses and offenders? What cultural conflict was involved which might tend to explain particular crimes? If offenders were children of foreign parents or Negro parents was there anything in their status or social position, such as exclusion from the town's juvenile activities, that might explain their misconduct? Were they regarded as "the crime problem?" If so what measures were taken to handle this situation?

XV. *Social Problems and Reform*
1. Poverty and poor relief
2. Crime and punishment
    Crime conditions, and moral attitudes
    Types of punishment
    Penology and institutions
3. Drunkenness and drug addiction
4. Prostitution
5. Slavery (a topic needing detailed treatment in the South)
6. Handicapped classes
    Orphans and aged
    The insane and feeble-minded
    The deaf, dumb, blind, and crippled
7. Health and disease
    Medicine and doctors
    Disease conditions
      Endemic
      Epidemic
    Public health control
    Folk medicine and practice
    Quackery and medical sects
    Relations to regular medicine
    Public medical services
8. Social reform movements
    Anti-slavery, temperance, women's rights, etc. (each of these can be treated in relation to a particular problem above)

This topic is of obvious importance. All American communities provide such institutions as government, the home, and the church to try to keep society moving in a normal and healthy manner. In spite of this, things go wrong—there is drunkenness, crime, poverty, and disease. These unfortunate conditions must be honestly described, not just minimized or ignored for the sake of the local reputation. Then, in each case, the story of the efforts made to remedy these conditions should be surveyed—in terms of both institutions (like jails) and of general reform movements like the temperance drive.

Many of our forefathers were convinced that God sent them crosses to bear. One instance was insanity in the family. No one would consider sending the crazy member to an institution. This was the punishment for past sins. When and how did the change occur in your town which led to sending such unfortunate members to public institutions? In a Maine village, within the last five years, an insane fifteen year old girl was chained to a stake in the front yard. She was her family's cross to bear. The sociologist uses the term *secularization* to explain the change from a "cross to bear" to utilizing specialized institutions for the care of such people. As John Morley tells us in his life of Voltaire, where the Sun is the object of veneration it is probable that it will be a crime to study the laws of heat.

On the credit side of the ledger, medical science and physicians always touched the daily life more closely and vitally than did any other science or scientist. The whole story of medicine, of medical practice, or quackery and folk practice, etc., is always of interest to readers. In large towns the "old family doctor" becomes less significant than the development of hospitals, medical schools, and medical research. Do not overlook the medical sects (*e.g.*, homeopathy, osteopathy, Christian Science, and others now forgotten such as Thomsonianism or "botannic medicine," and "hydropathy" with its "water cures"). The auxiliary services, like dentistry, veterinary medicine, and nursing (both "home" and "trained nurses") are also worthy of attention.[12]

XVI. *Recreation*
      1. Utilitarian recreation—corn huskings, house raisings, spelling bees, etc.
      2. Indoor games
      3. Outdoor sports—amateur and professional
      4. (See also literature, libraries, theaters, movies, radio, etc.)
      5. Vacations—public "resorts," "amusement parks"
      6. Immigrant contributions

A people's recreation may at first seem a more trivial matter than political or economic developments. It is now known, however, that recreation is essential to a people's morale. What people enjoy, their sense of humor, etc., are also a good clue of their character. If, for example, they enjoyed brutal sports like dog-fighting, this tells much about their nature.

Early Americans took their fun largely in connection with their necessary labors, in "utilitarian sports." Later they had more time and leisure for formal games, and still later for commercialized amusements. Outdoor sports had a great revival after about 1850. Do not overlook the influence of religion on amusements (Puritanism discouraged some of them); and also the influence of special European peoples—*e.g.*, the introduction of team games from English tradition, or of beer gardens by the Germans.

---

[12] See articles on early medical and dental practices in Ohio in October-December issue of the *Ohio Archaeological and Historical Quarterly* for 1941, 1942, and 1943.

XVII. *Folklore*

1. Superstititons of various sorts
2. Local beliefs about births, deaths, weddings, and funerals
3. Ghosts, charms, haunted houses, hidden stairways, secret closets
4. Strange and unaccounted-for happenings
5. Eccentric characters—inventors, cranks, prophets, gamblers, murderers, spies
6. Spite fences, churches, school, towns, and railroads
7. Odd decisions made by the flipping of a coin, etc.
8. Irreverent, odd, and interesting jingles on tombstones
9. Odd and obsolete punishments, ordinances, etc.
10. Local sayings, maxims, proverbs, and ballads
11. Dialect and words peculiar to the neighborhood
12. Local sports, feasts, fairs, etc.

Every community has its legends of epoch-making events, outstanding persons who were born or lived there, areas with fearsome powers resident in them, village nitwits, village drunks, village blacksheep, departure of lepers, rumors that brought disunity, fear of religious groups, reports of mysterious peddlers, persons with psychic powers, oft told tales of striking clocks and baying dogs presaging death. All these folk beliefs, fears, peculiarities, even the very name of the community will yield real pay dirt to the historian who is prepared to follow clues even though these lead him into dead end alleys. In other words, the most promising lead may turn out to be a waste of time but even so this labor has been of great value because it means that the chance was taken and proved of no value for your story.

Another source which might prove both valuable, rewarding, and challenging is folk sayings of your region or community. The origin of sectional accents has been fairly well analyzed but why certain expressions are found in one place but not a few miles away remains purely a conjecture. The "hurry-back" of the Georgian, the "I got potatoes in the cellar" in Maine, "the white water ahead" of New Hampshire, the "goodbye now" of Massachusetts, the "tonic" of New England, but "pop" elsewhere, imply at least a relation to the attitudes of the region, the tradition of the region, or perhaps a relation to some person or group, or even a belief.

In one New England city there are several acres of land willed to Jesus Christ who presumably is to take possession upon his second coming. No one knows whether piety and religious convictions motivated the bequest or hatred for real estate taxes.

The local historian frequently will find that the names given to children express clearly the religious or political attitudes of the period being studied. For example such names as Oh Be Joyful Johnson, or Praise God Ballou, or Hate Evil Hall or County Referendum Wilson (all names that have been given children) permit the inference that while the parents were concerned about the welfare of their offspring, they also unconsciously believed that names, by some sort of word magic, would influence them in the direction such names implied.

This chapter should be the most varied and yet, possibly, the most interesting of the whole volume. It should contain those interesting items of local lore which are too important to omit but which will fit in at no other point. Do not, however, include here items which can clearly go into earlier topics—*e.g.*, stories under "2" above can often be better discussed in relation to Religion or the Family. Probably nothing will show the peculiar character of your community more than the local folklore. Almost anything can be included in this chapter, from old remedies to fires, storms, and tempests. In dealing with items, 4, 5, 6, 7, and 8, it is probably best to confine your remarks to those persons and events which have had time to mellow with the passing years. To bring your compilation too near to the present might involve you in difficulties. The older stories will soon be forgotten, moreover, unless they are recorded now. It is also advisable to label as legend and hearsay rather than as authentic history anything which cannot be verified.

XVIII. *Technical Format*
    1. Preface
    2. Table of contents
    3. Lists of illustrations, charts, and maps
    4. Introduction
    5. Chapters of text
    6. Footnote citations
    7. Appendices
    8. Bibliography
    9. Index

These various components of what go to make up the composition of nearly every serious piece of writing will be discussed in detail in the succeeding two chapters. Once you have all the information you want for item number 5 (the chapters of your text) you are ready to devote your attention to the writing of your book and after you have completed the writing of your chapter narratives you will want to frame them in the proper technical setting in order to make your work a genuine piece of professional writing.

Chapter IX

COMPOSITION AND TECHNICAL DETAILS
IN HISTORICAL WRITING

GENERAL SUGGESTIONS

While it is true that literary style cannot be acquired and is best when original, there are, nevertheless, certain obvious" handles" which should be useful to the beginning writer of local history. One of these is to try to write so that one sentence easily leads to the next and one paragraph becomes related to another. A new paragraph or a complete change of subject should not be thrust upon the reader with bomb-like unexpectedness. Readers do not relish jumping in confusion from one idea to another. They will not mind new ideas, however, if these are introduced gradually, with some relationship to the preceding paragraph or the aforegoing subject. They also appreciate help in following the time element of the story by frequent insertion of dates, seasons, or epochs.

Transitions:

A few sample phrases that achieve such relationship or transition are the following:

The above
Ten days later
Several times that summer
When the leaves fell
During the next year
Meanwhile
Meantime
In due course
Not only was the aforegoing true, but
In addition to
By the early eighties
After several months
In this as in other things
Thus it happened that
In 1806
Then
In summary
Furthermore

Such "handles" are especially useful to knit together your bits of note-card information derived from many sources and bearing the traces of many styles. Avoid the bad practice of beginning your sentences with "and," "but," "too," or "however."

Sometimes it is necessary to go over your rough draft and "smooth" out the sentences that do not seem to relate one paragraph to the next. The examples below illustrate what improvements may be made with slight changes in phrasing:

Instead of:

An attempt may be made to summarize the conclusions arrived at in this study.

The same object is achieved in a more preferable form by:

In summary it may be said that . . .

Too obvious attempts at transition such as:

To get back to our chronology . . .

May be avoided by:

Meantime other events had contributed to . . .

Inversion is permissible if its purpose is to introduce a time element:

In June of the same year, the Missouri Democratic State Convention . . .

Instead of:

The Missouri Democratic State Convention of 1910 . . .

Othewise a direct sentence:

Bryan wrote about this tariff to several of the Democratic leaders.

Is preferable to an inverted one:

To several of the Democratic leaders, Bryan wrote about this tariff.

Beginning a paragraph with a page number:

On page 321 of the . . .

Is not as good as:

In a work entitled *Memories of Long Ago* there is a passage (p. 321) . . .

REPETITION OF WORDS

One of the most common flaws in writing is the repetition of the same word or words throughout a number of paragraphs. This may result from your habitual use of a certain term—of which you may be quite unaware. Or you may be discussing a particular topic like "feminism" through several pages, and so keep on using that particular noun. In any case, the reader will often be mildly irritated by seeing the given word over and over again. It is therefore wise to reread your pages with the purpose of watching for such repetitions, and in order to find synonyms wherever possible.

CLARITY WITHOUT REPETITION

It is not a simple task to assemble source materials and weave a multitude of styles and topics into one connected story. The material in your notes may seem clear enough to you but when you attempt to put it down in writing you are faced with the necessity of translating these thoughts into simple present day language and the result is often a badly muddled garble that fails to convey any thought to the reader. There is no rule of thumb whereby you can learn to write with clarity and understanding. A thorough digesting of one's material plus considerable practice in writing are indispensable prerequisites. For the first, paraphrasing was recommended in preference to quoting, in the process of taking notes. For the second, the following may give a little "first aid."

Direct sentence structure is generally clearer than inversions:
For example, instead of: The party was able to elect for governor its candidate, Charles Lynch.
The meaning is clearer thus: The party was able to elect its candidate, Charles Lynch, for governor.
Similarly: In a letter Hammond unburdened his opinions . . .
Reads more clearly thus: Hammond unburdened his opinions in a letter . . .
Sometimes too much brevity does not achieve enough clarity:
For example; instead of: Then as now current events affected speech.
The meaning is clearer thus: Then as today new expressions of speech were often the result of current events.
On the other hand too much elaboration does not always assure clarity:
For example, instead of: Naturally the common speech was less used by the educated, and those of wider contacts, yet there was always a tendency for even those classes to speak with somewhat less of grammatical correctness and propriety of diction than they had knowledge of.
The meaning is clearer if expressed thus: Even the better educated were discouraged from revealing their knowledge of grammatical correctness and refrained from practicing refined conversation.
Unnecessary repetitions are confusing instead of helpful:
For example, instead of: It is probably only . . .
All that is necessary is: It is probably . . .

CONCISENESS WITHOUT DRABNESS

While conciseness should not be employed at the expense of clarity or colorfulness, it is to be preferred to unnecessary phrasing and flowery expressions.

For example, instead of: As will be shown in due course, however, the files of the party journals at this time are burdened with editorials and articles.
The omission of unnecessary phrases improves the sentence thus: The files of the party journals at this time are burdened with editorials and articles.
Too much inversion plus unnecessary phrasing such as: So far as the Whig party of Mississippi is concerned no guardian angels presided at its birth.

126

Can be improved if stated directly thus: No guardian angels presided at the birth of the Whig party of Mississippi.

The choice of the proper word not only helps make the meaning more clear but makes the wording more concise:

For example: At the same time when . . .

Really should be: At the very time when . . .

Again: A significant counterpart of American political thought . . .

Is better expressed thus: A significant phase of American political thought . . .

Smoothness and greater conciseness may be achieved at times by tying two short sentences into a single sentence and thus avoiding the use of "and" or "but" at the beginning of a sentence:

For example: There is almost complete lack of evidence to substantiate these ideas. And, more important, there is the failure on the part of Americans . . .

May be improved thus: There is not only almost complete lack of evidence to substantiate these ideas, but, what is more important, there is the failure on the part of Americans . . .

PARAPHRASES AND QUOTATIONS

Historical composition consists of something more than the stringing together of quoted passages or parts of passages. Careful paraphrases are, in general, preferable to lengthy quotations. Too frequent and too long quotations not only break the continuity of the narrative but also make the reader suspicious that the author is lacking in critical ability and interpretative ingenuity. Quotations, therefore, should be limited to those words, phrases, or sentences actually containing the kernel of the passage and should be employed to give color and meaning to the narrative.

How to introduce a quotation:

The writer's own words are needed to introduce a quotation in order that these quoted portions may become an integral, understandable, and logical part of the connected narrative. An effort should be made to improve the style of the narrative by varying the wording in these introductory phrases. It becomes very dull for a reader to have every quotation introduced with, "He said."

Examples:

The following letter to the editor of the *Southern Cultivator* of October, 1851, is significant:

The planter at Pleasant Hill was, he said,

That he was not affected by sectional controversy, is evidenced by a letter of July 1, 1845:

He also included a statement of the condition of his own orchard:

In 1850 he wrote:

How to work a quotation into the text:

When one commences a sentence with a quotation, the first word in the quotation should be capitalized, whether it was originally in capitals or not.

Example:

"The further benefits" that he expected included an appointment as a federal examiner.

Similarly, if the quotation has the status of a complete sentence, its first word should be capitalized, even if it was not originally capitalized.

Example:

He suggested:"The question is whether acknowledged evil is not better than a mixture of good and evil."

If, however, the quotation is only a phrase incorporated into the rest of the sentence, its first word takes no capitals even if it happens to be capitalized in the original.

Example:

Wilson denounced him as a politician, a nullifier, and an abolitionist "who would have no objection to the blacks resisting the threats of the whites."

Not:

Wilson denounced him as a politician, a nullifier, and an abolitionist "Who would have no objection to the blacks resisting the threats of the whites."

When incorporating a quotation as part of a sentence in the text the writer must take care that the tense and the person in the quotation does not disagree with that of the rest of the sentence.

Examples:

In the same year he informed that paper that he had "lost five superior Berkshire pigs in twelve hours, by eating the berries of the Chinese trees."

Or:

In the same year he informed that paper: "I have lost five superior Berkshire pigs in twelve hours, by eating the berries of the Chinese trees."

But not:

In the same year he informed that paper that "I have lost five superior Berkshire pigs in twelve hours, by eating the berries of the Chinese trees."

Lengthy quotations:

A quotation of considerable length (more than five or six typewritten lines) may be set off from the rest of the text by single spacing. Such a quotation omits the use of quotation marks both before and after the quoted passage. When printed it will generally appear in smaller type than the text proper.

Example:

He also included a statement of the condition of his own orchard:

I have been giving attention to fruit culture for eight years, and have quite a variety of apples, pears, and peaches. I find the Bartlett pear to be the very best I have, a very healthy and vigorous growth, bears early, and seems to be free from all disease. Finer fruit than I have at this time on a small tree you could not find anywhere, I have examined fruit in the markets of all the northern cities, and never saw better. The apples that do best here are all the June varieties, the horse apple, maiden's blush, Bevan apple, fall pippin, and I have one called the Davis apple, purchased at Hatch & Co.'s nursery, Vicksburg, that is fine, ripening very late, and will keep through the winter.

Quotations with Omissions:

Omissions at the beginning or end of a quotation may quite properly be disregarded since, unless one quotes either the opening or the closing sentences of a letter, article, or book, a quotation is in the majority of instances but a portion of the whole work. In your notes it was important to indicate omitted portions at beginning and end, but when you are incorporating the material into the text this is no longer so important.

Example:

"I wish that more of your northern farmers and mechanics could be induced to settle among us."

Not:

". . . I wish that more of your northern farmers and mechanics could be induced to settle among us . . ."

Otherwise, any omissions within a quotation are indicated exactly the same way in your local history as in your note-cards.

Punctuation and Quotations:

The comma and the period are placed within the closing quotation marks instead of without, regardless of the punctuation of the original quotation. The semi-colon, however, is placed outside the closing quotation marks.

Examples:

Comma:

He now asked the latter "to attend to a small matter," the *"restoration"* to the family's Steubenville paper of the printing of the United States laws in eastern Ohio.

Period:

He made more than one trip to the capital and received the coveted printing with "some intimation of further benefits."

Semicolon:

One concerned the Indian boundaries on the frontier; while another forbade any person to "sell, or barter any ardent spirits, arms or ammunition"; while still another authorized that the "Governor adopt such measures as may be necessary to protect the frontiers from Indian depredations."

Interrogation marks and exclamation marks, when not an actual part of the quotation, should be placed outside the closing quotation marks.

Examples:

The trend in taxation has been to shift the burden from these best able to pay over to "those least able to pay"!

But when an actual part of the quotation:

Jackson proposed the toast: "Our Federal Union; it must be preserved!"

When a parenthetical expression follows the closing quotation marks, however, all punctuation (except a period indicating abbreviation) is transferred after the closing parenthesis:

Examples:

1. This, under "Churches" (p. 381), is a paragraph of cross references to 209 individual churches.
2. Oftentimes the news is "tampered with and exploited for the deliberate purpose of warping the human mind" (p. 17).
3. He found his material "among the Schurz, Bryan, and Roosevelt MSS." (p. 212).

When there is occasion to use a quotation within a quotation the comma and period is placed within both sets of closing quotation marks, but a semi-colon is placed outside both sets of closing quotation marks.

Examples:

Comma:

"I shall certainly be under the necessity of disposing of my goods the best way I may, shutting up my shop, mounting a Vide Poche Cart, and crying 'Marche donc,' " he warned.

Period:

"He achieved national prominence . . . 'as a journalist, novelist, and short-story writer extraordinary.' "

Semi-colon:

"He achieved national prominence 'as an experimental farmer, traveler, lecturer, and writer in agricultural subjects' "; the reviewer of his biography also says that he was a journalist, novelist, and short-story writer extraordinary.

IDENTIFICATION OF PERSONS

The writer of historical narrative should make it a practice to identify completely, that is with given name or at least initials as well as family name, every person, the first time that person's name is mentioned. This is particularly important for the names of obscure individuals, and simplifies the later task of indexing.

Example:
Eli J. Capell
Not:
Capell

It is bad form in historical writing to use the title Mr. for an individual already deceased. Mr. is reserved for those living today.

Example:
Alexander Hamilton

But:

Mr. James Smith, the history instructor.
The title Mr. need not be used with the name of a person still living if that person is well known as a public character.

Example:
Franklin D. Roosevelt
Herbert Hoover

INDICATION FOR FOOTNOTES

Footnote indications in the text should be noted in arabic numerals and should run consecutively throughout an article or essay. These numerals, called "superior figures," are placed slightly above the line, on a level with quotation marks and apostrophes. The normal position for these figures is at the close of the sentence which contains a statement or quotation requiring a citation. If only part of a sentence requires footnoting, the figure should be placed at the end of that particular part. Never place the footnote indication at the beginning of a paragraph, sentence, quoted passage, or title.

Examples:

When the entire sentence needs citation:

Paul Dudley, son of Governor Joseph and Rebecca (Tyng) Dudley, was born at Roxbury, Massachusetts, in 1675.[10]

If the quotation needs citation:

He described in detail the types of wood preferred by one of his neighbors, "an old experienced wagon maker."[29]

If but a part of the sentence relates to the citation:

Henry Clay, against whose nomination Lincoln had used his influence before the meeting of the Whig National Convention of 1848,[4] had been a lifelong friend of Secretary Ewing.

THE COMPONENT PARTS OF A LOCAL HISTORY

Study the makeup of any good volume of history and you will find that it consists of various features. First, comes the title page, which, as its name suggests, contains the complete title of the book. On this page there is also the name of the author, and at the bottom, the name of the publisher or printer and the date of publication. The reverse is generally the copyright page, on which is indicated the name of the person or company, the place, and date of copyright. Following this, most books carry another page, on which is given the title in a shortened form. This is known as the half-title page.

The next component part of a local history will be your preface. In this you can make a brief explanation as to why you have written the book and give due acknowledgment and thanks to all individuals and institutions which have helped you make the work possible. It is time to write the preface after you have finished writing the rest of the book. When you have taken information from recent works it is wise for you to secure permission from the authors or publishers (depending upon which ones hold the copyright) to quote their material. Some writers include these acknowledgments of permission in their preface; others make a separate item which follows the preface.

In addition to the preface some books contain an introduction. This introduction may be written by the author himself or by a more distinguished authority whose name and words of approval lend dignity and importance to the work. When the introduction is written by someone other than the author, it generally precedes the table of contents. If it is merely an introduction by the author, it can be considered as an opening chapter and should follow the table of contents.

The table of contents, as it implies, is a table or itemized list of the contents of your book. It may contain only the numbers of the chapters and the beginning pages for each one, or it may list the titles of each chapter as well as the numbers. Again it may be even more detailed and give under each chapter heading the various subdivisions. It will not be a replica of your outline but your outline should be your guide in drawing up your table of contents. Study the table of contents included in this book and compare it with those in other books you have used in your research. Decide on one which seems best to apply to your local history and use it as a model. The table of contents is generally compiled after the chapters of the history are written and you have definitely determined their order of arrangement.

If you are planning to include maps and illustrations you will need to have either a combined list of these or two separate lists (depending upon the number of each)—for example, if you have a dozen illustrations and only two maps it would be best to have one list. If, however, you have ten maps and eight illustrations you might want to make two separate lists. Arrange the illustrations in the order in which you intend to have them appear in your book, decide upon the descriptive legends for each one and list these legends, indicating the page number, or opposite which page number, each one appears in the history. Do the same thing for the maps.

Now as to the chapters themselves. Your chapter headings may be the same as the main subject headings of your outline and your guide cards. Sometimes, however, after you begin writing you will find that you can combine several main subject headings into one chapter. Try to make your chapters balance. That is, while it may be impossible to have them all the same length, do not have one twice the length of another. If this happens, it might make better reading to break the chapter at a logical point and make two separate ones out of it, or if you have two short chapters they might be combined into one longer one.

Your chapter headings need not be the exact wording of your main subject headings. They should convey the same idea but should strive for a bit of the unusual and colorful rather than the prosaic and humdrum. For example, instead of having a chapter called "Blanktown in 1800," you might achieve the same idea and be more original if you called it "Log-Cabins and Coon-Skins."

THE FOOTNOTES

A few hints have already been given you on how to write the chapters of your local history. As you write, interpret, and quote you will constantly be using the words, thoughts, and expressions of other writers. For your own protection as well as to inform your readers where you got your information you will want to have footnote citations for your statements. You may, in addition, want to make explanations which are not important enough to include in the text and these, too, will be placed among your footnotes.

When writing your first draft place your footnotes at the bottom of each page and number them consecutively throughout each chapter. When typing the final copy, you or your typist may find it simpler to type all the footnotes on separate sheets and to place them at the end of each chapter.

You will want to give a citation for every direct quotation, for paraphrases, and for controversial statements. You will not need to footnote commonly accepted statements of fact. If several quotations or paraphrases from the same source occur in one paragraph, group these under one footnote.

Unfortunately, the historical world has not yet decided on a definite form of footnoting and in your research you will have ample evidence of a hodgepodge in styles and methods. The important thing for you to remember is to adopt a simple method and to use it consistently throughout your chapters. In general, the following few rules should stand you in good stead for footnote practice.

Capitalization

Capitalize all nouns, verbs, adjectives, and adverbs in a title.

Example:

William F. Gephart, *Transportation and Industrial Development in Middle West* (New York, 1909), 156–157.

Volumes, parts, and pages

Indicate volume numbers in Roman numerals; give the identification of the part, if you have both a part and a volume, and use arabic numbers for pages. Do not use vol., v., for volume, or p. or pp. for page unless absolutely necessary (for example, when another arabic number precedes, such as a date, and it may be confusing, it is best to insert the abbreviation p. or pp.)

Examples:

Lawrence Lowell, *The Government of England* (New York, 1909), I, 147.

But: Annual Report of the American Historical Association, 1909, p. 36.

The first time you cite a published volume, spell out the author's name in full, do not invert; follow with a comma, then give the complete title of the book, which should be underlined (this indicates that it is published); follow this with the place and date of publication in parentheses, another comma, the volume number, if there is one, and the page or pages.

Examples:

[1]John Sherman, *Recollections of Forty Years in the House, Senate and Cabinet* (New York, 1895), II, 674–675.

²Emilius O. Randall and Daniel J. Ryan, *History of Ohio* (New York, 1912), I, 170.

³Edward and Annie G. Perritt, *Unreformed House of Commons* (Cambridge, England, 1903), I, 171 ff.

⁴Dumas Malone, ed., *Dictionary of American Biography* (New York, 1928–1936), IX, 210.

⁵Louis F. Snow, *The College Curriculum in the United States* (n.p., n.d.), 23.

⁶Theodore C. Pease and James G. Randall, eds., *The Diary of Orville Hickman Browning* (Springfield, Ill., 1925), I, 677.

After citing a work in full once it is sufficient to use a shortened form for later references. If the second reference immediat›ly follows the first you can use the abbreviation *ibid.* (meaning in the same place) for as much of the citation as is a repetition.

Example:

¹John Sherman, *Recollections of Forty Years in the House, Senate and Cabinet* (New York, 1895), II, 673–674.
²*Ibid.*, I, 356.

If, however, there is an intervening reference it is best to repeat the last name of the author and as much of the title as will distinguish it for recognition.

Example:

¹John Sherman, *Recollections of Forty Years in the House, Senate and Cabinet* (New York, 1895), II, 673–674.
²Peter Cartwright, *Autobiography* (New York, 1857), 164.
³Sherman, *Recollections*, I, 356.
⁴Cartwright, *Autobiography*, 160.

When citing articles in periodicals, papers in various historical reports and proceedings, include the author's name in full, then the title of the article in quotation marks, then the publication underscored, the place of publication in parentheses, the volume number in Roman numerals, the year in parentheses, and finally the page or pages.

Examples:

¹George H. Bates, "Some Aspects of the Samoan Question," *Century Magazine* (New York), XV (1899), 299.
²Margaret Lefever, "Story of Early Life in Michigan," *Collections of the Michigan Pioneer and Historical Society* (Lansing), XXXVIII (1912), 673.

As for citations to entire volumes, later citations to articles need repeat only enough to identify these to the reader.

Example:

[1]George H. Bates, "Some Aspects of the Samoan Question," *Century Magazine* (New York), XV (1899), 299.

[2]George A. Root, "Ferries in Kansas," *Kansas Historical Quarterly* (Topeka), IV (1936), 380.

[3]Bates, "Samoan Question," 298.

[4]Root, "Ferries in Kansas," 379.

When citing newspapers give not only the complete title of the paper but precede it with the name of the city, even if this is not in the title; follow with the month, day, and year, and if you want to make the search still easier for your reader, note also the page and column.

Examples:

[1]Columbus *Ohio State Journal*, April 26, 1877.

[2]Des Moines *Daily State Register*, March 27, 1862, p. 4, col. 3.

If there is some doubt as to the location of the city, include the state in parentheses, as illustrated:

[1]York (Pa.) *Democratic Press*, May 15, 1868.

When citing unpublished materials do not underscore or put in quotes any titles. Give as much exact information as you can.

Examples:

[1]Ohio Annual Conference Reports, Methodist-Episcopal Church, Samuel Williams MS. Collection (Department of Documents, Ohio State Archaeological and Historical Society Library), Box XI, Folder 4, item 36.

[2]John Jones to William Smith, January 14, 1895, William Smith Papers (William L. Clements Library), Box XLI, No. 65.

The above examples and directions, of necessity, will not serve as illustrations for every type of citation you may wish to indicate. They only describe the most general of four kinds of materials: the published volume, the article, the newspaper, and unpublished or manuscript material. The public records, business records, and church records you have used may be either of the published or unpublished variety; the diaries and old letters you have examined are, of course, unpublished and so are the cemetery inscriptions and the interviews you may have had with old residents. If you have used any microfilm or photostatic copies of materials you will want to note that fact in your citation. The main thing to remember is that you want to inform your reader in as simple and as complete a form as possible what you have used and where it may be found and that you want to give your information in the same way throughout your local history. If you adopt these rules and follow them religiously you will save yourself, your publisher, and your readers a great deal of grief.

After you have written your first draft and supplied sufficient footnote citations to protect yourself and inform your readers, you will find it necessary to reread this material over which you have spent so many laborious hours in order to see it in the larger perspective. It is helpful, often, to read your copy out loud. Sentences and paragraphs that seemed passable enough when examined silently may stand out as incongruous and impossible if subjected to the combined test of ear and eye. Phrases may have to be rephrased, sentences reworked, and perhaps, whole passages shifted, before you will be completely satisfied with your composition.

Your next test will be to ask a friend, your local librarian, minister, or English teacher to read your chapters. Do not expect them to find it 100% perfect. If they do, then they are only being kind but not helpful. Expect unfavorable criticism, but ask them to be specific, so that you can try to iron out the weaknesses they find and benefit by their suggestions on these completed chapters.

CHAPTER X

BIBLIOGRAPHY, ADDENDA AND INDEX

YOUR chapters are now completed and you will be ready for the final steps in the preparation of a local history.

BIBLIOGRAPHY

The first of these final steps in the preparation of your local history is the compiling of a bibliography. When you began to take your notes you were advised to make carbon copies of your call-slips and use these as bibliographical data. If you did this faithfully and have all your slips, the compilation will not be very difficult. A bibliography is merely an organized reading list which informs your readers of the amount of research you have done on your subject and serves as a guide to them should they want to find material of the same sort. A bibliography may include references not cited in your footnotes, but it should represent an honest record of your search and should not be padded with a long and impressive list of works which you barely examined or did not study at all.

A bibliography may be either a formal list or a critical essay. In the critical essay type of bibliography you not only list materials examined but you offer comments about the scope and value of each item.[1] Such a bibliography is arranged by topics, and each topic is discussed in sentences grouped in paragraphs. Bibliographical items are not inverted and, of necessity, there is considerable duplication and repetition of information. While useful for its comments, such a bibliography makes it hard for the reader to sift single items from the compact paragraph form.

The formal bibliography, which merely lists materials, is much easier to compile and simpler to use. If your research was limited to no more than a dozen or fifteen different works it will be sufficient to list these alphabetically by inverting the author's name and giving all other data necessary.

Example:

Koerner, Gustave, *Memoirs*, 2 vols., Cedar Rapids: The Torch Press, 1909.
Winsor, Justin, ed., *Narrative and Critical History of America*, 8 vols., Boston: Houghton Mifflin Co., 1884–1889.
Wisconsin State Historical Society, Collections, Madison, 1854–

---

[1] An excellent example of the critical essay type of bibliography is the "Critical Essay on Authorities" at the close of Arthur C. Cole's *Irrepressible Conflict* in the *History of American Life* series.

138

If, however, your research was more extensive and varied, you will want to organize the different types of bibliographical items and group the various works alphabetically under each type. You will probably have something to list under each of the following classifications:

A. Personal Interviews and Correspondence

B. Unpublished Materials
   1. Letters and Diaries
   2. Church Records and Cemetery Inscriptions
   3. Addresses and Sermons
   4. Unpublished Public Records
   5. Unpublished Business Records

C. Published Materials
   1. Family Histories and Biographies
   2. Autobiographies and Collected Works by Contemporaries
   3. General, Regional, State, and Local Histories
   4. Official Published Public Records
   5. Newspapers
   6. Periodicals and Special Articles in Periodicals
   7. Miscellaneous Collections

D. Atlases, Gazetteers, and Maps

E. Pictures

F. Museum Specimens

Try to be consistent in giving information on each item. Below are hypothetical samples of the forms to use:

A. Personal Interviews
   Baker, Arthur F., aged 83, native and life-long resident of Centerville, former mayor, interviews with writer at Baker's home, Jan. 10–11, 15, 1942.
   Johnson, Mrs. Jessie Koons, aged 75, former early resident of Centerville, daughter of first superintendent of schools, correspondence with Mrs. Millard Thomas, eldest daughter, with whom Mrs. Johnson resides, at Piketown, Feb. 14, 18, 26, 1942.

B. Unpublished Materials
   1. Letters and Diaries
      Baker, Arthur F., letters to and from various politicians and business men, 1870's, Centerville, Piketown, and Washington, D. C. In private possession of Mr. Baker.
      Koons, Frederick, diary, 1842–48, while superintendent of Centerville schools. In possession of daughter, Mrs. Jessie K. Johnson, Piketown.

2. Church Records and Cemetery Inscriptions
    Centerville First Presbyterian Christening Records, 1803–53.
    In Manuscript Department of Pike County Historical Society.
    Centerville Old Presbyterian Cemetery, Ridge Road, tomb-
    stone inscriptions of Koons, Baker, and Platt families.
    Centerville New Presbyterian Cemetery, Doddridge Pike, tomb-
    stone inscriptions of Koons, Platt, and Howard families.
    Centerville Methodist Cemetery, Billings Corners, tombstone
    inscriptions of Williams, Ellsworth and Haley families.
3. Addresses and Sermons
    Baker, Arthur F., July 4, 1872, address at dedication of new
    auditorium. In private possession of Mr. Baker.
    Koons, Hiram, notebook of 35 sermons for special occasions,
    while pastor of Centerville's First Presbyterian Church, 1813–
    37, including funeral sermons of early distinguished citizens.
    In possession of Mrs. Jessie K. Johnson, Piketown.
4. Unpublished Public Records
    Platt, Benjamin L., notes while Surveyor of Pike County Lands,
    1803–20. In MS. Department of Pike County Historical Society.
    Wills and Probate Records, Centerville Probate Court Records,
    1817–
5. Unpublished Business Records
    Baker, Allen A., Account Book, General Store, Centerville,
    1830–49. In MS. Department, Pike County Historical Society.
    Howard-Ellsworth Correspondence, 1842–65, Big Darby Flour
    Milling Company of Piketown Road. In Centerville College
    Library, custody of Dr. Evans Howard, History Department.

C. Published Materials

1. Family Histories and Biographies
    Johnson, Mrs. Jessie K., and Thomas, Mrs. Millard, *Koons
    Family History*, 2 vols., Piketown, privately printed, 1929.
    Brown, Lawrence, *Life of Benjamin Platt*, Chicago: Business
    Biography Publishers, 1923.
2. Autobiographies and Collected Works by Contemporaries
    Koons, Frederick, *My Life and Times*, Centerville: privately
    published, 1856.
    Belding, John D., *Early Notables of Piketown and Its Vicinity*,
    New York: Universal Publishers, 1843.
3. General, Regional, State, and Local Histories
    Hart, Albert B., ed., *The American Nation: A History*, 28 vols.,
    Boston: Houghton Mifflin Co., 1884–1889.
    Wittke, Carl, ed., *The History of the State of Ohio*, 6 vols.,
    Columbus: Ohio State Archaeological and Historical Society,
    1939–1944.

Belding, John D., *Centerville of Long Ago*, New York: Universal Publishers, 1845.

4. Official Published Public Records
Census of the Terriory of Arizona, 1864, in mimeograph form, Historical Records Survey, 1938.

5. Newspapers
Cincinnati *West and South*, July 4, August 29, 1868.
Piketown *Herald*, July 1–November 14, 1872.

6. Periodicals and Special Articles in Periodicals
a. *North American Review*, Boston, 1815–1877; New York, 1878–.
b. Farmer, Hallie, "The Economic Background of Frontier Populism," *Mississippi Valley Historical Review*, Cedar Rapids, X, 1924, pp. 406–427.

7. Miscellaneous Collections
Michigan Pioneer and Historical Society, Collections, Lansing, 1877–1917.

D. Atlases, Gazetteers, and Maps

Adams, James T., and Coleman, R. V., eds., *Atlas of American History*, New York, Charles Scribner's Sons, 1943.

Thompson, Zadock, *A Gazetteer of the State of Vermont; Containing a Brief General View of the State, a Historical and Topographical Description of all the Counties, Towns, Rivers, and etc., together a Map and Several Other Engravings*, Montpelier, E. P. Walton and the author, 1824.

Centerville in 1845. Topographical Map of County Surveyor's Office, 12″ × 18″, scale of 1″ to 1 mile. In Pike County Historical Society.

E. Pictures

Baker, Arthur F., photograph at age of 35, badly faded, size 5″ × 8″. In private possession of Mr. Baker.

F. Museum Specimens

Gavel used by Arthur F. Baker, while presiding over town council meetings during 1870's.

APPENDICES

It may be that you have come across certain statistical data, genealogical tables, or other important materials which you do not want to omit yet you cannot very well weave into the general story you are telling. These materials are too lengthy to be inserted as footnotes and too specialized to deserve a separate chapter. The logical place for them will be at the very end of your local history, either before or after your bibliography, but preceding your index. Here may be placed explanations as to varying spellings of proper or place names, a glossary of Indian or French colloquialisms of the time and their locations; a calendar list of certain letters quoted in your chapters, genealogical data, statistics, and other kindred agenda.

INDEX

Now that you have organized your chapters, properly annotated them with footnote citations, prepared your bibliography, inserted the maps and illustrations in their proper places, compiled a list of each as well as a table of contents, and have even written a preface to your magnum opus, your next task is that of preparing a minute inventory to the storehouse of material which you have garnered, and arranging that inventory so that your reader can, on a moment's search, find any fact, name, or other detail in your mass of paragraphs, pages, and chapters. First you have broken down the information of others into tiny bits, and after putting these bits on note-cards, you have erected from them a complicated structure of your own. Next you must analyze your own literary edifice and make enough keys to each item you have related for the curious searcher to find any detail he wants without too much difficulty. You have used indexes of others in your search for material and have undoubtedly been pleased with the ease with which some of these supplied you with the desired facts or irked by the inadequacy of others which were too sketchy or perhaps even inaccurate.

The making of an index is a laborious job but a good index is indeed a joy to its users. Your first task is to read your material sentence by sentence. It is advisable to use your carbon copy rather than the original pages for indexing. While you read, underline all words or phrases which require indexing; these will include the names of all local persons, places, business firms, organizations, schools, churches, newspapers, wars, political parties and events, etc., etc. While it is not essential to index items that are mentioned only incidentally or are very general and vague in nature, it is best to err on the side of overinclusiveness rather than to omit important items. While you go through your copy with an eagle-eye and a figurative fine-comb you will find, perhaps, that you have failed to give names of individuals in full the first time such names are mentioned. Now is the time to remedy such oversights, for your index must be complete in so far as possible. In addition to the underscored key words you may find it necessary to write in on the margins certain other words which do not actually appear on the pages but the ideas about which are conveyed in slightly different phraseology. After you have completed a chapter of underscorings it may be a good stopping place to change over to the next step—that of writing the index slips. Cards or slips of $3'' \times 5''$ size are generally the best for these (ordinary scratch pads may be used). If you know someone willing to assist in this laborious task now is the time to enlist his aid. Index slip-writing merely means copying key-words onto slips and indicating the page number where such a word appears. Do not try to put more than one key-word and one page number on a single slip at this stage. Combinations and correlations cannot be done satisfactorily until all the slips are written. Do not alphabet the slips either. Just write and keep them in the order of the pages upon which the words appear.

Example:

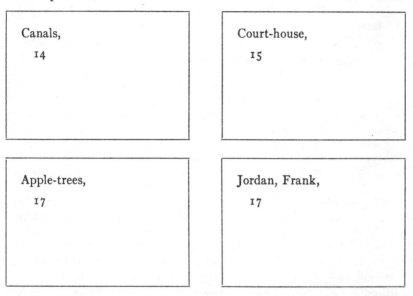

Continue chapter by chapter until your entire volume is marked and slip-written. Do not forget to make entry slips for illustrations, maps, and material in addenda. Do not index the bibliography. It is a moot question as to whether you should index the footnotes—most indexers don't, though your readers may thank you for going to this extra trouble.

Next, check your slips carefully with the marked text; this is especially important if someone else wrote your slips, but is not to be ignored even if you were your own scribe. Errors and oversights are easy to creep in and can be eradicated with little difficulty at this stage, but may be very difficult to find later.

The next step is to alphabet all your slips. This is most easily done by first putting all the A's in one pile, all the B's in another, etc. This is called "rough" alphabeting. Then within each letter you may arrange exactly in alphabetical order all the cards found in that category. When you do this you will find that certain slips will have the same key-words with different page numbers. For example, you may have six slips for "canals," three for "court-house," four for "apple-trees," and ten for "Frank Jordan." Of these, some may be just casual references and have the page number only, but others may be more detailed and have a subentry as well as the key-word entry. For example, your six slips bearing the word "Canals" may be something like this: (1) Canals, 14; (2) Canals, federal aid for, 15; (3) Canals, 16; (4) Canals, commissioners appointed, 17; (5) Canals, dedication of first in Piketown, 20; (6) Canals, 27. When organizing this material put all the casual references together in order of pagination, and then list the subentry references also according to page order. This will make your final coordinated card look something like this:

> Canals, 14, 16, 27; federal aid for, 15; commissioners appointed, 17; dedication of first in Piketown, 20.

Clip your individual slips and put them aside. Insert your coordinated slip with the slips that require no further coordination (single items) in proper alphabetical order. For problems of filing, arrangement of proper names, etc., follow the *A. L. A. Rules for Filing Catalog Cards*, prepared by a Special Committee, Sophie K. Hiss, Chairman (Chicago, American Library Association, 1942), which, though especially prepared for arrangement of dictionary catalogues, is equally helpful in filing index material.

When coordinating slips you will find that in a number of instances you will have made entries under related or similar subjects, some more general, others more specific, and in certain cases entries that are almost synonymous may occur, as, for example, there may be "waterways," "transportation," "canals," "canal-construction," "canal boats," "travel," and "navigation"; or "apple-trees," "trees," "fruit," "horticulture," and "fruit-growing." You will have to decide which entries you wish to retain and for the others you will suffice with a cross-reference that will read something like this: "Fruit-growing, *see* horticulture." Sometimes you will want to include both entries and yet inform the user of your index that there is more than just that reference to look for. In such a case you may have what is called a "see-also" entry. For example, "Fruit, apples, 10, 15, 26. *See also* apple trees."

After all your slips are completely alphabeted and coordinated for multiple items, you are ready to type your index or to have it typed by someone else. Type in block formation, single-spacing within an item and triple spacing between items. Make two columns to the page. Example:

Canals, 14, 16, 27; federal aid for, 15; commissioners appointed, 17; dedication of first in Piketown, 20.

Jordan, Frank, 17, 19, 29; justice of peace, 21; mayor, 26–8; state representative, 30; death, 32.

This is, to all effects, a complete index to your typewritten copy. It may be that your book will never be printed and this typewritten form is final and the one which you will have bound and deposited at some library for safekeeping. It will be doubly valuable with an index. If, however, you have reasonable hopes and expectations of getting your book published, it is advisable to wait until the material is in its final stages (page-proof for printed material) before constructing the index.

An index made from typed copy may be transformed into the later-stage index by some extra labor. The slips that have been alphabeted must be unscrambled and rearranged by page number again—the un-coordinated duplicate slips reinserted in place of the multiple-coordinated entries. Then the slips are compared with the printed pages and page numbers are changed to correspond. After that, the slips have to be re-alphabeted, corresponding changes made on the coordinated entries and the new arrangement typed. This may seem very complicated but except for some lost motion in alphabeting it is not very difficult to make the page changes.

For strictly genealogical material it is of some advantage to have a separate index for names of individuals and perhaps another one for places, but for local history and historical material of a more general nature the single index with one alphabet for all indexed items is the preferable one to prepare and will be the most useful.

PART III

PUBLISHING LOCAL HISTORY

CHAPTER XI

VARIOUS MEANS OF PUBLISHING LOCAL HISTORY

Now that your volume is written your next concern is how to get it published. You will never make a fortune publishing a local history. It may even cost you more than the sale may bring in. Nevertheless, it is possible for you to get your book into circulation *in some form*, if perhaps not in the form you most desire. There are about half a dozen ways of reproducing material and these will now be considered.

PRINTING

Printing a book is an expensive proposition, more expensive than you may think. The late Robert C. Binkley, who made a thorough investigation of the cost of various methods of reproducing material, wrote in 1936:

> In analyzing the composition, the area and the running costs for producing a book by straight printing, in Chicago as an example. A book of 50,000 words in an edition of 250, on 128 6″×9″ pages, could be made for $246.57. Taking these figures as an illustrative sample, it appears that for composition and printing a book, about 50% of the cost goes for composition, about 32% for make-up, 12% for make-ready, and 6% for actual printing in a minimum edition.
>
> . . . .
>
> Running costs are not decisive in small editions. The difference between the cost of printing 50 and 100 copies is so small that firms often quote the same price for both. It is thus possible to have an overprint, which can be left in sheets until needed, at a very slight additional cost.[1]

This same investigator further points out that ordinary printing of a book as done by the big commercial publishing firms "will take care of any material desired by 2000 paying customers."[2] If, therefore, you are sure of 2,000 purchasers of your local history, you can think of ordinary commercial publishing as a possibility. Do not, however, be misled regarding the number of sales for your volume. One local history which met with what was considered marked success was printed in an edition of 1,000 copies, for a city of 6,000 residents. This volume had 207 pages, cost $900.00 to publish, and sold for $1.50 a copy, so that a small profit was realized.[3] Kingsport, Tennessee, with a population of 35,000 in its immediate area, published a local history recently, printing an edition

---

[1] Robert C. Binkley, *Manual of Methods of Reproducing Research Materials* (Ann Arbor, 1936), 17.

[2] *Ibid.*, 183.

[3] Eleanor Iler Schapiro, "Publishing a Local History," *Social Education*, January, 1939, pp. 25–29 and *passim*. Pledges of 800 subscribers were received in advance of publication. A total of about 75 copies of the 1,000 printed remained unsold at the time of writing. The local history in question was *Wadsworth, Center to City*.

149

of 7,500 of which about 4,800 were sold to subscribers. Others were sold until only about 300 copies remained two years after publication.[4]

Mount Morris, Illinois, a town of about 2,000, had a local history published in 1938, a 464-page book profusely illustrated and well arranged and edited. The author, who is also the head of a large publishing company which did the printing, writes:

I did not publish this book with the idea of making any money out of it, and up to date the cost has been about $1,000.00 in excess of the revenue. I printed 1,000 copies and had 600 copies bound of which I sold approximately 550 copies at $3.00 per copy. I have now had the remaining 400 copies bound in a cheaper cloth which I expect to sell at $2.00 per copy. The total cost not counting any of my time was somewhere between $2500.00 and $3000.00.

No charge was made for biographical sketches . . . .

It might be possible to make a book of this kind pay but I made no effort to do so because I wanted to include in the book only material of historical interest . . . .

I am quite sure that the principal factor in the sale of my book was due to the many illustrations and especially the old pictures. The best source for pictures of this kind is the morgue of the local newspaper, and I was particularly fortunate here because of the fact that we have had an engraving department for many years and used illustrations quite liberally in the Mount Morris Index.[5]

Unless a good deal of effort is put into the selling of a local history, it is doubtful whether as many persons as one in ten in the population will buy a copy. The three examples given above are exceptional. The first had a school behind it, the second a Rotary Club, and the last a local publishing firm. Not one had the intention of making money out of the publication. The first made a small profit, the second a large profit (though it must be remembered that the Rotarians sponsored it and that the publishing was done at cost), and the last will amost "break even."

In estimating the probable sale of a local history many things have to be considered, such as the confidence the prospective readers have in the author's ability, the interest of the public in the subject, the sale price of the book, the color and kind of binding, the number of pages, the number of maps and illustrations, and also often the attention paid to individuals who may be prospective buyers. You can roughly estimate the possible sale by dividing the total population within the scope of your history by ten, or safer still by twenty. Large commercial publishing firms are reluctant to undertake the printing of a book unless they can expect a sale of a couple of thousand copies, or unless the printing is subsidized by the author or others. Therefore, unless you live in a very large community, a

---

[4] Letter of W. V. Pierce, ex-president of the Rotary Club of Kingsport, Tennessee, July 27, 1939. The printing was done by an active Rotarian at cost. The book contained 248 pages, sold for $1.00 a copy, and a net profit of about $1,800 was realized. The history was promoted and compiled by the Rotary Club as a service project and promotional scheme.

[5] Letter of H. G. Kable of Mount Morris, Illinois, July 24, 1939.

city of 10,000 or more, you can hardly expect a commercial publishing firm to agree to print your local history on the usual terms whereby it bears all the expense and risk, and returns to you a percent of the receipts (if any).

In a small city you might find a publisher who would be willing to print your book under an arrangement whereby both of you would share the expense, risk, and possible profits. The smaller the city or town, the more expense and risk you will have to bear. It may be, however, that a local publisher has enough local pride to make some very favorable arrangements which will relieve you of all or part of the financial burden. Certainly you should visit your local publishers first and see what they have to say. Ask them for advice. Be prepared, however, for rebuffs on various scores. It may be that your local printer does not have sufficient type for book work and may lack other equipment for the production of a creditable looking volume.

Perhaps you have sufficient means to finance the printing of the book regardless of cost and other considerations. There have been local historians of this sort, though their number is small. It may be that you can work out a plan by yourself, or with the advice of the printer, by which the book will be sold by subscriptions taken in advance for the most part. Agents may be employed to go throughout the expected sales area and solicit subscriptions. Letters can be sent to former residents of the town. In this way the printer can know in advance how many copies should be printed. Moreover, he can suit the quality of his work and the number of pages, illustrations, and maps to the expected receipts.

There are several other ways by which a local history, printed or in some form, can be financed. There may be a sufficiently large number of public-spirited businessmen and citizens, such as the members of Rotary, Kiwanis, Lions, or other civic clubs, who would be willing to give enough money in gifts to enable the work to be done. Local organizations, historical societies, churches, fraternal orders, and women's clubs might be willing to help defray the cost of publication. Dublin, New Hampshire, voted to produce a town history in 1904; a committee was appointed, and in 1920 the history was published at the town's expense. In 1919 the New York legislature passed a law authorizing the mayor of each town in the state to appoint a local historian and the local authorities to levy taxes to publish the town's history.

You might resort to the method used years ago, selling space at so much per page for biographical sketches of "leading" citizens. These sketches could make "Part Two" of your book, leaving your own local history separate and unquestioned as to its integrity. Still another method might be to solicit advertising from local businessmen. The advertising should be placed toward the end of the volume and not interspersed with your own material. A plan somewhat like this was followed in the book published by the Rotary Club of Kingsport, Tennessee. If the people of your community have faith in you and your work, it is difficult to believe that they will give no assistance and let your history—their history—remain unpublished To be sure, they may need prodding, and for this some publicity in the local newspapers regarding your work may help.

Assuming that some arrangements have been made for the publishing of your book, you may think that your labors are completed and that you can relax somewhat until the printed volume appears. Alas, that is far from what will happen. Work is still unfinished. If you employ a small private printer you will find it necessary to instruct him in all the details that go to make up a good book and it will be imperative for you to acquaint yourself with these niceties before you make any decisions. There are four divisions in the manufacture of a book: paper, typesetting, presswork, and binding.

On the first, much will depend on the price you are willing to pay and the arrangements you are making for illustrations and maps. Certain papers will print illustrative material while others will not. In general those that will are a smooth or glossy finish while the dull finish will make a clear impression for type but not for illustrations. If you decide on the latter and have maps and illustrations these will have to be inserted on separate pages at intervals throughout the book, at the beginning or at the end of the volume. For durability it is advised that you invest in paper that is at least 80% rag content and weighs seventy pounds to the ream.[6]

The size of the page most commonly used is 6×9 inches, if the work runs less than 500 pages; if more than that it might be a saving to make the pages larger in size. As for the type and format, examine other history books and select the one that you like best because the margins are just right, the type is distinct, and the headings are well-balanced. Ask your printer to look at this model and let him show you what type faces he has available. Select one which most nearly matches your model and tell the printer to make you up a sample page or two for visual analysis. Show the sample to some of your prospective reader-friends for criticism. Finally, decide on what headings you will want in solid capitals, the sizes of the type, whether these are to be boldface or not, the width of the margins, and other typographical details. Make your decisions and stick to them. Changes later will be expensive.

Ask your printer the name of the type you have selected and the various sizes you will use for the text, the headings, the footnotes, etc. Mark these down and before turning over your copy, mark in colored pencil the various type faces and sizes. Your printer has other jobs besides yours and unless you are careful to mark all your type sizes and faces and indicate where you want more space and what should be in capitals and what

[6] Stetson, *Art of Ancestor Hunting*, 247–250, and *passim*.

in italics, you will later face the necessity of arguing as to whose fault it was that your material was not set up properly. If you are having your book privately printed you must be your own editor and you must, therefore, be doubly vigilant.

As for ink, you should insist on his using the best grade that will make the most distinct copy on the page you select. The binding, also, is of importance. The folded sheets should be sewed with good linen thread and have double reinforced backs and head boards. The boards for covers should be of the best quality and covered with a durable cloth or buckram. The backbone, the front cover, and the title page should be attractive and dignified in appearance.[7]

If you are using illustrations or maps that are smaller than a full page and have selected a paper which reproduces equally well for both type and illustrative material, it is advisable to decide exactly what position on the page your small illustration or map will have so that the printer may set the type in short lines around the illustration.

First you will receive a galley proof, long strips of three or more pages per strip, which you should read carefully, indicating all the corrections of printer's errors and your own changes. It is advisable to use different colored pencils for each so that there will later be no argument as to the resetting of how many lines (most book printing is done on a linotype machine and every word changed means the resetting of a line) you are willing to pay for. Make all your changes in the galley proof. Changes in page proof are more costly.

After the galleys are returned to the printer he will set the type into pages and send you page proof. This again should be read carefully. You should now also have an engraver's proof of the maps and illustrations you are including.[8] Check your legends. See that your footnotes are properly placed so that the text indication and the footnote reference occur on the same page. Try to have your pages look well balanced. Do not have one or two words of a last line beginning a new page. If this occurs fill the line by adding a few words either there or somewhere before this break occurs. Also do not have a chapter ending with too few lines. These are minor matters but if you want a well-made book you must take such details into consideration.

Now you are ready for the making of your index. If you have already followed the instructions on indexing in chapter X you will have your slips already made and all that you need to do at this stage is to insert the proper page numbers from your page proof. Then alphabetize and coordinate your index slips according to the instructions given in chapter X, type the slips on sheets of paper and have the printer set the copy

---

[7] *Ibid.*

[8] There are three common types of "cuts" for illustrations: the zinc etching, the zinc half-tone, and the copper half-tone. The first two are not as expensive as the third but do not produce as well on smooth finish paper.

into type, generally in a much smaller point type (in the interests of economy and not for any other reason) and in double column. On the index too you will receive a proof which should be checked carefully with your sheets and checked back to the text wherever any queries occur.

The book is now ready for final printing and binding, except for one step, and that is the securing of a copyright. By copyrighting your work you make certain that no one else can print it and claim it as his own. On the reverse of your title page you should have printed the following: "Copyright, *date*, by *your name*. All rights reserved. This book, or part thereof, must not be reproduced in any form without permission of the author." The registration fee costs two dollars, the notary fee a dollar or less, and two printed copies of the book have to be sent to the Copyright Office, Washington, D. C., and will eventually be deposited in the Library of Congress. Books printed or reproduced in any of the newer forms discussed later in this chapter may also be copyrighted.

One way of getting your history before the public is through the medium of the local newspaper. If the editor is a wideawake man he will realize the value of local history and the interest people have in it. "Almost any newspaper can make a success of historical stories as a regular feature, for they are both popular and constructive," according to one writer on the subject, who points out that the local historian may even receive money compensation for the articles he writes for the local newspaper.[9]

Publication of your articles in the local newspaper may provide the means of getting your local history in book form. Since the type will have to be set up for the newspaper articles, and since the composition usually accounts for about half the cost of printing, you will be saved this cost of type-setting. You may reach some agreement with the editor by which he will agree to keep intact the type used for your articles until enough has been assembled for four, eight, sixteen, or even thirty-two book-size pages. With very little time, labor, and expense this type can be set up to run off a section of a book before it is distributed. You will have to have an understanding respecting the length of a line on a page. It may be that the local newspaper editor will be willing to set up your articles with a line two columns wide, which length is much more easily changed later into book-page proportions. Whether a one or two column line is agreed upon, however, a book can be made to suit either length. Questions of bookstock paper, running expenses, number of copies, type of cover, illustrations, and maps, will have to be investigated just as thoroughly as if no previous arrangements were made with the newspaper. The personnel of the newspaper office, however, is in an excellent position to secure these estimates for you and may help you with your selections.

Your book, though printed in "signatures" of four, eight, sixteen, or

---

[9] Weicht, *Local Historian and the Newspaper*, 52, 53.

thirty-two pages from time to time, could finally be published when all the chapters are issued. Many people would have become acquainted with your history through the newspaper articles and this would serve as an advertisement and advance notice for them to secure the whole series in book form. The books could be sold by subscription. It might be that the editor would desire you to "slant" historical articles in a journalistic style. He will probably have to show you how this can be done.[10] Newspaper publication is an avenue not to be overlooked in your search for publication.

Perhaps you cannot afford to have your local history printed yourself and the newspaper editor is not interested. What then can you do? Another method is the multigraph, which can be made to look like regular print but is only about one-half as expensive as straight printing. The multigraph is a small rotary printing machine, seen most often in offices where it is employed chiefly for printing form letters and circulars to look like regular print as found in a book, or like typewriting. Its appearance is never quite as good as a printed page and it is most economical when using paper $8\frac{1}{2}'' \times 11''$ in size. Pictures cannot be included on the same page with printed matter, but a book which is multigraphed can have the pages with pictures at the end of the volume or scattered through the book. The late Dr. Binkley suggests, "The mimeoform process of multigraph printing is useful for the production of . . . books when the edition is in the region of 100 to 500. Considerable savings over ordinary printing are here effected because composition costs are reduced."[11] According to his figures a book of 50,000 words (100 typewritten sheets of the customary 500 words to a page) by the mimeoform process of multigraphing would cost about one-half of what it would by straight printing.

LITHOPRINTING AND PLANOGRAPHING

If either printing or multigraphing is found to be too expensive, you can resort to a process which is frequently applied to book production when the number of copies in the edition is not greater than a few hundred. This process is known by various names: photolithography, photo-offset, lithoprinting, offset printing, planograph printing, etc. The same Dr. Binkley explains:

The process . . . has developed in the last thirty years from the combined application of the principles of lithography and photography, together with a new type of printing press . . . . A photography image is transferred, via a negative, to a metal plate covered with a light-sensitive emulsion . . . . An exposure to an arc light hardens the portions of the emulsion under the transparent parts of the negative so that they remain on the plate after development as an image of the copy to be reproduced.[12]

---

[10] Bleyer's *Newspaper Writing and Editing* has already been referred to as a helpful guide for this purpose.

[11] Binkley, *Reproducing Research Materials*, 19.

[12] *Ibid.*, 21. The plate is flat and must be put in a special offset press.

The most economical size of sheet to use with this process is $8\frac{1}{2}'' \times 11''$, though it is possible to make ordinary book-size pages of $6'' \times 9''$ or $5\frac{1}{2}'' \times 8\frac{1}{2}''$. With the larger size of sheet, it is possible to put from 500 to 900 words on a page and still have the type legible. The number recommended, however, is 700 words to the page. It is possible, too, to have a single or a double column of words on a page. The double column is said to give less strain to the eyes. Only the single column format is used when the sheets are $6'' \times 9''$ in size.

One extremely desirable feature of a planographed book is that illustrative material, such as photographs, maps, drawings, and charts, all of which are very expensive to include in a printed book, can be incorporated with no more additional expense than a typewritten sheet. Too, the typing and illustrative material can appear on the same page, something which is impossible in multigraphing and often difficult in printing. Thus a local history may be profusely illustrated if the manner of publication is either lithoprinting or planographing. Edwards Brothers, one of the pioneer firms doing this type of work, state:

> There are virtually no limitations on the type of material which can be included with a manuscript for Lithoprinting or Planographing. Anything that can be photographed in black and white can be Lithographed or Planographed, and the reproduction will be as perfect as the original.
>
> Drawings, charts, diagrams, etc., made with India ink on good paper, reproduce perfectly, and can be incorporated in the text precisely at the desired points. Further, there is no extra charge for illustrations of this nature . . . .
>
> In addition to charts or diagrams, pages or extracts from other books can be reproduced. This includes all illustrations as well as the text portions. Such reproductions are a clear and faithful facsimile of the original copy . . . .
>
> Original photographs can be reproduced satisfactorily.[13]

Lithoprinters can use your own manuscript, but unless your typing has been exceptionally well done, it is best to have the lithoprinters or at least a competent typist re-type it to insure perfect "master copies."

A substantial saving can be made if you do your own typing, *i.e.*, prepare the master copy, and special instructions will be supplied you in the event that you wish to prepare the master copy for your book in your own office.

MIMEOGRAPHING

Cheaper than lithoprinting and planographing, but inferior to these in appearance and readability, is mimeographing. Binkley supplies the estimate "that multigraphing is about 30% higher than mimeographing, and that printing is about 70% higher than mimeographing."[14]

---

[13] *Manual of Lithoprinting and Planographing* (Ann Arbor, Mich.: Edwards Brothers, Inc., 1939), 4. This 90-page manual is an example of the process it describes and will be sent free upon request to anyone interested.

[14] Edwards Brothers declare that the cost of lithoprinting is actually less than mimeo-

Mimeographed work if expertly done is attractive as well as readable. With some instruction, the average typist can learn to cut satisfactory stencils on his own typewriter. In normal times it is even possible to rent a mimeograph machine and run off your own stencils, performing all the production work except the binding.[15]

The foregoing indicates how inexpensive it normally is to produce a book by the use of the mimeograph. Stencils and paper should be bought in large quantities in order to obtain them at a low cost. The paper should be about 20 lb. stock, though 16 lb. or 24 lb. may be used. Mimeographing is usually done on only one side of the paper, but by increasing the quality of the paper used, and by "slip-sheeting," mimeographing can be done on both sides of the sheet. This reduces the paper cost from one-half to one-third, and cuts in half the size of the bound volume, making it more easily handled. If you do not feel equal to the task of cutting the stencils and running them off, you should turn your whole manuscript over to the expert staff of a letter service company which specializes in this type of work.

On the binding of mimeographed, hectographed, lithoprinted, and planographed material, Binkley has a few suggestions.[16] Thus, from all these suggestions and from estimates which can be obtained locally, it should be possible for you to figure quite accurately the expense involved in reproducing your local history manuscript in mimeographed form. It should be mentioned that simple maps, charts, drawings, and sketches can be reproduced on a mimeograph machine. The better way, however, is to have these done by lithoprinting and the sheets with illustrations can be inserted at the desired positions in the mimeographed material, or all may be placed at the end of the volume. This applies equally well to the next process of reproducing material, that of hectographing.

---

graphing in practically all cases where 300 or more copies are required. They point out, too, that mimeographing often is not very satisfactory, as so much depends upon the quality of the paper, stencils, typewriter, mimeograph, and the typist and operator of the machine. *Manual of Lithoprinting and Planographing*, 1–2.

[15] By the mimeograph process a wax stencil is inserted in your typewriter, the ribbon spools are removed, and the typing is done almost as simply as ordinary typewriting. The wax stencil can be used for making up to 500 good copies, though 600, 700, or more can be made. Or you could turn over your final draft to a commercial letter service firm for reproduction.

[16] If your published material does not exceed 40 or 50 pages and you desire to bind it inexpensively, you can resort to wire stapling. Machine stapling, including a suitable paper cover, is available at a cost of a few cents a copy and will take care of booklets up to one-fourth of an inch in thickness. Spiral binding, increasingly common for notebooks, is a possibility but is not to be recommended. The cost of a good library binding for a book about one and half inches thick, 8½" x 11" in size, is about $1.25 a copy, whether 25 copies are bound, or 500, or 1000. A considerable saving can be made if copies of books are offered for sale in two styles, bound in good cloth, or unbound or with a small paper binding. Plastic binding is becoming popular for some types of work.

Hectographing is less expensive than mimeographing. At the same time it is less permanent and less attractive in appearance.

By the hectograph process "approximately 100 to 150 copies of a document may be reproduced in methyl-violet dye from a single master sheet." There are two processes which may be used in hectographing, the gelatin and the liquid, the latter being preferable. With the use of the liquid process the decrease in legibility begins after 100 to 150 copies have been made. The hectograph process has rarely been used to reproduce a long manuscript. Dr. Stanton L. Davis of Cleveland, Ohio, however, used it to produce fifty copies of a 350 page book, *Pennsylvania Politics, 1860–63*, at a cost of $1.95 per copy. The additional expense for binding amounted to $32.50. He found that the total hectograph costs of this book, exclusive of binding and mailing ($6.72 to 18 libraries), for an edition of fifty were only $47.10 more than the cost of the typewritten draft and one carbon copy.

If worst comes to worst, and you find all attempts to print, lithoprint, planograph, mimeograph, multigraph, or hectograph your manuscript impossible you can still bind the typewritten pages as well as the carbon copies, and deposit one or more in the local library with instructions to allow the material to be used. One copy, perhaps the original, you will want to keep yourself as a reminder of a labor well done, of which the workman need not be ashamed. La Porte, Indiana, has a *History of One Hundred Years*, consisting of only seven copies of 2,039 typewritten pages. It has 256 articles written by several hundred contributors, 90 illustrations, and an index of 160 pages. The seven copies of this unique local history have been deposited where they can be consulted, four in La Porte and three elsewhere.

One more suggestion remains regarding the publication of your local history. The American Documentation Institute, which operates the Bibliofilm Service referred to in an earlier chapter, has a plan for unpublished materials: You submit your manuscript to, let us say, the journal of your state historical society with the request that the journal publish it in its entirety (which it certainly cannot afford to do), or print a summary (which the journal may ask you to write for it). In the latter case the summary will have a note attached to it that the complete manuscript is available from ADI (American Documentation Institute) as Document No. ——, at a cost of —— cents in microfilm or —— cents in photoprint. The editor of the journal forwards to the ADI the complete manuscript with the deposit form filled out, giving the author's name, the title, and the issue of the journal in which the summary will appear. ADI receives the manuscript as a permanent deposit, gives it a Document Number and fixes the price for a copy, at its regular cost copying rates, and at once advises the editor of the Document Number and the price.

Reprints of the manuscript deposited with ADI may be obtained by the author in unlimited number from ADI at its usual cost rates, either in microfilm or photoprint. Or if the author wants to order a definite number reproduced by printing, or any of the modern methods such as offset printing, blueprint or black-on-white print, ADI will be glad to make such an edition for him on a nonprofit basis. Thus, failing to have your local history reproduced by any of the more common methods, you have through the facilities of the ADI a means of getting your work before a wider reading public than that of your local community. All this can be done at no cost whatever to you. Correspondence concerning this method of "publication" should be addressed to the American Documentation Institute, care of the Offices of Science Service, 2101 Constitution Ave., Washington, D. C.

Whatever form of publication your local history may take, you are certain to receive an exultant thrill when the first copy of your book is delivered to you. The delight of actual authorship which accompanies the sight of your work is one of the goals of literary desire. It is a partial payment for the diligent work that has gone into the gathering and writing of a local history. Steel yourself, however, against derogatory book reviews, for the best volumes often receive scathing treatment. Enjoy the compliments, but do not grieve over the unfavorable criticism. Retain a sane balance and dignity and you will come out of the experience of authorship a wiser and better individual.

CHAPTER XII

COOPERATIVE LOCAL HISTORY

LOCAL history may be gathered, written, and published either by an individual working alone or cooperatively with a group of interested people. The first eleven chapters of this book have been directed to the individual local historian, but an individual may work with others in the local history field, or a group may work as a unit, cooperating in every phase of the work of gathering, writing, and publishing the local history.

A number of local histories have been cooperative projects and much is to be said for this type of undertaking. While the individual local historian may have, or may lack "unflagging industry and unswerving honesty in seeking out the truth, imagination to interpret it aright, literary art to bring it home not only with conviction but with welcome to men's minds and bosoms,"[1] other members of a cooperating group may have just those qualities he may lack. One individual may find that he makes a good gatherer of local history, but that he cannot write in a pleasing and attractive manner. Another may be a good gatherer and writer of local history but may lack all business sense in handling the very important financial affairs in connection with publication. What one member of a group may lack in ability will, therefore, be compensated by the good qualities of another, or of several others.

Whether the cooperating group is a local history society, a class of students, the community in general, a library, a club organization, a church, or some other aggregation, it will usually be found that one or two individuals have to take the leadership in planning the work which the others are to perform.

THE LOCAL HISTORICAL SOCIETY AS A COOPERATIVE ENTERPRISE

If your community has a wide-awake historical society, it is fortunate. If it does not have one, new life should be infused into what passes for such a society, or an entirely new group should be formed.[2]

---

[1] Fortescue, *Writing of History*, 72.

[2] About 1885 there were only 128 historical societies (omitting Ohio, which in 1890 had 18) in the entire United States, and only five in all of Canada. Probably three-fourths of these could be classified as local societies. By 1890 the number had grown to 182 for the United States; with five for Canada. The *Magazine of Western History*, I (1885), 351–353; XII (1890), 109–113. Thereafter, the interest in local history rose rapidly, if one can judge by the number of societies formed. By 1904 the number was between 400 and 500. Henry E. Bourne, "The Work of American Historical Societies," *Annual Report of the American Historical Association, 1904*, 119. A little over 300 of these were listed in the report of the Association for 1905. By 1930 local historical societies were common in the New England and middle western states. Massachusetts alone had more than two hundred such organizations. Edmund M. Conaway, "A Historical Society and Museum for the Public

The membership of a local historical society should include those who are actively interested in collecting and preserving information about every phase of community life. As members, or as honorary members, old residents may well be included as well as local history teachers, newspaper men, ministers, important community officials, and others.

It is a good plan to have a chairman who will appoint committees and assign to each committee a particular task and a special line of investigation. Thus, one committee can do research on one phase of local history as suggested in the model outline. Another can devote its time and energy to another field, and so on. At the monthly meetings reports should be given of progress made in these various fields of research. Each member ought to be allowed to choose, so far as possible, his own sphere of activity and interest, for it must be realized that an individual works best on that in which he is most interested. At intervals, as the work of gathering historical data continues, the membership of committees may be changed to suit the needs. If a committee feels that nothing more of value can be learned, a new line of activity can be assigned to it, or the committee can cease to exist and re-form in a new grouping.

Every community has individuals who are interested in genealogy. A member with such an inclination may very profitably be assigned to record his own family history, or the history of the community's "founder," or the genealogy of all the early settlers. A camera fan may be given the pleasant task of photographing all the old houses, buildings, historical sites, and other interesting local views, such as early mills, covered bridges, pioneer cemeteries, important early manuscripts, old musical instruments, samplers, needlework pictures, ox-yokes, flails, shepherds' crooks, poke bonnets, smocks, and kindred articles of everyday use in days gone by. Similarly a lover of art may be asked to collect examples of early local art. A member interested in drafting may be given the work of drawing sketches of early buildings and may be requested to construct a map of the community showing the area as it looked at the time of settlement as well as other maps indicating growth at intervals of a decade or a quarter century. Other members may be interested in manufacturing, agriculture, public and private morals, churches, schools, local politics, or public improvement and will find plenty of opportunity to follow their particular bent. The fact that their efforts will be appreciated by the group will be an added incentive.

School," *School and Society*, XXXI (1930), 431. A recent compilation of historical societies lists over 500 in the United States and Canada. The *Historical Societies in the United States and Canada, a Handbook*, (Indianapolis, 1936). Copies sell for $1.50 each and can be obtained by addressing the American Association for State and Local History, Box 6101, Washington, D. C. A new edition of the handbook is now in press, prepared by the Association. By 1932 Canada alone had over sixty societies. D. C. Harvey, "Importance of Local History in the Writing of General History," *Canadian Historical Review*, VIII (1932), 243.

In a number of places the school, or an American history class or club in the school, has taken the lead in gathering, writing, and publishing the history of the locality. Mrs. Schapiro, for five years head of the English department in the high school at Wadsworth, Ohio, tells how their school published a local history. Oddly enough, the enterprise started in the most unexpected way.

Casting about for a theme for their year book, the class of 1938 of the Wadsworth High School decided that the current Northwest Territory Celebration could be localized very suitably to fit a high school annual in an old Northwest Territory town such as theirs. Consequently the pupils in the five senior English classes, which numbered about one hundred and twenty-five, began to inquire into the history of the town among their parents and friends. Very soon a great deal of time in the English classes was appropriated to animated extemporaneous discussions of various phases of Wadsworth history. Pupils began to bring old photographs, newspapers, books, letters, and other relics resurrected from family attics. Each new contribution was eagerly examined by all the classes. Each stimulated the others to find more. Very shortly the teacher and the classes discovered that they had altogether too much material to use in the limited space of an annual, but they were loath to allow it to return to the secluded obscurity of the village garrets. Therefore, the group decided that it wished to publish an entirely separate history of Wadsworth in order to use the material.

The next step was to announce in the two town newspapers that the senior class was considering the possibility of publishing a history of Wadsworth, provided that the people showed interest enough to warrant it. The teacher then presented the idea to the local printer, whose equipment was adequate to getting out such a book . . . .

In order to learn approximately how many copies of the book could be sold, the publisher offered to print subscription blanks at her own expense. These the members of the class circulated in the town. A subscriber pledged himself to purchase a copy of the book if and when it appeared. It was decided to offer two types of bindings, a heavy paper cover to sell at one dollar a copy and of cloth covered edition for one dollar and a half. In spite of the fact that the depression hit the town during the spring with great force and caused the lay-offs of hundreds of factory workers, the seniors still were able to get about eight hundred pledges to buy their history. Everyone concerned was elated at the response of the public. The publisher decided that eight hundred pledges warranted the printing of an edition of one thousand books.[3]

Meanwhile, the classes began collecting historical material in a systematic manner, interviewing old residents to the number of almost three hundred, consulting available written sources, such as newspaper files, old magazines, old letters, diaries, and books. Citizens offered highly treasured family records, such as letters, diaries, and genealogical data belonging to their ancestors. The pupils had profitable experiences in going to the libraries, newspaper offices, city halls, and court houses of their own town as well as those of nearby cities.

[3] Schapiro, "Publishing a Local History," 25–26.

While the seniors were collecting all this material, the office-practice classes typed it. The classes held a "cutting and pasting bee," as they called it. All the information on one topic was clipped from the various interviews and from other sources and pasted together on sheets of uniform size . . . . In this way the information for all sixteen chapters of the book was organized in rough preliminary form. Thirty of the better prepared English students then re-wrote the history, dividing themselves into committees to work on each chapter. The teacher finally edited the material and prepared it for printing. The office-practice classes typed the manuscript for the local printer.

To illustrate the book, two pupils in the senior class made twenty-four pen- and-ink sketches from photographs representing buildings no longer standing but once important in the life of the town.

Wadsworth, Center to City contained sixteen chapters dealing with the pioneers, town government, churches, education, industry and business, transportation, hotels, publications, recreation, library, racial groups, cemetery, old houses, military affairs, and sketches of professional men. It included also a bibliography, a list of contributors of information, and a foreword. This volume of two hundred and seven pages had been seventeen weeks in preparation, from the time the first systematic collection of historical data was begun in February until the book was printed and and ready for the subscribers late in May. The students disposed of around nine hundred copies, receiving enough to pay the printer's bill and leave a small surplus, Since the town of six thousand was then undergoing the financial difficulties of the late thirties, such a showing may be called most satisfactory.

The Wadsworth town history is not an isolated instance of a local history gathered, written, and published by a group of students. *Marion County in the Making* was produced in much the same way by the J. O. Watson Class of Fairmont High School of West Virginia, in 1917. It is an excellent example of a school-sponsored local history, produced under the direction of the head of the history department of the high school. It is printed in excellent style and is well illustrated with household and farm implements, utensils, tools, and relics of the past, the drawings having been made by members of the class.

On a much less pretentious scale, a small high school in Kansas gathered, wrote, and published in mimeographed form the local history of the county. The project was financed by selling advertising space to the local merchants.

There may be some who are inclined to doubt the ability of high school students to gather and write local history, but little doubt exists in the minds of teachers who have directed activities along this line. It must always be remembered that an adult with a good eduction, well trained in historical methods, is essential as the directing mind behind the students' efforts. To gather stories from old residents may be relatively easy;

to obtain authentic and connected historical data from local archives is admittedly much more difficult; yet this, too, can be done under proper supervision and guidance.

In this connection it is worth noting that the Board of Education of Great Britain has printed a pamphlet, entitled *Village Survey-making, an Oxfordshire Experiment* which aims to provide elementary school students with proper guidance in making community surveys. In the United States courses in state and local history have been introduced into many high schools and have resulted in a more pronounced interest in local history. Several states have published pamphlets directing the students' activities in assembling historical data and objects.[4] Several state historical societies have offered prizes to the counties for the best high school student's essay on the history of his community.[5]

Occasional articles which have appeared from time to time tell how interest in local history has been aroused among high school students.[6]

In conclusion, it is worth nothing that when the town of New Rochelle, New York, desired a local history which could be used in its public schools as a textbook, it turned over the assignment to the faculty of the high school and in 1938 there was published a beautifully printed and profusely illustrated local history designed for classroom use just in time for the celebration of the town's two hundred and fiftieth anniversary.[7]

LIBRARY-SPONSORED COOPERATION

In some localities the library has become the logical depository for local historical documents and relics. Many libraries have a nucleus collection of historical objects such as old pictures, maps, letters, pamphlets, and relics, and these have a tendency to attract others. Some libraries keep a scrapbook containing clippings which refer to the local history. Other libraries make an effort to secure a copy by gift or purchase of every book referring to the community history. When a book cannot be obtained, a bibliographical note is generally kept, so that there is at least

---

[4] Wisconsin has a mimeographed pamphlet: *Teachers' Pictorial Survey of Rural Wisconsin a Century After the Black Hawk War*, sponsored by the State Historical Society in consultation with the College of Agriculture of the University of Wisconsin, the State Superintendent of Public Instruction, and the *Wisconsin Journal of Education*.

[5] *Cf. Indiana State Bulletin*, XV (1938), 357. Indiana requirements state that emphasis is to be placed on research, accuracy, and information not contained in the printed county and state histories. Michigan also is known to offer prizes for students' historical essays and the winning essays are published by the state historical society.

[6] A few worth noting are: (1) H. E. Wilson, "Look Around You; How to Make a Community Survey," *Scholastic*, XXX, (1937), 19-20. This tells what a high school class did in making a survey of its community and in studying its local history. (2) Conaway, "Historical Society and Museum," tells how to promote high school local history societies and how to collect material for a museum. (3) Murdock, "Giving the Past a Future," tells how to decorate a history club room.

[7] Herbert B. Nichols, *Historic New Rochelle* (New Rochelle, N. Y., Board of Education, 1938).

a record of all works referring to the community. The library may also compile an inventory of old local manuscripts, letters, diaries, account books, and the like. If the owners of these are unwilling to deposit them in the library, at least the library can direct interested persons where to go to consult then. The same treatment may be accorded historical relics. A list compiled giving the location and nature of each such object will be useful and, where no local museum exists, a photograph may be taken and kept in the library. Such a centralized storehouse can lead to later coordination either by members of the library staff themselves or by an interested outside group cooperating with the library.

COMMUNITY-SPONSORED COOPERATION

New York State has done as much to encourage local communities to gather and publish their history as any other state. In 1919 the state passed the following law:

A local historian shall be appointed, as provided in this section, for each city, town or village, except that in a city of over one million inhabitants a local historian shall be appointed for each borough therein instead of for the city at large. . . . Such historian shall serve without compensation, unless the governing board of the city, town or village for or in which he or she was appointed, shall otherwise provide. . . . The local authorities of the city, town or village for which said historian is appointed, may provide the historian with sufficient space in a safe, vault or other fireproof structure for the preservation of materials collected.[8]

The law further provides that the mayor may appoint the local historian and that the local authorities may raise by taxation the necessary funds to publish the town history.

Royal Oak, Michigan, a decade ago appointed a city historian to gather and write the history of the town.[9] A number of New England towns have appointed local historians or committees to gather and publish the story of their past. They have also granted funds to defray the cost of publishing the histories.[10]

NEWSPAPER-SPONSORED COOPERATION

Newspapers often promote interest in local history, or can be the means by which various community organizations promote that interest. Editors should and very often do show considerable interest in preserving and publishing local history. As a consequence a large number of local histories have been written and published by newspaper men and print-

---

[8] *Handbook of Historical and Patriotic Societies in New York State, Including List of Local Historians* (Albany, 1926), 3. This handbook lists 103 historical societies in New York State, most of them for towns and counties.

[9] *American City*, January, 1931, p. 157.

[10] *The History of Dublin, N. H.*, resulted in this way from a committee appointed in 1904, though the history was not published until 1920.

ers. Part of this interest is perhaps due to the fact that such individuals have access to the back files of newspapers. It is not surprising that a day-by-day or week-by-week chronicler of a town's life often looks upon himself as the guardian of the town's written records, and desires to make these records known.

The newspapers can arouse interest by publishing in their columns the accounts of old residents and the pictures of bygone days. Such stories and pictures prompt others to tell their stories and loan their old pictures. Newspapers also arouse interest by having a query column which asks for names, dates, and other specific information difficult to locate. Seeing these, an old settler may come forward with the desired information. Often addresses of former residents can be discovered in this way. Such individuals not only may have information needed in the writing of the local history but they are nearly always good buyers of a town history.

Newspapers will also often cooperate with local historical societies, schools, churches, clubs, and museums in printing articles which deal with the community's past.

The collector of local history, whether an individual or an organization, should use the local newspapers to the utmost in keeping the community acquainted with the progress of work on the local history. Fortescue says that people seldom reflect upon their local history until a well is sunk exposing a ruin, or a gale blows trees down and exposes the remains of an early building.[11] The collector of local history should be careful to take advantage of everything that may catch the popular interest. If you find a rare old map of your community, write an article about it for the newspaper; the article may bring other maps and pictures from readers. If you discover a valuable old diary or packet of old letters, let the public know about your find and what you intend to use it for, and you may be the recipient of other old diaries, letters, and records of whose existence you never dreamed. Keep constantly in mind that you are building up a buying public, one eager to subscribe in advance to your book or to buy it as soon as it is on sale. The newspaper and the historian or history club, working together, can accomplish a great deal.

CLUB-SPONSORED COOPERATION

Cooperation in collecting, writing, and publishing local history may be sponsored by a club or organization whose primary object and interest is anything but history. The work of the Rotary Club of Kingsport, Tennessee, has previously been mentioned and serves as an excellent example of this sort.

In some counties in England the Women's Institutes have taken the gathering of the local history as a special responsibility. It is possible that your community has a woman's organization which would be willing

[11] Fortescue, *Writing of History*, 4.

to undertake the task as a major or a minor interest. Often the Daughters of the American Revolution, the American Legion, or other patriotic organization would lend their active support and cooperation to a project contemplating the publishing of a local history.

Perhaps there may be a number of such clubs or societies, each of which could be induced to cooperate in its particular sphere. The Parent-Teachers' Association might agree to study the community's educational history; the Chamber of Commerce, the Rotary Club or Lions Club, the early business life and business ethics; the patriotic societies, the military history; the various church groups, their own church history. If the project were carried out in this way, each group would be studying the field in which it is most interested, and yet each club or organization would be cooperating in producing a real history of the community. The more organized cooperation of this sort you can secure, the less your own task will be, the more interest you will arouse in the entire project, and the more copies your published history can eventually be sold. Cooperation in gathering and writing the history of each phase of community life should naturally lead to cooperation in sharing the expenses of publishing the history if subsidy becomes necessary.

The attempt should be made to enlist cooperation from clubs in the direction of their natural interests. Boy Scouts, interested as they are in Indian lore, might be induced to study local Indian mounds, relics, pioneer life, Indian fighting, animal hunting. Their patriotic pride might be enlisted to secure the copying of fast-fading inscriptions of pioneers in the local cemeteries. Their interest in the mysterious might lead to the discovery of every ghost house, secret stairway, and false hall in the entire town. Their propensity for mapping might be guided into production of community maps showing development at various stages. Girl Scouts, Girl Reserves, 4-H Clubs, and other youth organizations might be induced to turn their energies into useful channels leading to cooperation in gathering local history and relics. If they can be interested in the gathering, they may become interested in efforts to sell the local history when published. Boys' and girls' clubs often take hikes. Their interest in local history may be aroused by pilgrimages to local historic spots, and perhaps in the erection of historical markers at historic sites within their own boundaries. Of all the organizations in a community, the youth clubs, by whatever name they are known, can be depended upon to have more latent energy and enthusiasm which may be turned into useful channels than any other group.

Needless to say, to enlist cooperation of this sort requires the utmost tact, perseverance, and imagination. Some are endowed with the ability to fire the imagination, create enthusiasm, and secure active cooperation on the part of many; others are not. If you are not fortunate enough to be a good "salesman," team up with someone who can do the public relations work while you do the research and writing.

167

Churches have produced more local history than any other organized group and the number of church histories is steadily increasing. While nearly all such works devote most of their space to their own church life, a considerable amount of local history of a general sort must be introduced in order to give the proper background for the strictly church history.

Church sponsored histories are probably more easily sold than any other kind of local history for local pride is united with church pride, church loyalty, and religious fervor in inducing members to give both time and money to the gathering, writing, and publishing of a history of their particular denomination.

Miss Helen M. Wright, the successful author of two church histories, offers the following sound advice.:

In general a church history should not be written without the support of the congregation, at least in part. An interest in the financing of such a project stimulates an interest in the sales. This is an ideal situation. On the other hand, very few of the early churches in America seem to control enough wealth even to consider anything classed as so great a luxury as a history; the publication of the records themselves is almost unthought of. Therefore, when a history is proposed, it is usually the work of one, two, or three, perhaps a few, persons who assume the responsibility financially. Some of the smaller historical booklets are financed by appeals for advertisements which are printed on the fly-leaves. This, however, increases the cost of production as well as the cost of distribution and it usually detracts from the appearance of the book. When subscriptions and advertisements are taken, the book is usually given away. When a few individuals back the project, the book is sold as easily as possible, and the balance needed to clear the cost of production is met by those interested.[12]

A truly cooperative church or parish history should be in the hands of a committee representative of all the various organizations of the church, such as the session, the trustees, the council, the Sabbath School, the adult organizations, and the young people's clubs. The chairman of the committee should be an individual well qualified for the position by education and training, tact, business acumen, and the ability to elicit enthusiasm and cooperation. While each organization should be responsible for its own history and list of membership, the chairman, or one appointed by him, should edit all the material handed in and give it a unity which it otherwise would lack. A truly cooperative history of this sort would probably have little or no difficulty in finding a means of financing publication. If necessary, each organization would find a way of appropriating or raising funds to bear its proper share in publishing the church history.

---

[12] Letter of Helen M. Wright, Jersey City, N. J., August 6, 1939. Miss Wright is author of the history and records of the Methodist Episcopal Church and the Presbyterian Congregation, both of Mendham, Morris County, New Jersey, published in 1938 and 1939 respectively.

Another form of cooperative church history would be to have each church in a community to agree to publish the history of each denomination in a single volume. The account of each such church would necessarily have to be much shorter than that contemplated in the preceding paragraph, yet a fairly adequate treatment of each denomination could be published. An agreement could be reached by which each church would be entitled to a number of pages in proportion to the money appropriated or raised for the project. Cuts could be as numerous as each church desired, under an arrangement by which the cost would be borne by the organization concerned. Such a cooperative history could have a part of the book or several chapters devoted to the general history of the community as a setting for the various church histories. The cost of this part, too, could be shared under some arrangement fair to all. With all the churches of a community cooperating and sharing in the production of such a local church history, it is difficult to believe that the project could be a failure from the financial standpoint.

ANNIVERSARY-INSPIRED COOPERATION

An examination of many of the local histories contained in the large libraries of this country reveals the fact that numbers of them were written in anticipation of an anniversary celebration, or as a result of the enthusiasm aroused by such a celebration. The local historian, the local historical society, and other individuals and groups should take advantage of each such occasion to gather, write, and publish local historical material. One should strike while the iron is hot, or, perhaps better, strike while it is getting hot—while the anniversary is in the immediate offing. It is easier to finance a local history or local church history at the time of an anniversary than at any other period. However, you need not wait for a perfect anniversary date to celebrate. There is no reason why the ninetieth anniversary of a town should not be celebrated as well as the hundredth. The 25th, 50th, 75th, 100th, 125th, 150th, etc., are favorite occasions for anniversary celebrations, but the multiples of decades are often celebrated as well, such as the 30th, 40th, 50th, 60th, and 70th. Do not be too particular about what anniversary you celebrate. If the settlers moved into your region in 1832, you are obviously too late to plan for a centennial of their arrival, but by hunting about you may find that the community was not officially named until, let us say, 1847. You can fix upon the anniversary to commemorate the centennial of the corporate life of the town which began in 1847. Again you may find that settlement begin in 1800, the town was incorporated in 1815, but changed its name to another about 1849. You can take the convenient date as the one whose contennial is to be celebrated.

Two recent anniversary-inspired local histories come to mind, though many could be mentioned. One is about one hundred and forty-five pages in length, bound in stiff paper covers, and written as a cooperative project by twenty or thirty authors. Each of the ten churches of the community, for instance, has a separate history written by its own historian and occupying about two pages each. The pictures are all grouped together at the end, doubtless for economy. The city fathers appointed a committee to write the local history and prepare as well for the approaching centennial celebration.[13] The second anniversary-inspired local history was not so pretentious, sold for twenty-five cents, and included a pageant of the community's past.[14]

It is probably best to link any contemplated local history with an anniversary celebration if at all possible. One should not, however, wait idly around until an opportune date is not far off.[15]

There are, thus, various avenues, ways, and means for the writing of local history and to him who has the will and the endurance, the lasting enthusiasm and the unflagging patience, the painstaking meticulousness and the constant inspiration, the field is fertile and, in many instances, hardly trail-blazed. Go forth, willing searcher, and may the reward of Clio's benediction be yours to guide your steps along the long but enticing paths of local history writing.

---

[13] *Geneseo Centennial History, 1836–1936* (Kewanee, Illinois, 1936).

[14] Tippecanoe County Historical Association, *Pageant Celebrating the Establishment of the Northwest Territory, Souvenir Program with Local History of Lafayette and Tippecanoe County, Indiana*. It was published at Lafayette, Indiana.

[15] An anniversary-inspired history of a larger scope is the six-volume set of *The History of the State of Ohio* being issued under the auspices of the Ohio State Archaeological and Historical Society and inspired by the Sesqui-Centennial Celebration of the Northwest Territory.

WRITING THE WAR HISTORY OF COMMUNITIES

IN time of war, when the national effort is directed toward a common goal and news or anticipation of critical events steadily attends us, when the daily lives of virtually the whole population are affected directly or indirectly by the struggle and the personal tragedy of battle, leaving its indelible impression upon civilians at home, a popular interest soon develops in recording the events and conditions of these memorable years for the satisfaction of the participants as well as for the enlightenment of posterity. As this interest found expression, for example, during the American Civil War and World War I, so it is recurring at present to a greater degree than ever before. The following comments on writing war history of individual communities are made with emphasis upon narratives composed during or shortly after the conflict and thus affected in numerous ways by the nearness of the events themselves. Some of these observations, however, may be applicable likewise to historical accounts of communities at war in the more distant past.

Let us inquire at the outset when the history of the present war should begin. Is December 7, 1941 the best date to serve as a starting point? Is it well to use a specific date except by way of a brief introduction to capture the reader's interest? If the continuity of history commands our respect, we recognize that, whatever the subject or period treated, it cannot be divorced from what preceded without impairing its meaning. When the community goes to war, its manner of going is determined to a considerable degree by prewar conditions. This relationship is well illustrated by the sequence of events before the United States entered World War II. The transition from peace to declared war was a period of "defense" and in such phrases as defense program and defense work directed against aggressor nations it continued as a household word long after Pearl Harbor. It seems fairly obvious that the story of such a transition is an essential prelude to any war history. So, too, the aftermath of war as reflected in the local scene merits consideration to provide at least a thoughtful summary and conclusion on postwar problems as viewed at the close of the conflict.

Patriotism has always been a dominant motive in writing war history. The will to fight engenders the urge to write and enthusiasm for one's subject is by no means to be despised. When the patriot becomes historian, however, he must base his narrative as far as possible upon original contemporary records. Assuming that he knows how and where to find them, we may predict that his quest will yield some conflicting evidence requiring critical judgment to arrive at or most nearly approach the truth of the matter. Although it is gratifying to recount the best efforts put forth in behalf of the cause, the records of shortcomings and failure along the way cannot be ignored in the historian's obligation to tell the whole truth. "Business as usual," "too little and too late," were undeniable indictments early in the present conflict. War is not all sacrifice and glorious achievement. The historian should have sufficient courage to say as much in the light of evidence at hand, although the closer he is to events and persons discussed the more hazardous his task.

In preparing the history of a community in wartime the center of focus would seem to be self-evident. It should be the community. The story of Middletown or of Union County in World War II which devotes detailed chapters to the Battle of Europe, American diplomacy, or national mobilization betrays faulty perspective and misdirected emphasis. On the other hand, local events do not transpire in a vacuum, detached from state, national, and even international developments in this age of radio. Such broad developments may serve as background from which some appropriate thread is woven now and then into the local scene to point up the narrative and maintain that essential relationship between immediate incidents and far reaching causes and effects. To achieve this balance and maintain the proper focus is one of the most difficult problems in writing local history, especially when events beyond our own horizon are of overwhelming significance. Yet in one sense of the word all occurrences are local, and those of widespread importance which happen in one's own community can be given special emphasis, both factual and interpretive, in the war history. The author should keep in mind the idea of writing for the community. However much others may consult his work, local residents will comprise most of his readers. Can he not cultivate an interest in their own history by giving them not merely what they expected about men and events but something of more enduring value?

In centering such a historical study on developments in the community with due regard for their relation to outside forces, it follows that two aspects of the subject must be considered. In the face of national emergency the community marshals its human and material resources for winning the war. But these efforts are only part of the story. Equally important is the impact of war upon the community in countless ways that make for profound changes in everyday life. This second aspect involves an analysis of economic, political, and social conditions along with a clear presentation of the main sequence of events. Changes in population, proximity of army camps or naval bases, establishment of new industries, war relief work, food and fuel supplies—these are examples of outward manifestations of the community at war; but public opinion on questions of the day, the psychological reaction of various social groups under the stress of war, and readjustment of peacetime habits and modes of living call for investigation, if a well rounded picture is to be provided.

Here, then, is an attempt to present war history as social history. If this approach needs justification, it may be offered in the fact that no war is fought exclusively on the field of battle, that successive modern wars have affected ever increasing proportions of the population, and that we have generally accepted "total war" today as a reality. The Civil War history of many a southern locality dealt chiefly with military events in the immediate area, and quite properly, although, in most cases, too exclusively so, from the historical viewpoint of our own time. But in recent years all American communities fortunately have been far removed from the scene of battle and therefore military aspects of war have a bearing on local history only within quite narrow limits. Men and women in the armed forces from the community play their decisive part in the war elsewhere. Since they are scattered over the face of the globe, their service becomes a series of personal records which can be compiled and published in a memorial volume, but their individual experiences are not an integral part of the community's war history.[1] This point is made with full recognition of their primary importance to winning the war. What they have done in active service abroad can be effectively summarized; the significance of the contacts maintained between them and the people at home can be portrayed by illustrations from available correspondence and other sources.

In viewing war history in its social manifestations, it should not be assumed that the role and impress of outstanding personalities in the community or from without are to be overlooked. Most persons are inclined to think of history too exclusively in terms of careers of national leaders and their accomplishments. In contrast to them the common man seems a drab, inarticulate mass or, as an individual, a local nonentity. This is not the place to argue whether the great man determines the course of history or whether he is essentially the product of his times. The influence of environment in historical evolution is generally recognized and that environment is primarily local. The social historian finds abundant evidence of the common man's expression through the social group. The democratic way of life has encouraged this expression and the leaders who have emerged have in turn been influenced by it. Social history is concerned with action and reaction among various social groups as well as between the individual and the group or between rival individuals. Thus the nature of a community's leadership is of vital concern especially when wars and rumors of wars disseminate conflicting ideas and cast suspicion upon cherished ideals. The war historian might undertake to evaluate this leadership in relation to prewar problems, wartime issues, and anticipation of postbellum conditions.

To consider more specifically how the war history of a community might be developed, the following outline is presented as one of several possibilities. The scheme is a combination of chronological and topical

---

[1] Such experiences would appear more appropriately in histories of military, naval, or other units of the war.

treatment. It aims to be essentially narrative in form, but a topical discussion of the impact of war upon the community seems preferable. Although this plan may entail some repetition, skillful handling of the material can render this feature unobjectionable and, in fact, utilize it at certain points for emphasis. If sufficient information is available, it is suggested that occasional comparisons might be effectively drawn between conditions, incidents, or reactions in the community during the two world wars.

I. INTRODUCTION: THE PREWAR YEARS
  A. Brief Survey of Economic Conditions and Outlook, 1938–1939
     1. Chief factors determining occupations and living conditions
     2. Vestiges of the great depression and recovery
     3. Relations between private enterprise and government
     4. How reflected in political and social life
  B. First Year of the War in Europe, 1939–1940
     1. Reaction in the community to prewar crises abroad and conflicting ideologies
     2. Reaction to American neutrality program
     3. Degree of public interest or apathy—population origins in relation to war questions
  C. The Period of Defense, 1940–1941
     1. Changing attitude toward preparedness and aid to Britain
     2. Forces of unity and disunity—influence of propaganda
     3. Participation in the national defense program, military and economic
     4. Political and social repercussions

II. THE COMMUNITY ON THE HOME FRONT IN WORLD WAR II, DECEMBER, 1941–194—
  A. The Shock of Pearl Harbor and Its Effect upon the Community
     1. Crystallization of public opinion on defense and war
     2. Reality or unreality of global war, its duration, and meaning for the individual and the group
     3. First efforts in transition from defense to war activities
  B. The Community in Relation to the Progress of the War and to National and Statewide Developments
     1. Chief local events concerning mobilization, production, salvage, bond purchases, civilian defense, war relief, etc., in 1942
     2. Same for 1943 and 1944, with some comparative comments
  C. Other Important Events More Purely Local in Character during the War
     1. Political
     2. Military
     3. Economic and social
          Note: Section C might be combined with Section B.

III. MEN AND WOMEN OF THE COMMUNITY IN THE ARMED FORCES
   A. Men in the Army and Navy
      1. Summary comments on volunteers in various branches for successive periods
      2. Summary comments on draftees
      3. Men in non-combatant service
   B. Women in the Army and Navy
      1. Summary comments on numbers in various branches for successive periods
      2. Women in medical service
   C. Contacts Maintained with the Community
      1. On leave and furlough
      2. Reflections on home and community through correspondence
      3. Beginning of veterans' return to civilian life
   D. Leadership and Distinction of Certain Individuals
      Note: This section might be combined with Sections A and B.

IV. THE IMPACT OF WAR UPON THE COMMUNITY
   A. Population Changes
      1. Immigration and emigration—net results
      2. Labor supply in various categories
      3. Racial and nationality factors
      4. Military population—proximity of camps, bases, etc.
   B. Economic Problems
      1. Agriculture
      2. Manufacturing, new and revamped industries
      3. Trade and commerce, financial, wholesale, and retail
      4. Labor—relations with employers and government
   C. Political Issues
      1. Local expression on national questions; the elections of 1942 and 1944
      2. Party politics on state and local questions
      3. Evaluation of political leadership
   D. Intellectual Aspects
      1. Changes in education
      2. Libraries—reading interests of the public
      3. Lectures, public forums, etc.
   E. The Arts in Wartime
      1. Creative work
      2. Public appreciation under stress of war
   F. Religious and Social Life
      1. Influence of churches and other religious organizations
      2. War work of emergency organizations
      3. Activities of older organizations under abnormal conditions
      4. The role of women on the home front

G. Public Opinion
    1. Influence of the press, radio, and movies
    2. Pressure groups and patriotism
    3. Attitude toward war regulations and restrictions
    4. Optimism regarding the outcome of the war
    5. American ideals—"what are we fighting for?"
H. Observations and Interpretive Comments on Civilian Life and Activities
V. CONCLUSION
    A. End of Military Campaigns
        1. Relaxation of wartime regulations
        2. First effects of demobilization
    B. Public Interest in Postwar Problems
        1. Concepts and anticipation of a "return to normalcy"
        2. Local problems of readjustment
        3. The United States and world peace

This outline requires a few comments to try to anticipate some questions that will doubtless be raised. Details given in the subheadings are not intended to imply complete coverage of the subjects to which they relate. Additional subjects will be important features in the histories of some communities; others will find certain points in the present outline irrelevant or inapplicable. If a general survey of the war years is undertaken, as proposed in Part II, discriminating use should be made of worldwide and national events so that they supply momentum to the narrative without overshadowing the local scene and its action. Sections B and C of Part II may be enriched by selecting important data from various subjects in Part IV to weave into the story. Some of these facts could be used effectively again in the topical sequence. The five principal headings are not meant to suggest a limit of five chapters. The relative amounts of material gathered on various subjects and their final arrangement will help determine the division by chapters. Part III might well constitute a single chapter. Data on individuals in the form of biographical sketches would mar the continuity of the text and therefore should, along with rosters and other lists, appear in an appendix. The conclusion of the outline is of necessity somewhat speculative in character.

The collection of war records, in which a few research libraries were engaged before Pearl Harbor, developed steadily in the states after America entered the war. In some states special projects were organized with support from their Offices of Civilian Defense or from educational, historical, and archival institutions; in others these institutions expanded their normal programs to give attention to war materials. A survey of this movement to the end of 1943 has been published.[2] It includes some

---

[2] L. J. Cappon, "War Records Projects in the States, 1941–1943," American Association for State and Local History *Bulletins*, I, no. 8 (March, 1944).

discussion of the variety and extent of the records and of methods of collecting them, with illustrations from state and local programs. Writers of war histories are advised to get in touch with these projects or with affiliated institutions. A list of these agencies was published in *The War Records Collector*, I, no. 1 (March, 1944), issued by the Committee on State and Local War Records, American Association for State and Local History.

The following categories of war materials are presented for consideration in their bearing upon community history. In this connection the reader should consult the corresponding items in Part I of the present *Guide*.

1. Governmental archival records (normal and emergency), state and local, including certain federal war records of the locality (see ch. 4 above)
2. Records of economic, political, social, and religious organizations, whether emergency in character or permanent with wartime activities (see chs. 5 and 6)
3. Newspapers—wartime papers of army camps, hospital units, special industries, etc., and normal dailies and weeklies (see ch. 3)
4. Personal papers—manuscripts (see ch. 2)
   Letters, diaries, reminiscences, etc., of persons in military service
   Similar original materials of persons in civilian life or government service—publicists, scholars, war correspondents, artists, business men, politicians, etc.
5. Books and periodicals pertaining directly or indirectly to the war effort, especially state and local (see ch. 1 for certain items)
6. Posters, maps, music, professional and amateur films and photographs, and other miscellany (see ch. 1)
7. Museum objects (see ch. 2)
8. Data compiled by questionnaire, interview, special investigation, etc. (see chs. 1 and 2)
   Sociological
   Personal service records, rosters, etc.

Most of these types of materials are self-explanatory. A few comments seem advisable, however, because we are dealing with recent and current records widely scattered and often not readily accessible. Federal records in the states and localities are subject to war restrictions and government orders and may be removed later to Washington or elsewhere. Since they fall eventually under the jurisdiction of the National Archives, this agency becomes the best source of information on how federal archives can be used and what they contain. State records go into the custody of the state archival agency, where such exists under an effective system of operation; where none exists, the fate of the records is uncertain. Local archival records usually remain in the community and too often are inadequately preserved. Since most governmental records are voluminous, an understanding of the nature of their content and the functions of the agency which produced them is prerequisite for using them without untold loss of time.

Valuable war materials will be found among the original papers of organizations representative of all aspects of social history. The war records projects have shown great interest in this type of material and are taking steps for its preservation. Most of it will not be accessible for research until after the war; many organizations will retain their own records. Therefore the investigator will have to seek them beyond the confines of research libraries and other public collections. The same is true of personal manuscripts, although some institutions are already obtaining original letters or copies, especially those of persons in the armed forces. Correspondence and other original accounts by civilians are equally valuable and, being uncensored, are often more informing.

Work in recent history offers opportunity for securing information by oral testimony of participants to supplement written records. Some of the projects have persuaded key persons in various organizations to put in writing statements of their war activities with critical comments on policy and accomplishments. Such statements provide limited data long before official records are accessible, and the only first-hand data if the records are destroyed or withheld indefinitely. The highly subjective character of material created in this fashion must be taken into account by the historian.[3]

In a state with an active war records project or with capable historical agencies, the writer of a community history will find considerable material already available. By the end of the war he should find these collections greatly enriched and steadily growing. He must not overlook, however, the sources remaining in offices of organizations and in private hands. Faced with an abundance of material, he needs skill in selection, sound judgment in interpretation, and a facile pen in writing. Whatever the merits or faults of his work, he may as well accept the view that no historian has ever said the final word on his subject.

---

[3] For more detailed comments on types of war records see American Association for State and Local History, *Bulletins*, 207–218; and L. J. Cappon, *A Plan for the Collection and Preservation of World War II Records* (New York, Social Science Research Council, October, 1942), 14–22.

Bibliography

TECHNICAL WORKS ON WRITING AND PUBLISHING
PUBLISHED VOLUMES

Binkley, Robert C., *Manual of Methods of Reproducing Research Materials*, Ann Arbor, Michigan: Edwards Bros., 1936.

Bleyer, Willard Grosvenor, *Newspaper Writing and Editing*, New York: Houghton Mifflin Co., 1932.

Edwards Brothers, *Junior Models for Lithoprinting and Planographing*, Ann Arbor, Michigan: Edwards Bros., 1939.

———, *Manual of Lithoprinting and Planographing*, Ann Arbor: Edwards Bros., 1939.

Fortescue, John, *The Writing of History*, New York: Longmans, Green and Co., 1926.

Hiss, Sophie K., Chairman, Special Committee, *A. L. A. Rules for Filing Catalog Cards*, Chicago: American Library Assoc., 1942.

Historical Records Survey, *Instructions for Using the County Records as Source Material*, 2d ed., Nashville, Tenn.: Historical Records Survey, 1939, mimeographed.

Hockett, Homer Carey, *Introduction to Research in American History*, New York: Macmillan Co., 1935.

Humphreys, A. L., *How to Write a Village History*, Reading, England: A. L. Humphreys, 1930.

Hutchinson, Lois Irene, *Standard Handbook for Secretaries*, New York: McGraw-Hill Book Co., 1936.

Josephson, Bertha E., *Manual of Style for Publications of the Beveridge Memorial Fund*, New York: D. Appleton-Century Co., 1940.

Preservation of Business Records, Boston: Business Historical Society, Inc., 1940.

Spahr, Walter Earl, and Swenson, Rinehart John, *Methods and Status of Scientific Research; with Particular Application to the Social Sciences*, New York: Harper and Bros., 1930.

University of Chicago Press, *A Manual of Style Containing Typographical Rules Governing the Publications of the University of Chicago Together with Specimens of Type Used at the University of Chicago Press*, Chicago: University of Chicago Press, 1937.

Village Survey-Making, an Oxfordshire Experiment, Oxford, England: Board of Education.

Vincent, John Martin, *Historical Research*, New York: Henry Holt and Co., 1911.

Wake, Joan, *How to Compile a History and Present Day Record of Village Life*, 3d ed., rev. and enlarged, Northampton, England: Northamptonshire and Soke of Peterborough Federation of Women's Institutes, 1935.

Young, Pauline V., *Scientific Social Surveys and Research*, New York: Prentice-Hall Inc., 1939.

ARTICLES AND PAMPHLETS

Cheyney, Edward P., "Thomas Cheyney, A Chester County Squire. His Lesson for Genealogists," *Pennsylvania Magazine of History and Biography*, Philadelphia, LX, 1936, pp. 209–228.

Evans, Luther H., "Archives as Material for the Teaching of History," *Indiana History Bulletin*, Indianapolis, XV, 1938, pp. 136–153.

Foster, C. W., "Suggestions for Work on Local History," *Local History: Its Interest and Value*, Lincoln, England: Lindsey Local History Society, n.d.

Goss, Dwight, "Methods of Securing Information for Local History," *Michigan Pioneer and Historical Collections*, Lansing, XXXVIII, 1912, pp. 56–59.

Harvey, D. C., "Importance of Local History in the Writing of General History," *Canadian Historical Review*, Toronto, VIII, 1932, pp. 244–251.

Holbrook, Franklin F., "Some Possibilities of Historical Field Work," *Minnesota History Bulletin*, St. Paul, II, 1917, pp. 69–81.

Luce, Robert, "Town and City Histories," *Granite Monthly*, Concord, N. H., VII, 1884, pp. 306–327.

Mahan, Bruce E., *State and Local History in the High Schools, Bulletin of Information Series*, No. 12 (1924), of the State Historical Society of Iowa, Iowa City.

Michigan Historical Commission, *Bulletin* No. 10 (1919), Lansing.

Murdock, Henrietta, "Giving the Past a Future," *Ladies' Home Journal*, Philadelphia, LIV, February, 1937, p. 99.

Osterhus, Grace, "What to Collect and How," *Wilson Bulletin, A Magazine for Librarians*, New York, VII, May, 1933, pp. 571–573.

Phillips, Hubert, "History at Its Source," *Survey Graphic*, New York, XVI, February, 1930, pp. 524–525, 544–545.

Savelle, Maxwell Hicks, "History, Photography and the Library," *Library Journal*, New York, LX, November 15, 1935, pp. 876–877.

Schafer, Joseph, "Documenting Local History," *Wisconsin Magazine of History*, Madison, V, 1921, 3.

Schapiro, Eleanor Iler, "Publishing a Local History," *Social Education*, Boston, III, January, 1939, pp. 25–29.

Weicht, Carl L., "The Local Historian and the Newspaper," *Minnesota History*, St. Paul, XIII, 1932, p. 51.

Williams, Alice, "The Value of a Local History Collection," *Public Libraries*, Chicago, XXV, December, 1925, pp. 556–557.

Wilson, H. E., "Look Around You; How to Make a Community Survey," *Scholastic*, Pittsburgh, XXX, 1937, pp. 19–20.

SOURCE BOOKS AND GUIDES

Adams, George Burton, and Stephens, H. Morse, *Select Documents of English Constitutional History*, New York: Macmillan Co., 1904.

American Handbook of Learned Societies and Institutions, Washington: Carnegie Institution, 1908.

Beers, Henry P., *Bibliographies in American History: Guide to Materials for Research*, New York: H. W. Wilson Co., 1942.

Bourne, Henry E., "The Work of American Historical Societies," *Annual Report of the American Historical Association*, 1904, Washington.

Bowker, Richard R., *State Publications*, 4 vols., New York: Publisher's Weekly, 1899–1909.

Bradford, Thomas L., *Bibliographer's Manual of American History*, ed. and rev. by S. V. Henkels, 5 vols., Philadelphia: Henkels, 1907–1910.

Brigham, Clarence S., *Bibliography of American Newspapers, 1690–1820, American Antiquarian Society Proceedings*, Worcester, XXIII–XXXVII, 1913–1928.

Channing, Edward; Hart, Albert Bushnell; and Turner, Frederick Jackson, *Guide to the Study and Reading of American History*, rev. and augmented edition, Boston: Ginn and Co., 1912.

Checklist of American Newspapers in the Library of Congress, 1901.

Cheyney, Edward P., *Readings in English History Drawn from the Original Sources*, Boston: Ginn and Co., 1908.

Childs, James B., *An Account of Government Document Bibliography in the United States and Elsewhere*, Washington: Government Printing Office, 1927.

Coulter, Edith M., *Guide to Historical Bibliographies*, Chicago: University of Chicago Press, 1927.

Coulter, Edith M., and Gerstenfeld, M., *Historical Bibliographies*, Berkeley: University of California Press, 1935.

Crittenden, Charles, *North Carolina Newspapers before 1790, The James Sprunt Historical Studies*, Chapel Hill: University of North Carolina, XX, 1928, No. 1.

Fox, Dixon Ryan, "Local Historical Societies in the United States," *Canadian Historical Review*, Toronto, VIII, 1932, pp. 263–267.

Gregory, Winifred, ed., *American Newspapers, 1821–1936: A Union List of Files Available in the United States and Canada*, New York: H. W. Wilson Company, 1937.

Gregory, Winifred, ed., *Union List of Serials in Libraries in the United States and Canada*, New York: H. W. Wilson Co., 1927 and supplements.

Griffin, A. P. C., comp., *Bibliography of American Historical Societies, Annual Report of American Historical Association*, 1905, Washington: Government Printing Office, 1906.

Griffin, Grace Gardner, comp., *Writings on American History, 1908–*, New York: Macmillan Co., 1910–1921; at Washington, D. C.: Government Printing Office, from 1921 to 1941. (Future volumes to be published by the Beveridge Memorial Fund of the American Historical Association.)

Handbook of Historical and Patriotic Societies in New York State, Including List of Local Historians, Albany: University of the State of New York Press, 1926.

Hart, Albert Bushnell, and Curtis, J. G., eds., *American History Told by Contemporaries*, 5 vols., New York: Macmillan Co., various dates.

Hasse, Adelaide R., *Index of Economic Material in Documents of the States of the United States*, 13 vols., Washington: Carnegie Institution, 1907–1922.

Historical Societies in the United States and Canada, a Handbook, Indianapolis, Conference of Historical Societies, 1936.

MacDonald, William, ed., *Documentary Source Book of American History, 1606–1926*, New York: Macmillan Co., 1926.

MacDonald, William, ed., *Select Documents Illustrative of the History of the United States, 1776–1861*, New York: Macmillan Co., 1927.

McLaughlin, Andrew C., Slade, William A., and Lewis, Ernest D., *Writings on American History, 1903–1907*, Washington: Carnegie Institution, 1905–1908.

Monthly Catalogue of United States Public Documents, Washington: Government Printing Office, 1910.

Monthly Check List of State Publications, Washington: Government Printing Office, 1910–.

Publisher's Weekly, New York, 1872–.

Readers' Guide to Periodical Literature, Minneapolis, 1901–.

Richardson, Ernest C., and Morse, Anson F., *Writings on American History, 1902*, Princeton: Princeton University Press, 1904.

Wheeler, Robert C., comp., "Selective Index to the *Centinel of the Northwestern Territory*," *Ohio State Archaeological and Historical Quarterly*, Columbus, LII, 1943, pp. 217–247. Also issued separately by the Society.

GENEALOGIES AND GENEALOGICAL AIDS

Allaben, Frank, *Concerning Genealogies*, New York: Grafton Press, 1904.

Allaben, Frank, and Washburn, Mabel, *How to Trace and Record Your Own Ancestry*, New York: National Historical Co., 1932.

Alphabetical Index of American Genealogies and Pedigrees, Albany, N. Y.: Munsell, 1886.

American Genealogist and New Haven Genealogical Magazine, New Haven: IX–, 1932–.

Doane, Gilbert Harry, *Searching for Your Ancestors*, New York: McGraw-Hill Book Co., 1937.

Durrie, Daniel S., *Index to American Genealogies and Genealogical Material Contained in All Works such as Town Histories, County Histories, Local Histories, Historical Societies, Publications, Biographies, Historical Periodicals and Kindred Works, Alphabetically Arranged*, Albany, N. Y., published in 5 editions, 1868, 1878, 1886, 1895, and 1900.

Grafton Index of Books and Magazine Articles on History, Genealogy, and Biography Printed in the United States on American Subjects during the Year 1909, New York: Grafton Press, 1910.

Heads of Families . . . 1800 . . . Vermont, Montpelier, Vt.: Vermont Historical Society, 1938.

Howe, Herbert B., *Jedediah Barber*, New York: Columbia University Press, 1939.

Jacobus, Donald Lines, *Genealogy as Pastime and Profession*, New Haven, Conn.: Tuttle, Morehouse and Taylor Co., 1930.

Jacobus, Donald Lines, ed., *Index to Genealogical Periodicals*, New Haven, Conn.: Published by author, 1932.

List of Titles of Genealogical Articles in American Periodicals and Kindred Works. Giving the Name, Residence, and Earliest Date of the First Settler of Each Family, Albany: J. Munsell's Sons, 1899.

New England Historical and Genealogical Register, Boston, 1847–.

New York Genealogical and Biographical Record, New York, 1870–.

Nichols, Jeannette P., *James Styles of Kingston and George Stuart of Schoolcraft*, Swarthmore, Pa., 1936.

Stetson, Oscar Frank, *The Art of Ancestor Hunting*, Brattleboro, Vermont: Stephen Daye Press, 1936.

Stiles, Henry R., *A Handbook of Practical Suggestions for the Use of Students in Genealogy*, Albany, N. Y.: Joel Munsell's Sons, 1899.

Virginia Magazine of History and Biography, Richmond, 1893–.

William and Mary College Quarterly, Historical Magazine, Williamsburg, 1921.

LOCAL, STATE, AND REGIONAL HISTORIES

Arizona, The 1864 Census of the Territory of, Historical Records Survey, 1938, mimeographed.

Barrows, John Stuart, *Fryeburg, Maine*, Fryeburg: Pequaeket Press, 1938.

Dailey, Mrs. Orville D., comp., *The Official Roster of the Soldiers of the American Revolution Who Lived in the State of Ohio*, II, Greenfield: Daughters of American Revolution of Ohio, 1938.

Davis, Stanton L., *Pennsylvania Politics, 1860–63*, hectographed in edition of 50 copies.

Dublin, N. H., History of, 1920.

Ellis, Roy, *A Civic History of Kansas City, Missouri*, Springfield, Missouri: Elkins-Swyers Co., 1930.

Ganser, Malcolm H., *History of the Evangelical Lutheran Church of the Trinity, Norristown, Pa., 1848–1938*, Norristown: Norristown Herald, 1938.

Geneseo Centennial History, 1836–1936, Kewanee, Illinois: Star-Courier Co., 1936.

Griffith, William, *History of Kansas City*, Kansas City, Missouri, 1900.

Hannum, Anna Paschall, *A Quaker Forty-Niner: The Adventures of Charles Edward Pancoast on the American Frontier*, Philadelphia: University of Pennsylvania Press, 1930.

Kansas City, 1900, Report of the Public Schools of, Kansas City, Missouri, 1900.

Kleber, Albert, *St. Joseph, Jasper, Indiana—Centenary: 1837–1937*, St. Meinrad, Indiana: St. Meinrad's Abbey, 1937.

Koenig, Samuel, *Immigrant Settlements in Connecticut: Their Growth and Characteristics*, Hartford: Connecticut State Department of Education, 1938.

[La Porte, Indiana], *History of One Hundred Years*, typewritten, 7 copies.

Marion County in the Making, published by the J. O. Watson Class of the Fairmont High School, West Virginia, 1917.

Nelson, William, "Church Records in New Jersey," *Journal of the Presbyterian Historical Society*, Philadelphia, II, 1904, Pp. 173–188, 251–266.

Nichols, Herbert B., *Historic New Rochelle*, New Rochelle, N. Y.: Board of Education, 1938.

O'Byrne, Mrs. Roscoe C., ed., *Roster of Soldiers and Patriots of the American Revolution Buried in Indiana*, Brookville, Ind.: Ind. D. A. R., 1938.

Official Roster of the Soldiers of the American Revolution Buried in the State of Ohio, I, Columbus: Daughters of American Revolution of Ohio, 1929.

Paxton, W. M., *Annals of Platte County, Missouri*, Kansas City, Missouri: Hudson-Kimberly Publishing Co., 1897.

Schafer, Joseph, *Four Wisconsin Counties, Prairie and Forest*, Madison: State Historical Society of Wisconsin, 1927.

———, *Wisconsin Domesday Book—General Studies*, 3 vols., Madison: State Historical Society of Wisconsin, 1922–.

Stone, William L., *History of New York City*, New York: Virtue and Yorston, 1872.

Teachers' Pictorial Survey of Rural Wisconsin a Century After the Black Hawk War, n.d., mimeographed.

Tippecanoe County Historical Association, *Pageant Celebrating the Establishment of the Northwest Territory, Souvenir Program with Local History of Lafayette and Tippecanoe County, Indiana*, Lafayette, Indiana.

Wadsworth, Center to City, Wadsworth, Ohio, 1938.

War of the Rebellion: A Compilation of the Official Records of the Union and Confederate Armies, 70 vols., Washington: Government Printing Office, 1880–1901.

Webb, Walter P., *The Great Plains*, Boston: Ginn and Co., 1931.

Whitney, Carrie Westlake, *History of Kansas City*, Chicago: S. J. Clarke Pub. Co., 1908.

Williams, Harry Lee, *History of Craighead County, Arkansas*, Published by author, c1930.

Wisconsin, A Study of Foreign Groups in, Bulletin of Information, No. 3, Madison: State Historical Society of Wisconsin, December, 1897.

Wittke, Carl, ed., *The History of the State of Ohio*, Columbus: Ohio State Archaeological and Historical Society, 6 vols., 1941–44.

NEWSPAPERS

Kansas City *Times*, 1872.
Parkville Industrial Luminary, Parkville, Missouri.

PERIODICALS

Agricultural Museum, Georgetown, D. C., 1810–1812.
American City, New York, 1909–.
American Farmer, Baltimore, 1819–1897.
American Historical Association, Annual Reports of the, New York, 1884–.
American Historical Review, New York, 1895–.
American Journal of Science, New Haven, 1818.
American Magazine, New York, 1939.
American Monthly Magazine, New York, 1833–1838.
Annals of Iowa, Des Moines, 1863–.
Daughters of the American Revolution Magazine, Washington, 1892–.
Emancipator, New York, 1834–1850.
Filson Club Publications, Louisville, 1884–.
Genius of Universal Emancipation, Mt. Pleasant, 1821–1839.
Genius of the West, Cincinnati, 1853–1856.